CRIMINAL MINDS

SOCIOPATHS, SERIAL KILLERS, AND OTHER DEVIANTS

JEFF MARIOTTE

WILEY

John Wiley & Sons, Inc.

This book is printed on acid-free paper. ∞

Copyright © 2010 by ABC Studios and CBS Studios, Inc. All rights reserved

Published by John Wiley & Sons, Inc., Hoboken, New Jersey
Published simultaneously in Canada

Design by Forty-five Degree Design LLC

Photo credits appear on page 285 and constitute an extension of the copyright page.

For general information about our other products and services, please contact our Customer Care Department within the United States at (800) 762-2974, outside the United States at (317) 572-3993 or fax (317) 572-4002.

Wiley also publishes its books in a variety of electronic formats. Some content that appears in print may not be available in electronic books. For more information about Wiley products, visit our web site at www.wiley.com.

Library of Congress Cataloging-in-Publication Data:

Mariotte, Jeff.
Criminal minds : sociopaths, serial killers, and other deviants / Jeff Mariotte.
    p. cm.
  Includes bibliographical references and index.
  ISBN 978-0-470-63625-1 (paper : acid-free paper); ISBN 978-0-470-77051-1 (ebk);
  ISBN 978-0-470-87218-5 (ebk); ISBN 978-0-470-87219-2 (ebk)
  1. Criminal minds (Television program) 2. Criminals—United States—Biography. I. Title.
  HV6785.M297 2010
  364.1092'273–dc22

                                                                        2010016889

Printed in the United States of America

10 9 8 7 6 5 4 3 2 1

He knows that part of my beauty is being alive,
but it's the dead me he wants.

— John Fowles, *The Collector*

CONTENTS

Introduction

CRIME TOUCHES US ALL. In ways large and small, direct and indirect, our lives are affected by the criminal acts of others. Our taxes support law enforcement and the judicial and penal systems. Retail prices factor in the expectation of a certain amount of shoplifting. Some of our pensions have been reduced or even eliminated because of white-collar crime in corporate boardrooms.

Then there are the more personal effects of crime, the kinds that happen one-to-one. In my life, I've had a few things stolen, and once in the 1970s I was mugged at knifepoint in a large city in California. The mugger left with seven dollars and change; I left with a little round hole in the back of my neck.

A girl I went to junior high and high school with became the first murder victim in our Virginia town. Another high school friend (at least, he was my friend until I decided he couldn't be trusted; the first time I used the phrase *pathological liar* was, I believe, in reference to him) became one of the most successful bank robbers in U.S. history; he died in a shoot-out with the police.

While researching this book, I learned that yet another high school classmate had probably been murdered by John Brennan Crutchley, who was known as the Vampire Rapist. I also discovered that the apartment complex in which my wife and I lived for a while in a second-floor unit was where serial killer and sexual predator Cleophus Prince took his first victim—from a second-floor unit—a couple of years before we moved in. You'll meet both the Vampire Rapist and Mr. Prince in these pages.

The CBS television series *Criminal Minds* deals with crimes like Crutchley's and Prince's, the heinous acts people commit against one another. It does so by telling the stories of profilers working in the Federal Bureau of Investigation's Behavioral Analysis Unit (BAU), a real entity that does spectacular work in bringing to justice kidnappers, rapists, murderers, and others. The cases depicted on *Criminal Minds* are fictional, but there may be elements that are similar to ones that have actually happened. In addition, during any given episode of *Criminal Minds*, one or more real-life criminals or crimes might be specifically mentioned as examples. Those true stories are what this book is about. (The book assumes that the reader has seen the episodes, or at least doesn't mind knowing the resolution, because sometimes in discussing the true crimes, the episode's mysteries must be unveiled.)

Some of the stories contained herein have been told many times, even fictionalized and filmed, with the result that the details are often murky or contradictory. Others have been told hardly at all, which means that there are few sources from which to learn about them. Wherever I found contradictions, I dug deeper still, looking for contemporary or firsthand accounts, settling on one version only when I could find multiple sources that agreed.

Details that are still not certain are described in that way. The reader should remember that some of the details of any crime are subject to interpretation—often the only people actually present were the criminal and the victim. The victim isn't talking, and the criminal is, in most cases, a liar; even detailed confessions are spun to achieve the criminal's own end. These accounts are as true and accurate as I could make them, given those uncertainties.

Criminal Minds is excellent television, with strong writers and one of the best casts in the business. Every actor is a standout, playing action scenes, tense interrogations, and tender character moments with equal credibility. Although the show focuses on solving crimes, the human aspects of the characters' lives and the effects of such a harrowing career are never shortchanged.

Just as important, the victims on the series are shown respect. In real life, it should also be that way. The bad men and women murder, rape, kidnap, and steal, but in the end it's the victims and their families, friends, and loved ones who have to spend the rest of their days in the shadow of those acts. The survivors and those close to them often show incredible courage and grit, whether they launch public anticrime initiatives or simply continue living their lives, refusing to be brought up short by a psychopath's heartless act.

Like the TV series, this book focuses on the crimes and criminals. But the victims and the survivors have not been forgotten, and this author dedicates the pages that follow to them.

First Glance

AT **FIRST GLANCE**, you don't see anything strange about the man. Maybe you don't notice him at all; blending in is part of his technique, after all, and he looks just like anybody else out there. He might be young, like Bill Heirens, the Lipstick Killer. He might be huge, like Ed Kemper, the Coed Killer. He's probably white, almost certainly male, most likely older than twenty but younger than forty. He might be staring directly at you, raising the fine hairs on the back of your neck. It's possible that he's unable to meet your gaze, so he glances away, pretending that his attention is elsewhere. Chances are he'll be alone, but he might have a partner nearby, perhaps even a woman whose task is to lure you into complacency so he can strike.

The man is a predator. He's driven by forces he doesn't understand, by urges he can tamp down but never quell. And by the time you realize what he is, it's probably too late.

Criminal Minds is about the worst of the worst: murderers, rapists, stalkers, kidnappers, molesters, predators of every sort. Avid viewers know that these criminals can be categorized in a number of different ways. There are organized and disorganized offenders. There are serial killers, spree killers, mass murderers, family annihilators. There are lust or thrill killers, visionary killers, mission-based killers, power or control killers. When we look at their crimes, it's important to consider which aspects are part of their modus operandi (MO) and which represent their individual signatures.

In subsequent chapters, we'll look at some of these real-life criminals in an organized fashion, grouping them by the types of crimes they commit, the types of victims on whom they prey, and so on. But we'll start with some who, for one reason or another, resist classification or who simply deserve to stand apart from their less accomplished fellows, and we'll allow them to demonstrate some of the characteristics of the categories above. Rarely do criminals fit exactly into one slot or another—for all their crimes, they're human beings, after all, and human beings tend to resist easy understanding.

I used the word *accomplished* in the previous paragraph with tongue somewhat in cheek; many of these people are, in fact, good at what they do and work hard at it, and they spend a lot of time and expend a great deal of energy and thought in pursuit of their avocations. Had they been willing to direct those resources toward useful goals, they might have contributed to society in some positive way.

Instead, they're the dregs, barely worth discussing, for the most part. However, they're fascinating to examine as case studies, in some perverse way—for the same reason we go to horror movies, one supposes, to see at a safe distance things we hope never to encounter in our own lives. As noted FBI profiler John Douglas points out in several books devoted to his work, the better we can understand these human predators, the better we as a society can protect ourselves from them and try to prevent them from doing the things they do.

Within the five seasons of *Criminal Minds* (as of this writing), there have been two fictional serial killers who avoided arrest the first time they appeared, only to become serious threats to two of the show's main characters. Readers familiar with the series will recall Frank Breitkopf; he was introduced in the episode "No Way Out" (episode 213) but escaped, only to return in "No Way Out II: The Evilution of Frank" (223) and kill a close friend of Supervisory Special Agent Jason Gideon.

Then there's George Foyet, known as the Reaper, who first appeared in "Omnivore" (418) as unit chief Aaron Hotchner's nemesis; he eventually murdered Aaron's wife, Haley. Aaron beat him to death with his bare hands, in the powerful 100th episode of the series, titled simply "100" (509).

As of this writing, Karl Arnold, known as the Fox, has also made more than one appearance; introduced in "The Fox" (107), he returned in "Outfoxed" (508), but he's in jail and not currently a threat.

Breitkopf and Foyet are both brilliant, brutal men, "ideal" killers with no real-life analogues. One possible parallel to Foyet might be one of the people most frequently mentioned on the series: David Berkowitz, popularly known as the Son of Sam, one of the most notorious serial killers of all time. The fictional BAU profilers on the series refer to Berkowitz in seven episodes: "Extreme Aggressor" (101), "Compulsion" (102), "Unfinished Business" (115), "A Real Rain" (117), "The Last Word" (209), "Lo-Fi" (320), and "Zoe's Reprise" (415). Only the names Ted Bundy and Charles Manson come up more often.

1 **DAVID BERKOWITZ** was determined to name himself to the New York Police Department (NYPD), but at first he appeared uncertain about what name he wanted to use. New Yorkers had started calling him the .44 Caliber Killer, because he was killing women with a Charter Arms .44 Bulldog handgun. In a letter addressed to NYPD captain Joseph Borrelli that was left at the scene of two murders, Berkowitz wrote, "I am the Son of Sam," but he also wrote "I am the 'Monster'—Beelzebub—the chubby behemouth." A skilled speller Berkowitz was not. He signed his introductory missive "Mr. Monster." He was indeed a monster, but Son of Sam was the name that stuck.

In the *Criminal Minds* premiere episode, "Extreme Aggressor," Agents Gideon, Hotchner, and Greenaway must profile a serial killer to find a missing woman before she becomes his next victim.

Berkowitz began his criminal career stealing from his adoptive mother, Pearl Berkowitz, and committing petty vandalism. He shoplifted things his parents would have bought him, and he poisoned his pet fish, fed rat poison to his mother's parakeet, and created a torture chamber for any insects unlucky enough to cross his path. Later in life, after Pearl had died and David's adoptive father, Nathan Berkowitz, moved away with his new wife, David became even more dangerous. Between September 1974 and December 1975, according to detailed diaries he kept, Berkowitz set 1,488 fires in New York City and pulled hundreds of fire alarms. He enjoyed the power, the ability to upend people's lives and to make the great city's resources respond to his will.

Common early indicators of serial murder are bed-wetting, fire-starting, and animal torture, sometimes called the McDonald Triad (after psychiatrist J. M. McDonald, who described it in a professional journal) or the triad of sociopathy. Berkowitz had two out of three.

His first murder attempt was a failure. On December 24, 1975, he took a hunting knife back to the apartment complex he had lived in with his adoptive father and stabbed a young woman in the back. Instead of dying in an appropriately cinematic fashion, she screamed. Berkowitz fled the scene, dissatisfied. His account of this stabbing has never been confirmed, and the victim has never been identified. A short while later, with the urge still strong, he crossed paths with fifteen-year-old Michelle Forman and took another crack at it. He stabbed Forman six times. Like his previous victim, she screamed but didn't die. After that, Berkowitz changed weapons. He wouldn't be a stabber after all, but a shooter.

His next attempt proved more successful. He had started to regularly cruise New York's streets, searching for victims. Early in the morning on July 29, 1976, he shot two teenagers, eighteen-year-old Donna Lauria and nineteen-year-old Jody Valenti, while they sat in Jody's car outside the Lauria home in the Bronx. Berkowitz claimed that he didn't know for sure if he had killed them until he read about the shooting in the newspapers, but he had managed to kill Donna and shoot Jody in the thigh. After the shooting, he returned to his apartment and slept soundly.

Most serial killers have a cooling-off period after a murder, and Berkowitz was no exception. By September, he had heated up again and returned to the hunt. His next target was Rosemary Keenan, eighteen, the daughter of a police detective who would later become part of the task force hunting Berkowitz. On October 23, Keenan and her friend Carl Denaro were parked outside her home in Queens. Berkowitz, using the Charter Arms .44 that would become his trademark, fired repeatedly into the parked car. Keenan, in the driver's seat, was unhurt, but Denaro was hit in the back of the head. He lived, but he had to have a metal plate put in his skull, and his air force career ended before it began.

Between then and the end of January 1977, Berkowitz struck twice more, killing Christine Freund, twenty-six, and injuring three others.

By this time, the police were beginning to suspect a connection among all these shootings. Although they were spaced out in time and there were no connections among the victims, they had all been shot with .44 bullets. Most of the victims were young women with long dark hair. In the cases in which Berkowitz had shot at men, they were with young women. Most were sitting in parked cars.

Things were changing in Berkowitz's life, too. Before the shooting rampage started, he had sent a letter to Nathan. In it he wrote, "Dad, the world is getting dark now. I can feel it more and more. The people, they are developing a hatred for me. You wouldn't believe how much some people hate me. Many of them want to kill me. I don't even know these people, but still they hate me. Most of them are young. I walk down the street and they spit and kick at me. The girls call me ugly and they bother me the most. The guys just laugh. Anyhow, things will soon change for the better."

After the murders, things looked brighter to him, at least for a little while. Berkowitz had worked menial jobs in construction and security and had then driven a cab, but shortly after he killed Christine Freund, he did well on a civil service exam, which enabled him to become a postal employee and earn the highest salary of his life. Like the fictional George Foyet and many real serial killers, Berkowitz was a man of above-average intelligence working at jobs below his real capabilities. Also like Foyet, although Berkowitz attacked victims of both sexes, he was most interested in his female victims.

Berkowitz ordinarily hunted late at night or early in the morning, but his next murder took place on March 8, 1977, at 7:30 p.m., not far from where he had shot Freund. He was on foot and saw Virginia Voskerichian, a nineteen-year-old student, walking toward him. He pulled his .44. Voskerichian held her books up to shield herself, and Berkowitz shot her in the face.

Two days later, Mayor Abe Beame joined the NYPD brass for a press conference, at which they announced the formation of the Operation Omega task force. Its only goal was to find the man or men doing these shootings.

About a month later, a letter was delivered to Sam Carr, a retired municipal worker who lived in Yonkers in a house behind the apartment building where Berkowitz lived. The letter complained about Carr's dog, Harvey, a black Labrador that was constantly barking. The importance of this communication wouldn't become known until much later.

The next incident, on April 17, was the occasion on which Berkowitz left the first "Mr. Monster" letter for Captain Borrelli. Berkowitz left behind the dead body of Valentina Suriani, eighteen. Her companion, Alexander Esau, twenty, held on for almost a day before he died.

Two days later, Carr received another letter that complained about his apparent unwillingness to control Harvey. "Your selfish, Mr. Carr," the letter said. "My life is destroyed now. I have nothing to lose anymore. I can see that there shall be no peace in my life, or my families life until I end yours."

On April 29, someone shot Harvey. Carr rushed the dog to a vet, who was able to save its life. Because the Borrelli letter had not yet been made public, Carr had no way to connect his own letters to the .44 Caliber Killer.

The existence of the Borrelli letter was not a secret for long. Columnist Jimmy Breslin wrote about it, noting that the writer—the so-called Son of Sam—habitually spelled women "wemon." The letter also referred to "father Sam," who got mean when he was drunk. There would be much more talk about Sam in the weeks to come.

For his attention, Breslin got a note directly from Berkowitz, who wrote the following:

Hello from the cracks in the sidewalks of NYC and from the ants that dwell in these cracks and feed in the dried blood of the dead that has settled into the cracks.

Hello from the gutters of NYC, which is filled with dog manure, vomit, stale wine, urine, and blood. Hello from the sewers of NYC which swallow up these delicacies when they are washed away by the sweeper trucks.

Don't think because you haven't heard for a while that I went to sleep. No, rather, I am still here. Like a spirit roaming the night. Thirsty, hungry, seldom stopping to rest; anxious to please Sam.

The publicity sold newspapers. Because Berkowitz preyed on brunettes, blond wigs sold out at stores all across New York. Thousands of worthless tips swamped the task force.

Berkowitz reached out by mail again in early June, when a New Rochelle man named Jack Cassara received a get-well note, ostensibly from Sam and Francis Carr in Yonkers. The note included a picture of a German shepherd and referred to Cassara's fall from a roof.

Cassara found this strange. He didn't know the Carrs, and he had not fallen from a roof. He found out that the Carrs were real people and gave them a call. Jack Cassara and his wife, Nann, and their son Stephen met the Carrs at the latter's home, where the Carrs described what had happened to Harvey and to a neighborhood German shepherd, which had also been shot. The Carrs' daughter, Wheat, a dispatcher for the Yonkers police, summoned officers Peter Intervallo and Thomas Chamberlain to look into things.

Something about the situation reminded Stephen Cassara of a strange man who had rented a room in the Cassaras' house in 1976. The man, David Berkowitz, had never liked the Cassaras' German shepherd, and he had moved out abruptly, never coming back for his two-hundred-dollar security deposit. Nann Cassara became convinced that Berkowitz was the Son of Sam but couldn't get the police to take her seriously.

Then another strange letter—this one to a deputy sheriff named Craig Glassman, a neighbor of Berkowitz's in the same apartment building—described a "demon group" that included Glassman, the Carrs, and the Cassaras. Intervallo and Chamberlain decided to check out this Berkowitz character. They found his current address, learned the registration number of his Ford Galaxie, and discovered that his driver's license had recently been suspended. That was as far as their investigation went, for the moment.

On the morning of June 26, 1977, Judy Placido, seventeen, had just left the Elephas disco with her date, twenty-year-old Sal Lupo. They were sitting in Lupo's car when the Son of Sam fired three shots into the car. Neither was seriously injured. Witnesses reported two people leaving the scene: a tall, stocky dark-haired man running and a blond man with a mustache driving a car without headlights.

The anniversary of Berkowitz's first killing (July 29) came and went without incident, but on July 31, he attacked Stacy Moskowitz and Robert Violante, both twenty. They were making out in Violante's car in a city park when Berkowitz opened fire. Moskowitz died in the hospital, and Violante lost one eye and most of his vision in the other.

There were several witnesses to this assault, but their stories were contradictory. Cacilia Davis, who had not seen the shooting, lived in the area, and two days later she told the police that she had seen an angry young man who resembled witness descriptions of the shooter take a parking ticket off the windshield of his car, a Ford Galaxie, which was parked too close to a fire hydrant. NYPD detectives didn't put much stock in her tale, but they accepted that the ticketed party might have been a witness. After a week, they finally reached out to the Yonkers police for help in locating the person who had been ticketed, and they were surprised when dispatcher Wheat Carr said that Berkowitz just might be the Son of Sam.

Officers Intervallo and Chamberlain had been busy. They had talked to Berkowitz's landlord and learned that Berkowitz had once been a security guard and had thus come into contact with guns. Chamberlain had responded to an arson report on Berkowitz's building filed by Deputy Sheriff Glassman. Someone had started a fire outside Glassman's apartment door and dropped two .22 rounds into the flames. Glassman showed Chamberlain the letters he had received from Berkowitz, who lived in the apartment above his, including one that said, "True, I am the killer, but Craig, the killings are at your command."

Meanwhile, Sam Carr had grown tired of the lack of police response to his complaints. He went to the headquarters of Operation Omega and gave them Berkowitz's name.

Finally the task force detectives decided to pay Berkowitz a visit. They had heard about his strange behavior from various cops in Yonkers. His presence near the Moskowitz and Violante shootings had been documented, and now they were hearing about him from Sam Carr.

On August 10, detectives saw Berkowitz's car sitting outside his apartment building. Inside the car they found a bag with a rifle sticking out of it and a letter addressed to one of the task force members promising more killings. They had their man, and they arrested him when he emerged from the building.

His story didn't end with his arrest, however. Berkowitz confessed to the killings in such detail that they knew he had really pulled them off. He told the story of his early life: born Richard David Falco on June 1, 1953, he was unwanted by his mother's married boyfriend, so his mother put him up for adoption before his birth. He was adopted by Nat and Pearl Berkowitz, but he was often a terror, bullying other kids, gripped by dark depressions, and threatening suicide. It all became worse after Pearl died. Nat and his new wife moved to Florida when David was eighteen, leaving him alone in the city.

He joined the army and became a proficient marksman. During his posting in South Korea, he had his one and only sexual encounter with a woman, a Korean prostitute, who gave him gonorrhea. He later wrote, "I think that if I were to have a good, mature sexual relationship with a woman I wouldn't have killed."

Berkowitz agreed to plead guilty to the murders in exchange for a sentence of life in prison instead of the death penalty.

Once in custody, he told stranger stories. The Cassaras' German shepherd, a noisy dog who howled a lot, was a demon. Other neighborhood dogs were, too—when they howled back, they were demons talking to one another, and to him. They wanted blood. Berkowitz wrote, "When I moved in the Cassaras seemed very nice and quiet. But they tricked me. They lied. I thought they were members of the human race. They weren't! Suddenly the Cassaras began to show up with the demons. They began to howl and cry out. 'Blood and death!' They called out the names of the masters! The Blood Monster, John Wheaties, General Jack Cosmo."

General Jack Cosmo, commander of New York's devil dogs, was Jack Cassara. Berkowitz fled that house and moved into a building near the Carrs, but that was no better. They had Harvey, the black Lab. This meant that the Carrs, and especially Sam Carr, were also demons. The "Sam" in Berkowitz's notes was Sam Carr. Sam, he sometimes believed, was Satan himself, and he, Berkowitz, was the Son of Sam. All of the murders that Berkowitz committed were commanded by these demons, particularly Sam Carr and Harvey.

Later, Berkowitz claimed to have been part of a satanic cult that included John and Michael Carr, Sam Carr's two sons. Both Carr brothers died within two years of Berkowitz's arrest. There were, he said, about two dozen people in the cult, whom he called the twenty-two disciples of hell. Police have found some evidence of cult activity in the area Berkowitz described, reported as early as five years before the first murder. That activity included pedophilia and child pornography, as he claimed, and also the ritual sacrifice of German shepherds. Witness reports described other people at and around some of the Son of Sam murder scenes, and some of the descriptions matched people who Berkowitz said were in the cult. He admitted that he was present at all of the murders, but he insisted that some had been carried out by other cult members. Yonkers officials were convinced enough to reopen the case, and it remains officially open to this day.

Still later, interviewed by FBI profilers Robert K. Ressler and John Douglas, Berkowitz admitted that the story about devil dogs had been fabricated in an effort to claim an insanity defense. The main motivation behind the murders was sexual after all. He hunted most nights, but on nights when he couldn't find an appropriate victim, he would return to the scenes of earlier shootings, then go home and masturbate.

Berkowitz named himself the Son of Sam well before his arrest, and his bizarre letters hinted at demonic cults. So was he a visionary killer, sent on missions of murder by a demonic dog? Or was he just a common lust killer? As so often happens with these people, the truth is probably somewhere in between.

Whatever the truth, Berkowitz was sentenced to six consecutive life terms in jail, and he refuses to be considered for parole. He remains incarcerated at the Sullivan Correctional Facility in upstate New York. He has converted to Christianity and claims to be repentant. He still sometimes blames demons for everything.

Berkowitz is, in many ways, a classic serial killer. He went out into the night hunting, determined to kill and looking for the right opportunity. He was organized enough to hold a job and keep his own apartment. Once he killed, the fantasy he had been building up to was satisfied for the moment, and he went through a cooling-off period while it built again. There was a similarity to his victims: people in parked cars, always with a young woman present, even if he also had to shoot a man at the scene.

Just as George Foyet's impact on Boston could be reminiscent of the Son of Sam's impact on New York, his relationship with Hotchner is reminiscent of the one Gary Charles Evans, a serial killer who befriended David Berkowitz in prison, had with a police detective named James Horton. It was not as violent as the fictional one, but for years Horton knew Evans, thought he was a small-time burglar, and even used him as an informant, without being aware of Evans's serial murders (including that of a former partner in crime named Michael Falco—coincidentally, the same last name Berkowitz had at birth). Evans, his biographer, M. William Phelps, says, was "a master escape and disguise artist."

2 **IT'S UNLIKELY THAT** there's ever been a living serial murderer with Frank Breitkopf's combination of folksy but sophisticated charm, his brilliant mind and vast knowledge of history and culture, and his cold-blooded, sadistic nature. The character, a psychopathic sexual sadist, may have killed hundreds of people from coast to coast in a thirty-year period.

A record like that brings to mind only one U.S. serial killer—at least, according to his own confessions. For his efforts, Henry Lee Lucas has been mentioned on the air a couple of times throughout the five seasons of *Criminal Minds*, in the very first episode and again in "Soul Mates" (412).

If Henry Lee Lucas, known as the One-Eyed Drifter, is to be believed—and he rarely is—then his early childhood seems to have been custom-made to create a serial killer. Even if one is skeptical of his reports of the facts of his youth, there are witnesses and other testimony that support at least the broad facts. He was born on August 23, 1936, in Blacksburg, Virginia, in a log cabin without plumbing or electricity. His childhood home was described in a report from the site of Lucas's first incarceration, the Beaumont Training School for boys, as a place that was "furnished with only necessities and is not clean or neat. There are four rooms, one of which houses two goats that belong to a roomer who is a half-witted man who owns a half interest in the house."

Lucas was the last of nine children. It's unlikely that even his mother, Viola Dison Wall Lucas, knew who his real father was, but the person he called his father was Anderson Lucas, who lived in the cabin with Viola. She told Henry that Anderson was not his real father; on one occasion, in town, she pointed out a stranger and claimed that he was Henry's father. That was most likely a lie meant to torture the boy.

Viola was a prostitute, and by all accounts she was a vicious, hateful woman. She forced Anderson and Henry to watch her having sex with clients. She beat them both with sticks and broom handles. Anderson, bereft after watching her entertain a client, got drunk, staggered out into the snow, and fell down on a railroad track. A passing train severed both of his legs, earning him the nickname No Legs and ensuring Viola's ability to control him. What little income he derived came from a still, which he taught Henry to operate, as well as to drink from, at the tender age of ten. Anderson also begged and sold pencils on the street. Still, compared to Viola, he was an angel, even sharing nickels and dimes with his son on occasion.

Viola, on the other hand, let her pimp, Bernie, live in the cabin with the family. She cooked for herself and Bernie but refused to feed the others. What they did manage to scrounge, they had to eat on the dirt floor.

Lucas described his childhood this way: "I hated all my life. I hated everybody. When I first grew up and can remember, I was dressed as a girl by my mother. And I stayed that way for two or three years. And after that I was treated like what I call the dog of the family. I was beaten; I was made to do things that no human bein' would want to do. I've had to steal, make bootleg liquor; I've had to eat out of a garbage can. I grew up and watched prostitution like that with my mother till I was fourteen years old." Viola did, in fact, send Henry to his first day of school dressed as a girl, with his long blond hair in curls. His teacher cut his hair and found some boys' clothing for him. Later that teacher fixed him the only hot meals he'd ever had and provided him with his first pair of shoes.

Everything young Henry loved, Viola destroyed. He claimed that he once had a mule. His mother asked if he liked it; when he said yes, she went inside, got her shotgun (which she had once used to shoot a client in the leg, spattering blood on young Henry), and shot the mule. Then she beat Henry for causing her the trouble and expense of having it hauled away.

Lucas's favorite relatives were his sister Opal and his older brother Andrew. It was Andrew who accidentally stabbed Lucas in the eye, severing most of the optic nerve. A local doctor partly repaired the damage, but then a teacher accidentally swung her hand into Lucas's head and knocked the eye out. This time, he lost the eye altogether and had to get a glass one. The work wasn't done well, however, and the eye socket drained pus, which, along with Lucas's dirty clothes, poor manners, and bad smell, made Lucas a pariah at school.

His mother hit him with a two-by-four on one occasion, so hard that he was unconscious for thirty-six hours, until Bernie, the pimp, fearing a police visit, took the boy to a hospital. That and other head injuries, most inflicted by Viola, might have contributed to permanent neurological damage. To add psychological scarring to the physical, Viola told Lucas that he was no good and predicted that he would die in prison. On that count, at least, she was right.

A half-brother taught Lucas the "pleasures" of having sex with dead animals. This, along with his mother's horrific example, surely destroyed any chance that Lucas might have a normal sex life. In fact, he committed his first murder at fifteen. Wanting to know what sex with a human was like, he grabbed a seventeen-year-old girl at a bus stop and tried to rape her. She screamed and struggled, and he strangled her to death.

In 1952, Anderson Lucas caught pneumonia after spending a drunken night outdoors, and died. Almost immediately, Andrew left to join the navy. Now Viola's rages were directed almost entirely at Lucas. He took to spending as much time as possible away from the cabin and was soon arrested for breaking and entering. He was sent to the Beaumont Training School, the first of many institutions that Lucas would grace with his presence. At Beaumont, for the first time in his life, he had regular meals, indoor plumbing, electricity, and television.

After a year at Beaumont, he did odd jobs, then was arrested and sentenced to four years in jail in Virginia. He served two and escaped from a chain gang. He fled to Ohio, where he got in trouble again and served thirteen months on a federal charge. Released from that prison, he went to live in Michigan with Opal. He had met a woman named Stella and planned to marry her, but then Viola showed up. According to Lucas, his mother couldn't stand to see her son happy or in love, so she drove Stella off. In the midst of a drunken fight, Lucas stabbed Viola and fled. By the time Opal came home, it was too late to save Viola; she was dead.

Lucas was convicted of Viola's murder and sentenced to twenty to forty years in prison in Michigan. After serving a couple of years, he tried to commit suicide twice, reported hearing voices, and was sent to the Ionia State Mental Hospital, where he spent the next four and a half years. There he was heavily medicated and subjected to electroshock treatments. He felt so brutalized by his experiences at the hospital and so frustrated by his doctors' refusal to understand his promises that if he ever got out he would kill again, that by the time he did get out he was even more vicious, ready to torture others to make up for the torture he had undergone.

Lucas spent four more years in prison after his release from the hospital and then was paroled in 1970, despite his insistence that he would kill again. He claims that to punish those who released him, he killed two women the day he got out and dumped one of the bodies within walking distance of the prison. This, like many other claims he has made, was never proven.

Lucas was in and out of Michigan prisons two more times in the next few years, but then came the period of his life that was subject to the most scrutiny—and, conversely, to the most uncertainty, because no one tells the same story, and even Lucas rarely told it the same way twice.

What's known is that he lived with various relatives for a while and eventually found himself in Jacksonville, Florida. There, at a mission, he met a man named Ottis Toole, who seemed to be his soul mate. Toole invited Lucas home, where he lived with his extended family, including his eleven-year-old niece, Frieda Powell, who went by the name of Becky. A female friend said that Toole liked to pick up men at the mission and bring them home for sex and that he also liked to watch the men he brought home have sex with her and with young Becky. Henry Lee Lucas fit right in.

In the next several years, Lucas and Toole drifted from state to state together. Sometimes they worked, and other times they robbed. If anyone gave them trouble, they killed. If they saw a woman they liked, they would murder her and have sex with her corpse. Sometimes they would rape her first, then kill her, and then have sex with her corpse. Many of their victims were horribly mutilated. Toole had a taste for human flesh, but although Lucas might have tried some, that was one habit he never shared with his friend and lover.

During some of these escapades, little Becky and her brother Frank accompanied the men. Finally, Becky and Frank were put into a juvenile home for their own protection. Lucas and Toole broke them out, but Frank didn't want to go with the men, so they left him behind and took Becky. They headed west, where they killed and beheaded a woman in Texas and then dumped the head in the Arizona desert. Toole wanted to return to Florida, but Lucas didn't. By now, Becky was Lucas's common-law wife, and she stuck with her man. Toole and Lucas split up.

Lucas and Becky wound up in California, where Lucas did some odd jobs for the Smarts, a couple who owned an antique store. They took Lucas and Becky to Texas with them so the pair could care for Kate Rich, Mrs. Smart's eighty-year-old mother. Kate liked them, but the rest of the family didn't, and after a while those family members demanded that Lucas and Becky leave Kate's house. On the road again, Lucas and Becky met Ruben Moore, a preacher whose small fundamentalist group, the House of Prayer, took them in. In exchange for room and board, Lucas agreed to do roofing work and day labor at the sect's little farm.

Becky took to the religious life and eventually decided that she wanted to return to Florida. Lucas didn't want her to leave, but he didn't want to lose her, either. On August 24, 1982, he relented, and the two set off, hitchhiking across Texas. They had made it only as far as Denton when they argued; Becky slapped Lucas, and he stabbed her to death. That done, he had sex with her corpse, then dismembered it. He cut her into enough pieces, he said, to fill three pillows from which he had torn the stuffing. Two weeks later he went back and buried one of the pillows.

Lucas claimed to feel remorse over this murder because he had truly cared about Becky. She was a quarter century younger than he was, but they had been together a long time, during which she had grown from a little girl into a young woman.

He returned to the House of Prayer and told Ruben Moore that Becky had accepted a ride from a trucker and left him behind. While he was there, Kate Rich heard about Becky's departure and called Lucas to tell him how sorry she was. The two agreed to go to a church service together. Lucas picked her up, but along the way they argued about Becky, and Lucas killed Kate. Following his usual routine, he had sex with her corpse, then cut her into pieces. He carried the pieces back to the House of Prayer and spent the night burning them in a stove.

Lucas realized that he was the last person known to have seen Kate alive. He fled, heading back to California, back to the antique store owned by Kate's daughter and son-in-law. The Smarts had been alerted by relatives that Kate was missing and to be on the lookout for Lucas. They contacted Sheriff Bill "Hound Dog" Conway in Texas, who asked them to keep Lucas there. California state troopers picked Lucas up and questioned him, but even though there was blood in the car he was driving, they couldn't prove that it wasn't his. They had to let him go. He returned to the House of Prayer, where Ruben Moore turned him in for possessing a firearm—a crime for a paroled felon.

In June 1983, Lucas was picked up on the weapons charge. After a couple of weeks in jail, he claimed to have experienced a religious conversion. He started confessing to his crimes, and he just wouldn't stop.

He asked for a pencil and paper and started drawing pictures of his victims—although he had never drawn before—adding pertinent notes about their dress or behavior and the details of his crimes. He remembered the most obscure facts, in many cases, and some of them were found to be true. In court, when a judge asked Lucas if he understood that by confessing to the murders of Kate Rich and Becky Powell he would probably ensure himself a lifetime behind bars, Lucas said that he did and that he had about a hundred other murders he wanted to confess to, as well.

Texas Rangers and other law enforcement officials from all over the country flocked to Lucas's cell. Before he was done, Lucas had confessed to—according to various reports—between 360 and 600 murders in twenty-six to thirty-six states. Some of these crimes were extremely unlikely; for instance, Lucas probably did not, as he claimed, kill Jimmy Hoffa. Nor did he deliver poison to Jim Jones in Jonestown (he said he drove to Guyana). Some of these confessions were clearly hoaxes, but they earned Lucas trips to other states on comfortable airplanes, stays in hotel rooms, and delays in his eventual and certain long stretch in prison. For a time, he claimed to have been part of a satanic cult called the Hand of Death, and he said that many of his murders were done for them; no doubt this was just another delaying tactic.

Other confessions were more convincing, however, and he was eventually convicted of eleven murders. He was sentenced to death for the murder of a young hitchhiker known as Orange Socks because that's what she was wearing when her body was found.

Yet another religious conversion led Lucas to recant all of his previous confessions except for three: the murders of his mother,

Becky Powell, and Kate Rich. Now he claimed that these were the only murders he had committed and that the rest of his confessions had been false. He had been supplied details by law enforcement and had used those details in his confessions. Still later, he recanted his recantations, claiming that he had been forced to make them and that he really had killed the 360 to 600 victims he'd originally claimed. He went back and forth so often that no one knew what to believe.

Even if Lucas did murder only three people, he's still, according to the standard definition, a serial killer. The term is generally applied to those who kill at least three people, with a cooling-off period between the murders. In 2005, the BAU set a new definition of serial murder as "the unlawful killing of two or more victims by the same offender(s), in separate events."

Some experts on Lucas's case believe that he killed between forty and sixty people—still enough to put him in the top ranks of overachieving U.S. serial killers. But others credit him with only the three that he's never denied.

After his sentencing, it was proven that he was out of the state when Orange Socks was murdered. George W. Bush, the governor of Texas at the time, commuted Lucas's death sentence to life in prison. This is the only death sentence that Bush ever commuted during his years in that office.

The One-Eyed Drifter died of natural causes in prison on March 13, 2001. The full extent of his crimes will never be known. Many of the hundreds or thousands of murders that he and others tried to pin on him will probably never be solved.

Lucas—at least, the Lucas who might have killed forty or so people—is a textbook lust killer. "Sex is one of my downfalls," he said. "I get sex any way I can get it. If I have to force somebody to do it, I do. If I don't, I don't. I rape them; I've done that. I've killed animals to have sex with them and I've had sex while they're alive."

What he said about animals also held true for people. With very few exceptions, people to him were simply objects who might provide sex. He killed because he didn't value human beings, and either it was easier to get sex after they were dead or he had raped them and didn't want them to say anything about it.

Lust-based serial murder doesn't necessarily run in families, but a distant cousin of Lucas's, Bobby Joe Long, was convicted in Florida of fifty rapes and the murders of ten women (although there might have been more of both). Long was born with an extra X chromosome, which caused him to grow breasts at puberty and created the fear that he was turning into a woman. After a motorcycle accident, he became hypersexualized, needing sexual release seven or eight times a day. He turned to rape, and then rape and murder, as a way to get what he wanted. He's currently on death row in Florida, serving twenty-eight life sentences, four ninety-nine-year sentences, one five-year sentence, and one death sentence.

3 **IF IT HADN'T BEEN** for George Metesky, there might never have been a BAU and thus never a *Criminal Minds*.

When Metesky, who earns a mention in "Extreme Aggressor" (101) when special Agent Derek Morgan explains that the BAU "cover[s] a whole spectrum of psychos," terrorized New York during the 1940s and 1950s, he was known as the Mad Bomber or as F.P. in the letters he sent. The Mad Bomber's first successful bomb exploded on March 29, 1951, inside Grand Central Terminal, near the Oyster Bar on the lower level. No one was hurt, but the commuters obviously were startled. Throughout the rest of that year, F.P. planted twenty-two more bombs. The man who had seemed like a harmless crank was beginning to look dangerous, after all. And mad he might have been, but he was an organized, mission-motivated offender all the way.

The world first heard from F.P. in 1940, when a pipe bomb was found inside a building owned by utility giant Consolidated Edison, which supplies most of New York's electricity. Wrapped around it was a note that said simply, "Con Edison crooks—this is for you." Police wondered why someone would wrap a note around a bomb;

had the bomb exploded, the note would have been destroyed. They did a perfunctory check of recently dismissed employees, but since no real harm had been done, they dropped the case.

Almost a year passed before another pipe bomb was found, this time on a street not far from another Con Ed building. Three months later, after the United States had entered World War II, a letter arrived at Manhattan police headquarters that said, "I will make no more bomb units for the duration of the war—my patriotic feelings have made me decide this—later I will bring the Con Edison to justice—they will pay for their dastardly deeds. F.P."

The Mad Bomber lived up to his word, and in 1951 he started planting bombs again. His technique had improved; although there were still some duds, many bombs went off. He planted them in very public spots: the Port Authority Bus Terminal, Radio City Music Hall, Macy's, Penn Station, the New York Public Library, and more. To plant bombs in theaters, he cut into the underside of a seat and placed the device in the stuffing. Between 1951 and 1956, he planted at least thirty bombs.

His last successful bomb exploded on December 2, 1956, in the Paramount Theatre in Brooklyn during a screening of *War and Peace*. Stephen P. Kennedy, New York's police commissioner, declared the "greatest manhunt in the history of the police department" to bring the Mad Bomber to justice.

For all those years and all those bombs, law enforcement had made little real progress. Because F.P. referred so often to Con Ed in his messages, the police believed that he was a disgruntled employee, past or present. There were many of those, however, and the employee records weren't always so orderly. The bombs themselves carried few helpful clues. Finally, in desperation, Inspector Howard Finney of New York's crime lab asked a friend in the Missing Persons Bureau for help.

That friend knew a criminal psychologist, Dr. James Brussel, who had done counterespionage work for the FBI and the U.S. Army's Criminal Investigation Division during the Korean War. Criminal profiling was in its infancy; noted profiler John Douglas has written that J. Edgar Hoover, the FBI's legendary director, considered it voodoo and wouldn't allow anything like the Behavioral Sciences Unit (later to become the Behavioral Analysis Unit) to exist under his regime.

But Dr. Brussel seemed to know his stuff. After reviewing the case file, he told Finney that the Mad Bomber was a male and a textbook paranoiac. Because paranoia peaks around age thirty-five, and the Mad Bomber had first been heard from in 1940, he was probably now in his fifties. Based on his neatly if oddly written notes, he was an orderly man with an exemplary work history. He had some education and was foreign-born. He was probably a former employee who believed that the company and the general public had done him harm. Most of his notes were written in block capital letters, but his W's were oddly rounded, suggesting a pair of breasts. That, his slitting the undersides of theater seats with a knife (which suggested sexual penetration), and the phallic shape of his pipe bombs led Brussel to believe F.P. suffered from an unresolved Oedipal complex. He probably had lost his mother when he was young, was unmarried, and lived with a female relative.

When the cops thought Brussel was done, they gathered their materials and prepared to leave. But Brussel, a man with more than a touch of the theatrical about him, wasn't finished. "One more thing," he said. "When you catch him—and I have no doubt you will—he'll be wearing a double-breasted suit." He paused, for dramatic effect. "And it will be buttoned," Brussel finished.

He suggested to the detectives that they publicize the profile and make the hunt for the bomber front-page news. With some reluctance, they did so. The expected onslaught of cranks and bad tips followed.

In response, the Mad Bomber sent more letters. Somehow he got his hands on Brussel's unlisted phone number and called him. "This is F.P. speaking," he said. "Keep out of this or you'll be sorry."

The *New York Journal American* published an open letter to the Mad Bomber, pleading with him to give up. He responded by mail, and the paper printed his response. In further correspondence, he went into more detail about his gripe against Con Ed.

Finally, a Con Ed employee named Alice Kelly found a file from a smaller company that had merged into the giant utility company. In 1931, an employee named George Metesky had inhaled gushing gas, which he blamed for the tuberculosis he later developed. He hadn't been able to prove his claim, and the company had refused to compensate him.

Metesky fit the profile, and the specifics of his case matched what F.P. had written to the *Journal American*. Kelly took the file to her superiors, who referred it to the police. On January 21, 1957, the police knocked on the door of Metesky's residence in Waterbury, Connecticut, where the fifty-four-year-old man lived with two older sisters. After he had been asked a few questions, he said, "I know why you fellows are here. You think I'm the Mad Bomber."

They did indeed, and he admitted it right away. They asked what F.P. stood for, and he told them it meant Fair Play. Metesky was in his pajamas and robe when the police came to the door at almost midnight, so he asked if he could get dressed before they took him in. They allowed him that, and he went upstairs. When he came back down, his hair was combed and he was wearing a double-breasted jacket—buttoned.

Metesky was ruled insane in April 1957 and sentenced to New York's Matteawan Hospital for the Criminally Insane. In 1973, the U.S. Supreme Court ruled that a mentally ill defendant could not be committed to a state hospital within the correctional system unless a jury had found him dangerous. Since Metesky had been committed without a jury trial, he was transferred in September 1973 to Creedmoor Psychiatric Center, a state hospital outside the correctional system. Here the doctors determined that Metesky was harmless, and because he had already served two-thirds of the twenty-five-year maximum sentence that he would have received at a trial, he was released in December 1973 on the condition that he make regular visits to a mental hygiene clinic near his home. He returned home to Waterbury, where he died in 1994.

Brussel's profile wasn't right in every respect. He put the bomber in White Plains, not Waterbury. He suggested that the man would have a facial scar and work nights. Metesky had no scar and didn't work at all. Brussel thought the target had been born and educated in Germany, but Metesky was a Slav. Brussel predicted that the bomber had heart disease, but Metesky had tuberculosis. Had it not been for Alice Kelly's careful detective work, Metesky might never have been found. Kelly turned down the twenty-six-thousand-dollar reward she was offered for the Mad Bomber's capture, saying she had just been doing her job.

But Brussel's story was what people remembered, particularly the bit about the buttoned double-breasted jacket. He became the first famous criminal profiler, and everyone who has come along since owes something to his work in helping to catch the Mad Bomber.

4 **JASON GIDEON** mentions Brussel's profile of Metesky when discussing the difficulties of profiling in the episode "A Real Rain" (117). In this episode, the unknown subject of the investigation (the "unsub," in FBI parlance) is a serial vigilante, killing people who have been acquitted of crimes but whom he believes to be guilty. Gideon worries that the case may become reminiscent of another vigilante folk hero, Bernhard Hugo Goetz, who in 1984 became famous for shooting four young black men on a New York City subway because he believed they were going to rob him.

Crime was a given in New York City in the early 1980s; the reported crime rate there was 70 percent higher than in the rest of the country. An average of thirty-eight crimes took place on New York subways every day.

In January 1981, three young black men had attacked Goetz at the Canal Street subway station. They smashed him into a plate-glass window and tore the cartilage in his knee. Only one of the three men was apprehended, and he spent three hours at police headquarters, charged only with criminal mischief for tearing Goetz's jacket. Goetz, clearly the victim, was at headquarters for six hours. He was almost as outraged by the aftermath as by the attack itself.

Later that year, Goetz went to Florida and bought a .38 revolver, since he couldn't get a pistol permit in New York.

The Saturday before Christmas in 1984, Goetz stepped onto a largely empty subway car. On board were four black youths, headed into Manhattan to steal money from video arcade machines. Two of them rose, blocking the view of Goetz from other passengers. Nineteen-year-old Troy Canty approached Goetz and demanded five dollars. Goetz stood up, unzipped his jacket, and asked Canty to repeat what he had said. Canty did. One of the other men made a gesture that Goetz interpreted to mean that he had a weapon. Goetz said that he mentally constructed his field of fire, drew his .38, and fired five times. One shot missed, but the other four found their marks, each hitting one of the young men. None died, but nineteen-year-old Darrell Cabey's spinal cord was severed, causing brain damage and paralyzing him from the waist down.

When a conductor entered the car, Goetz explained that the young men had tried to rob him. The train stopped before the next station, and Goetz slipped away into the darkened tunnel. Hurrying home, he packed a bag and hit the road for New England, where he dumped his clothes and disassembled his .38, tossing the pieces into the woods.

Goetz was an instant celebrity. Citizens bemoaned his lack of accuracy, not his vigilante approach. He traded on his notoriety, giving dozens of interviews, speaking about crime, and attending the funerals of crime victims. His supporters were all in favor of his actions, whereas his detractors called him a racist and accused him of skulking about the subway armed and looking for an excuse to shoot somebody, just to take revenge on any black youths for the wrong that had been done to him in 1981.

Goetz turned himself in to the police in New Hampshire and stayed at the police station until New York's finest came to pick him up. Back home, he was arraigned for attempted murder and illegal possession of a firearm, but a grand jury decided that his use of force had been justified, and the only charge he faced was for the unlicensed handgun. A second grand jury reversed that decision, and he stood trial. He admitted to the shootings but claimed self-defense. The jury acquitted Goetz of attempted murder and found him guilty of carrying a loaded, unlicensed weapon. He served eight months in jail. In a civil trial, a jury awarded Cabey forty-three million dollars, but Goetz has denied paying any of it.

If the idea that Goetz went "looking for victims" is valid, he would be considered a mission-based offender, someone who meant to rid New York of at least a handful of muggers. He's not a serial offender, though, or a spree offender, who takes his weapon and commits one crime after another until he's caught or killed. Someone who shoots multiple victims in a single event is called a mass offender and a vigilante, a breed that is scarce when the citizens of a society feel protected by institutional law enforcement but that is more common when they're afraid.

Although Bernhard Goetz left New York after the furor died down, he returned to the city and ran for mayor in 2001. He lost.

5 **YET ANOTHER** reference in the episode "A Real Rain" (117) is to the Zodiac Killer, who Spencer Reid suggests is similar to the unsub due to constant changes in the type of victim. One of the great unsolved serial-killer mysteries, Zodiac is also brought up in "Unfinished Business" (115) and in "Normal" (411).

Zodiac's first confirmed attack was on December 20, 1968, at Herman Lake in the Bay Area city of Vallejo, California. Two teenagers, Betty Lou Jensen and David Faraday, were parked in a remote spot, no doubt steaming up the windows of Faraday's station wagon. Witnesses saw them there at 11 p.m. The next time anyone saw them, Betty Lou was dead, several feet from the car, with five bullet holes in her back. David died en route to the hospital.

Shortly after midnight on July 5, 1969, Darlene Ferrin and Michael Mageau sat in Ferrin's car at a golf course a few miles from Herman Lake. A man drove up, got out of his car, and opened fire on the young lovers. Darlene died in the ambulance on the way to the hospital, but Michael survived and gave a description of their assailant.

At 12:40 a.m., the Vallejo Police Department received a stunning phone call from a pay phone. A male voice said, "I want to report a double murder. If you go one mile east on Columbus Parkway to the public park, you will find kids in a brown car. They were shot with a nine-millimeter Luger. I also killed those kids last year. Good-bye."

On July 31, three Bay Area newspapers each received part of a cryptogram allegedly sent by Zodiac, with a note warning of dramatic consequences if the newspapers did not print their respective parts. Proving once again that spelling is not a skill highly regarded by serial killers, Zodiac wrote, "I want you to print this cipher on your frunt page by Fry Afternoon Aug 1–69, If you do not do this I will go on a kill rampage Fry night that will last the whole week end. I will cruse around and pick off all stray people or coupples that are alone then move on to kill some more untill I have killed over a dozen people."

The cryptogram revealed that he enjoyed killing. "It is even better than getting your rocks off with a girl," he wrote. And he added, "the best part is thae when i die i will be reborn in paradice and all the i have killed will become my slaves." The idea that he was collecting slaves for the afterlife continued to be part of what would turn into a long and frustrating correspondence among the killer, the police, and the press. One of the symbols on the cryptogram was a cross inside a circle, like a gun sight, that would become his signature.

After the police announced that they had their doubts about the authenticity of these communications, the killer wrote again on August 4. This time his letter began, "This is the Zodiac speaking." It was the first time he had revealed the name he'd picked for himself, but it was a name that would remain in the awareness of Bay Area residents for decades to come. The letter also contained details about the first two shootings, confirming that the person who had committed those murders had written this letter.

On September 27, two college students, Bryan Hartnell and Cecelia Shepard, picnicking at Lake Berryessa in nearby Napa County, saw a man approaching them. He ducked behind a tree and emerged wearing a four-cornered black hood with a bib that extended down to his waist, with the Zodiac's crossed-circle design embroidered on it. On his belt he wore a knife in a sheath and an empty holster. With a gun in his hand, he walked up to the young couple and demanded money and their car keys. In the end, he didn't take much money, just pocket change from Hartnell, and he left the car keys behind. But he made Shepard tie up Hartnell with a clothesline, then he stabbed them both: Hartnell six times and Shepard ten. Hartnell survived the attack, but Shepard died two days later.

This time the Napa Police Department got the call. "I want to report a murder—no, a double murder. They are two miles north of Park Headquarters. They were in a white Volkswagen Karmann Ghia." The switchboard operator asked him to identify himself, and he said simply, "I'm the one that did it." Then he left the phone off the hook and walked away. He never again referred to this murder in any of his communications. The variations in MO and the fact that he didn't bring it up again led some people to believe that the murders were committed by a different perpetrator, someone trying to confuse the police by making reference to the Zodiac's crimes and his symbol, but the authorities believe that there are enough evidentiary links to attribute this one to the same man.

On October 11, a San Francisco cabbie named Paul Stine picked up a passenger in Union Square and drove him to the upper-class Nob Hill neighborhood. There the passenger shot him in the side of the head, took his wallet and keys, and removed a section of Stine's shirt, with which he mopped up some of Stine's blood. In later communications, Zodiac sent portions of the shirt to confirm his identity.

Stine's murder was the last death positively connected to the Zodiac Killer. After that, a long succession of letters arrived. In June 1970, Zodiac claimed that he had shot an unidentified man in a car. He didn't say precisely where or when that shooting took place, but the investigators believed that he might have been referring to the murder of a police officer in his car the week before. The last verified Zodiac letter showed up in 1974.

Police questioned and eliminated twenty-five hundred suspects without ever bringing charges against anyone. A man named Arthur Allen, a convicted pedophile with a collection of handguns and known interests in law enforcement and the criminal mind, was considered a serious contender, but no physical evidence ever connected him to the crimes, and he was eventually discounted.

In 2008 a man came forward to claim that while searching the belongings of his deceased stepfather, Jack Tarrance, he had found a bloody knife and the homemade black hood from the Lake Berryessa assault. In 2009, a Bay Area woman reported that her father was the Zodiac Killer and that at seven years of age, she had accompanied him on some of his crimes and had helped him write and mail his many letters. This woman has also claimed to be an illegitimate daughter of President John F. Kennedy and a witness to the assassination of Robert F. Kennedy.

These claims, and all of the other theories that have been offered throughout the years, have never been proven to anyone's satisfaction. Although the San Francisco Police Department has labeled the murder of Paul Stine an inactive case, Zodiac's other murders remain officially open and unsolved.

Zodiac was a classic power and control killer. He liked to have absolute control at his crime scenes; the Lake Berryessa assault is the most vivid illustration of this, but even at the other murders, he was the man with the gun and he was the one who decided who died and in what order. He also wanted to have power over the authorities who investigated his crimes and the press that reported the crimes—hence the constant communication. He was extremely organized as well, planning his murders, leaving few clues, and presumably holding a job throughout. He is a rarity among murderers in that he simply stopped; if this was because he was arrested on some other charge, he never confessed to his crimes. Another possibility is that he died after his last letter in 1974.

6 **JACK TARRANCE** isn't the only man to have a family member claim that he was a killer, of course. Retired Los Angeles homicide detective and writer Steve Hodel is convinced that his father is the Zodiac Killer, the murderer of Elizabeth Short (the victim in the famous Black Dahlia case in Los Angeles), and, for good measure, the real killer behind the crimes attributed to William George Heirens, Chicago's Lipstick Killer.

Heirens is mentioned in the first episode of *Criminal Minds* when a message he wrote with lipstick on the wall of one of his victims turns up on the computer of a victim in the show. While Heirens's name doesn't come up in "The Big Wheel" (422), an event in that episode could be reminiscent of the act that earned Heirens his nickname: serial killer Vincent Rowlings writing "Help me" at a murder scene. He's recording every moment of his activities, and the videotape gets into the hands of the BAU.

Bill Heirens was undoubtedly a troubled boy. He was caught burglarizing homes at the tender age of thirteen, when he worked as a delivery boy for a drugstore. He wore women's underwear that he had stolen, while he looked at pictures of Nazi atrocities. He liked guns and was once picked up for carrying a rifle on Chicago's South Side. Heirens was a smart kid; he was only seventeen at the time but was already in his second year at the University of Chicago, having skipped senior year of high school.

The first murder attributed to Heirens was that of forty-three-year-old Josephine Ross, a divorced mother who lived with her two daughters on the city's North Side. On June 5, 1945, Ross saw her daughters off to school, then went back to bed. Her daughter Jacqueline found her body when she came home for lunch at 1:30. The apartment had been ransacked; Ross's throat had been hacked open, a dress was wrapped around her head, and her body was sprawled on her bed. Her underwear was found in a pool of bloody water in the bathtub.

On December 10 of that year, Frances Brown, thirty-three, a former member of the U.S. Navy WAVES (Women Accepted for Volunteer Emergency Service), came home to her apartment, which was not far from Ross's, around 9:30 p.m. The next morning, a maid heard Brown's radio playing loudly and noticed that her door was open. The maid went into the apartment, followed a bloody trail into the bathroom, and found Brown's nude body slumped over the side of the bathtub. Her pajamas were wrapped around her head, she had a bullet hole in her skull and a butcher knife in her neck, and the following message was written on her living room wall in lipstick:

For heAVen's
SAke cAtch Me
BeFore I Kill More
I cannot control myselF

The apartment had been ransacked, but nothing was taken. One smudged, bloody fingerprint, presumably belonging to the killer, was found at the scene.

That won the Lipstick Killer his sobriquet, but it wasn't until he was accused of the brutal murder and dismemberment of a six-year-old child that he instantly became Chicago's best-known serial killer, a title he held until John Wayne Gacy stole it in 1978.

Chicago celebrated its first Christmas and New Year's after the war ended. On January 7, 1946, Jim Degnan went to wake his six-year-old daughter, Suzanne, for school. Her door was closed, her window was wide open, and she was gone. A ransom note demanded twenty thousand dollars for her safe return. The FBI investigators later found smudged fingerprints on the note, but it had already been handled by dozens of cops and reporters.

The police searched everywhere for the girl. An anonymous caller suggested that they check the sewers, and when they did, they found Suzanne's head. Not far away, they found more bits and pieces of her body. They discovered that the dismemberment had been done in the basement washtub; bits of flesh and hair clogged the drain.

Hundreds of suspects were interviewed and discounted. Months passed.

On June 26, 1946, Bill Heirens, still committing burglaries while attending college, was surprised as he was sneaking into an apartment. He ran, the police were called, and he was apprehended. During the scuffle, an off-duty police officer hit him on the head with three flowerpots, one after the other. Heirens was knocked out cold.

By the time he awakened, he was being accused of more than just petty burglaries. Police officers hit him, pinched him, and asked why he liked cutting up little girls. Heirens denied having anything to do with Suzanne Degnan's murder, so they just hit him harder. After days of being beaten and ordered to confess—without being allowed to see the lawyers his parents had retained—he was given Sodium Pentothal, or truth serum.

Under the influence of the powerful drug, Heirens blamed "George Murman" for the murders. Murman, it turned out, was a name he had given a fictional character in a school writing assignment. The police told the press that it was his version of "Murder Man." No transcript of the interrogation has ever surfaced, and in spite of the truth serum's use as a tool to pressure Heirens to confess, one of the two doctors present says that at no time did Heirens claim responsibility—either as himself or as George Murman—for the crimes.

Other attempts were being made to pin the murders on Heirens. Although the fingerprints discovered at the Brown murder scene and on the Degnan ransom note were smudged, and some investigators had determined that they didn't match Heirens's, others insisted that they did. Heirens's handwriting was said to match that of the message on the wall and the ransom note—or not, depending on which expert one consulted.

Heirens suffered through a spinal tap administered without anesthetic, apparently to rule out some mental deficiency, and then, without being allowed to recover first, he was given a polygraph test. The police declared it inconclusive. Later it was shown to be entirely conclusive, but the conclusion was not the one the police wanted. Anyway, it was argued, a coldhearted killer could beat a polygraph.

Six days after his arrest, Heirens was finally allowed to see his lawyers. He was arraigned, then he promptly collapsed from exhaustion, spending the next ten days in the hospital. His attorneys and his parents pressured him to accept the plea bargain that, he was told, was the only thing standing between him and the electric chair.

Finally he agreed. The police had been feeding every detail of the investigation to a voracious press—five daily Chicago newspapers competed for readers, and the slightest hint of an exclusive on the case skyrocketed circulation. When Heirens relented and accepted the deal, which required a confession, the *Chicago Tribune* jumped the gun, printing a fictionalized confession written by its own reporter with no input from the supposedly guilty party.

The response was enormous. Newspaper sales went through the roof, and the other papers picked up the story. All of Chicago read a confession that Heirens had yet to deliver. Heirens claimed later that he tried to match the *Tribune*'s phony confession, because when he tried to give his own version of the "facts" of the killings, if he deviated too broadly from the *Tribune*'s tale, his lawyers would guide him back toward that reality. His attorneys worked out a deal with State's Attorney William Tuohy for three life sentences, served concurrently; with good behavior, Heirens could be out in twenty years.

On July 30, Heirens was to give his confession in public, before the state's attorney. When the time came, he later explained, "after assembling all the officials, including attorneys and policemen, he [Tuohy] began a preamble about how long everyone had waited to get a confession from me, but, at last, the truth was going to be told. He kept emphasizing the word 'truth' and I asked him if he really wanted the truth. He assured me that he did. Now Tuohy made a big deal about hearing the truth now, when I was being forced to lie to save myself. It made me angry . . . so I told them the truth, and everyone got very upset."

Once again, Heirens denied the murders. Tuohy was furious, and the particulars of the deal changed. Instead of serving his life sentences concurrently, Heirens would have to serve them consecutively. Tuohy didn't have much of a case—the flawed evidence and the illegal treatment of the prisoner would all be picked over in court. Avoiding a trial by gaining a confession was the only way to guarantee Heirens a long prison term.

Under threat of the electric chair, Heirens agreed to the new terms and again made a full confession, pleading guilty to each count. His sentencing was scheduled for the next day. That night, he tried to hang himself in his cell, but a guard spotted him and saved his life.

In prison, Heirens continues to insist that he didn't murder anyone. He's been a model prisoner—the first in Illinois history to get a four-year college degree while incarcerated. He taught himself TV repair, then created a shop and taught other prisoners. He's been a counselor and has worked in the Catholic chaplain's office. Experts agree that he's completely rehabilitated, but despite his efforts over the years, he has never been freed. In prison since 1946, he has been incarcerated longer than any other prisoner in the United States.

Did Heirens do it? He said yes a couple of times, and he said no for decades. The better question might be this: Would the same person who killed two women, left their bodies naked and their heads wrapped in clothing, and urinated and defecated at both scenes also take a young girl from her home with her whole family present and strangle and dismember her?

The killer's signature in the first two instances is unmistakable. In the third, there are some areas of possible overlap, but there are vast differences as well. The killer may have washed Suzanne Degnan's body in the washtub, as the two older women were presumably washed in their bathtubs—but then again, he put Suzanne's head in a sewer, which seems to negate attempts at cleanliness; perhaps the washtub was simply to catch the blood of dismemberment. At the second and third scenes, some sort of written communication was left behind, but is a ransom note the same as a cry for help? Maybe Heirens did kill the first two but not Degnan, and his cry for help was answered: he was caught before he killed again.

FBI profilers John Douglas and Robert Ressler believe that Heirens is guilty. So do members of Degnan's family. A careful consideration of the known facts seems to cast some doubt on that verdict, but according to the laws of the state of Illinois, William Heirens is the Lipstick Killer, and he will be known that way when he finally dies in prison.

7 **BILL HEIRENS** is not the only youthful killer to be discussed by the members of TV's fictional BAU. In the episodes "Plain Sight" (14) and "The Eyes Have It" (506), Herbert Mullin's name comes up as an example of a serial killer who murders a variety of people.

Herbert Mullin was born on April 18, 1947. Significantly—to Mullin, at any rate—April 18 was the anniversary of the 1906 San Francisco earthquake and of Albert Einstein's death.

What might have been the next most significant date of Mullin's short life was February 13, 1973. On that day, while Mullin was picking up firewood for his family up in the redwood-covered hills outside the beach town of Santa Cruz, California, he believed that he received a telepathic message from his father: "Don't deliver a stick of wood until you kill somebody."

The day before, trap shooters had come across the body of Mullin's second victim, hitchhiker Mary Guilfoyle. Another serial killer, Edmund Kemper, had been making a career out of killing hitchhikers near Santa Cruz around this time, too, and the city was being called the Murder Capital of the World. Kemper's targets were so consistent that he was called the Coed Killer. Mullin's victimology was considerably more random.

Wanting to heed his father's supposed telepathic advice, Mullin stopped outside the home of retired boxer Fred Perez and fired one shot with the rifle he had taken from four hippies he had killed in the woods three days earlier. Perez fell down and died. Mullin backed out of the driveway and slowly drove away.

It was to be Mullin's last murder. One of Perez's neighbors heard the shot, saw the car, and phoned the police, who picked up Mullin before he got home. He didn't resist arrest. When he got to the police station, he wouldn't say a word, except to shout "Silence!" whenever he was asked a question.

Herb Mullin had always been troubled. Raised in and around San Francisco and Santa Cruz, he was diagnosed as a paranoid schizophrenic in his early twenties. He was in and out of mental hospitals five times, determined to be a danger to himself and others, but in California, under Governor Ronald Reagan, mental hospitals were being closed right and left. All but the most severely mentally ill were expected to take their meds, live in halfway houses, and attend group therapy sessions.

It was easy for a smart kid to skip those things and to just lose himself in San Francisco's counterculture or the redwoods around Santa Cruz. And Mullin was a smart kid, voted "most likely to succeed" by his high school class. A low point in his life came when his best friend, Dean Richardson, was killed in a car accident the summer after graduation. In despair, Mullin took to his room, built shrines to his pal, explored esoteric philosophies, and sought meaning in tragedy.

Jim Gianera, a buddy of Richardson's, ran into Mullin at the beach and offered him some marijuana. As they smoked, Gianera told him about the burgeoning antiwar movement. This was 1966, and the Vietnam War was escalating hot and heavy. Mullin's drug experimentation went further, and he eventually tattooed "Legalize Acid" across his belly. According to former FBI profiler Robert Ressler, drugs didn't cause Mullin's psychosis, but in combination with his paranoid schizophrenia they hurried him past the breaking point.

Mullin swung from one extreme to the other, trying on lifestyles like pairs of shoes. He was, at various times, a drug-addled hippie, a shaven-headed ultraconservative, a conscientious objector, a nonviolent boxer, a bisexual, a skid row resident, and a would-be marine who passed the psychiatric tests and was passed over only because he wouldn't finish the have-you-ever-been-arrested paperwork. In September 1972, after punching holes in his San Francisco apartment, he moved back in with his parents in Felton.

At exactly the worst time in his life for something like this to happen, someone predicted "the big one," the major earthquake that every Californian wonders about at one time or another. Most people disregarded the "prophet," but not Herb Mullin. He had, after all, been born on April 18. He knew it was coming. And he knew how to stop it.

On Friday, October 13, Mullin went for a drive. He saw a man walking along the road, a transient nobody would miss. Mullin passed him and stopped, pretending to have engine trouble. When the man, Lawrence White, offered to help, Mullin cracked his skull with a bat and shoved him over the embankment.

White, according to Mullin, looked like the biblical Jonah, without the whale. The telepathic message that Mullin heard him broadcast was "Hey, man, pick me up and throw me over the boat. Kill me so that others will be saved."

Next came Mary Guilfoyle, whom Mullin picked up while she was hitching to a job interview. Mullin had read about Michelangelo dissecting corpses to learn about human anatomy, so he decided to do the same thing. He stabbed Guilfoyle in the car, then carried her off into the woods and cut her open. When she was found almost four months later, she was believed to be another of Ed Kemper's coeds.

Father Henri Tomei was inside St. Mary's Catholic Church, over the hill in Los Gatos, on All Souls' Day, November 2. Mullin found his way to the church, hoping, he said later, to find the strength to stop killing. He began confessing to Father Tomei, then decided on a different course of action and stabbed the priest in the heart.

Mullin then tried to join the coast guard but was turned down. He planned to kill a friend, but there were too many people around and all he had was his hunting knife. He bought a gun, failing to inform the gun shop about his various mental hospital stays. On January 15, 1973, his effort to join the marines failed. He moved out of his parents' home and got a cheap apartment near the beach. There he decided that the next to die had to be Jim Gianera, who had ruined his life by introducing him to drugs and leftist politics.

January 25 found Mullin at a cabin near the kitschy tourist destination the Mystery Spot, where Gianera had lived. Kathy Francis, home with her two children while her husband was in San Francisco doing a drug deal, told Mullin that Gianera and his wife, Joan, had moved into town. Mullin went to the address Francis had given him, where Gianera let him in the front door. Almost immediately, Mullin shot Gianera. Wounded, Gianera made it upstairs to where Joan was taking a bath. Mullin followed him and shot them both in the head, then went to work on them with his knife.

Mullin realized that he had to return to the cabin. Francis had told him where the Gianeras lived, so when they turned up dead he would be the obvious suspect. He drove back up the hill, shot Francis and her two boys, then stabbed them.

He went back to his apartment and managed to maintain for a couple of weeks. But on February 10, he couldn't hold his urges in any longer. Wandering in the woods, he ran across four teenage boys who were camping illegally. He told them to pack up and leave; they refused. The next day, he came back and shot all four of them and took their .22 rifle, which he used a couple of days later to gun down ex-prizefighter Perez.

The police hadn't linked the various crimes because there were no obvious connections. The bludgeoned homeless man outside Santa Cruz didn't have any ties to the stabbed priest in Los Gatos. Mary Guilfoyle was found out of sequence, and Ed Kemper was the immediate suspect in any hitchhiker murder. The Gianera and Francis murders appeared to be drug-related. The four kids in the woods weren't found until a week after Mullin's arrest for shooting Perez. Mullin was the very picture of what is called a disorganized offender, except that he was capable of driving a car. Because his last ten murders were committed so close together, he blurs the distinction between spree killers (who kill one victim right after another) and serial killers (who have time gaps between their murders).

Mullin is a perfect example of the mission-based killer, one who truly believes that his murders serve a greater good.

The only connections among his victims were in Mullin's fevered brain. He had to kill, he explained, because "a minor natural disaster will prevent a major natural disaster." To prevent a major earthquake from striking California, a few people had to die. Because Mullin understood this, it became his mission to carry out those executions, and the victims themselves had telepathically given their blessing, inviting Mullin to murder them. Einstein understood—he had sacrificed himself on an earlier April 18 so that

Herbert Mullin might live in order to save California from disaster. The fact that "the big one" hadn't happened was proof of the success of his efforts.

Mullin was found mentally ill, but sane enough—in the legal sense of sanity, able to distinguish right from wrong—to stand trial. He was charged with ten murders—White, Guilfoyle, and Tomei had not yet been connected to him—and found guilty of premeditated murder in the cases of Jim Gianera and Kathy Francis and her children, and second-degree murder in the more impulsive killings of the others. Sentenced to life in prison, he won't be eligible for parole until 2025. He remains incarcerated at Mule Creek State Prison in Ione, California.

8 **WILLIAM HEIRENS** and Herbert Mullin didn't look like murderers. In "Natural Born Killer" (108), we're introduced to Vincent Perotta, a killer who not only looks like one but who has made it a career as well as a hobby by becoming a Mob hit man. Perotta, the BAU team discovers, has killed more than a hundred people, and he sometimes resorts to extreme overkill. He started hunting at a young age and showed extreme aggression with no fear or remorse. At one point, a homeless man found small-time mobster Freddy Condor's head in a Dumpster; the rest of Freddy turned up in other garbage bins close by. Perotta was captured after one of his murders drew too much attention to his Mob bosses.

If the fictional Perotta were compared to real-life Mafia hit man Roy DeMeo, Perotta would be a piker.

Exact figures are hard to come by, for obvious reasons, but DeMeo is suspected of between seventy-five and two hundred murders. A Neapolitan rather than a Sicilian, he grew up around mobsters in Bath Beach, Brooklyn, in the early 1940s, and he worked his way into their good graces. He was close to a Gambino family associate named Nino Gaggi, and with Gaggi's sponsorship eventually became a made man (someone officially inducted into the Mafia). As a young man he was violent, aggressive, and strong.

Working for the Gambino family, DeMeo put together his own crew, specializing in auto theft and drug trafficking (an activity of which Mob boss Carlo Gambino disapproved). At age thirty-two, DeMeo did his first hit, a simple execution: several bullets to the head, the body left in an alley.

DeMeo realized that some bodies shouldn't be found, so he developed a method to dispose of them that rivaled Henry Ford's advances in the mass production of automobiles. DeMeo owned a bar called the Gemini Lounge; it had an adjoining apartment, and the bathtub sometimes came in handy. Because his crew performed their grisly tasks there (sometimes referring to the place as the Horror Hotel), their technique became known as the Gemini Method.

When they had a victim whom they needed to disappear, he would be shot in the head. Immediately, another member of the crew would wrap a towel around the head to stanch the flow of blood. Someone else would stab the victim numerous times in the heart in order to make sure the victim was dead and stop his heart from pumping. He would be put in the bathtub, or hanged over it, so that the blood would drain into a controlled location and be easily washed away. The drained body was then beheaded, cut into pieces (DeMeo, once a butcher's apprentice, knew about chopping meat), wrapped in garbage bags, and tossed.

The first time DeMeo's butchers tried this method, they made a couple of mistakes. One of the crew put the victim's head through a compacting machine, an unnecessary bit of overkill. Once the victim was bagged, they tossed him into a Dumpster, believing that it would be emptied soon. When it wasn't, a homeless man came along and opened the bags, then fled. The next passerby called the police. After that point, the Gemini crew delivered packages directly to the garbage dump or buried them beneath buildings under construction. The disassembly crew enjoyed its work and was good at it. Between 1977 and 1979 these men plied their trade almost nonstop.

The FBI whittled away at the Gemini crew, and finally Gambino decided that DeMeo's habits were drawing undue attention to family matters. DeMeo, like so many of the people he had met in the last decade, was executed. He was shot seven times, and his body was left in the trunk of a car that was abandoned at a boat club. DeMeo wouldn't be allowed to disappear the way his victims had—he was used to send a final message.

DeMeo associate Richard Kuklinski, also known as the Iceman, would also put Perotta to shame. Kuklinski was ten years old when his alcoholic father, Stanley, beat his older brother, Florian, to death. Young Richard and his mother lied about Florian's cause of death in order to protect Stanley from the law. By age fourteen, Kuklinski had committed a murder of his own. Before his career came to an end, he claimed credit for at least 130; some sources put it closer to 200.

Kuklinski's favorite murder weapon was cyanide, because it was hard to detect postmortem. But he was flexible, so he also used guns, knives, chain saws, and even a crossbow on at least one occasion. In his nearly scientific quest for murderous perfection, he sometimes froze the bodies of his victims to disguise their times of death, thereby earning himself the nickname the Iceman.

Kuklinski died in prison in 2006, reportedly of natural causes, but he was preparing to testify against Gambino family underboss Sammy Gravano. After the Iceman's death, the charges against Gravano were dropped for lack of evidence.

Although people like Roy DeMeo and Richard Kuklinski— and the fictional characters Vincent Perotta and Tony "Basola" Mecacci, the Mob enforcers from "Reckoner" (503)—are not typically counted among the ranks of serial killers, they share many traits with them. Most notably, they suffer from a sociopathic lack of empathy. They feel no remorse about their victims, no sense of loss about lives snuffed out before their time. DeMeo and Kuklinski killed more for business reasons than personal ones, but they couldn't have racked up the body counts they did if they weren't supremely damaged human beings. In Kuklinski's case, especially, the cause of that damage is obvious. Both men were, as the title of the episode suggests, natural-born killers.

Sexual Predators: Female Victims

THE MOST FREQUENTLY encountered unsubs on *Criminal Minds* are sexual predators. This might be because their particularly heinous crimes make dramatic television. When sex and death are mixed up, the result can be prolific serial killers whose fantasies lead them to kill and who refuse to stop. Some serial sexual predators focus on women, whereas others prey on men. What they have in common is the overriding urge behind their actions. They're killing out of lust, and in most cases they're powerless to stop themselves.

1 **ONE KILLER** who broke that final rule—who stopped himself cold, once he had dispatched the person at whom his anger was really directed—was Edmund Kemper, the Santa Cruz contemporary of Herbert Mullin's. Kemper, the Coed Killer, is referred to by Aaron Hotchner as an example of a spree killer in the *Criminal Minds* episode "Charm and Harm" (120) and again, by David Rossi, as a killer with some characteristics similar to those of the unsub in "Penelope" (309).

Edmund Emil Kemper III was born on December 18, 1948, and it wouldn't be long until he killed his first victims—his own grandparents. Since his parents' antagonistic relationship had ended in divorce, Kemper's psychological problems—no doubt intensified by living with a mother, Clarnell Kemper, who constantly belittled and demeaned him—grew worse. He had two sisters, one older and one younger, and he used to play a death-ritual game with the younger in which he would pretend to be strapped into a chair in a gas chamber. She would release the poisonous gas, and he would struggle and writhe until he "died." When his sister teased him about a crush on a female teacher, he said, "If I kiss her I would have to kill her first." He was already, at a young age, beginning to have fantasies that interwove murder and sex.

When Kemper was an adult, he was six feet nine and weighed almost three hundred pounds. But when he was a child, his mother, fearing that her already oversized son would sexually assault his sisters, made him move his belongings into the basement and sleep there, locked in. Her various marital adventures didn't help; Kemper's successive stepfathers didn't know how to deal with the troubled boy. Kemper ran away and tried living with his natural father briefly, but he wasn't wanted there, either. When he was fifteen, he was sent to live on his paternal grandparents' remote California ranch.

Things went bad one day in August 1964 while his grandfather, the first Edmund Emil Kemper, was out. The boy was at home with his grandmother when an uncontrollable urge came over him. He shot her in the back of the head, then stabbed her several times. When his grandfather drove up to the house, Kemper decided to spare him the sight of his murdered wife and shot him to death before he ever made it into the house. Alone, Kemper called his mother, then the police. After he was arrested, he explained, "I just wanted to see

In "Penelope," Agents Hotchner, Reid, Prentiss, and Jareau gather to help Garcia (center) after she is targeted by a serial killer.

what it would feel like to shoot Grandma," and he expressed sorrow that he had missed the opportunity to undress her.

These murders resulted in Kemper being sent to Atascadero State Hospital, a maximum-security facility for the mentally ill. Testing showed him to be a paranoid schizophrenic and to have a near-genius IQ. Kemper hid his inner turmoil and became an assistant to one of the hospital's psychologists, even administering psychological tests on the doctor's behalf. What he learned about the testing was to stand him in good stead when it was time for his own examination. After less than five years in the hospital, he was deemed an acceptable risk and released into his mother's care.

By this time Clarnell had found a job on the campus of the University of California at Santa Cruz. She let Kemper move back in with her. He applied for a job with the California Highway Patrol, but he was too tall. Instead, he found employment with the state highway department and started hanging out at restaurants and bars frequented by cops. He was smart, had a good sense of humor, and could carry on a conversation, so he was accepted by the police officers he met.

The urges Kemper had felt earlier were returning, perhaps heightened by the fact that he was living with his abusive mother again. Finally he saved up enough money to rent a place in Alameda with a friend. During this time, he was building up to the acts that would make him infamous. He went out driving, picking up dozens of female hitchhikers—of which no shortage existed in early 1970s California—and learning how to put them at ease.

The time came to make his fantasies real. On May 7, 1972, Kemper picked up two college girls, Mary Ann Pesce and Anita Luchessa, who were hitchhiking to Stanford University. Kemper tooled around with them for a while, then pulled onto a deserted country road. There he handcuffed Pesce to the seat, locked Luchessa in the trunk, and stabbed them both to death. He hauled them up to Alameda, and in the privacy of his apartment he decapitated Luchessa. He removed Pesce's clothes and dissected her, cut off her head, and sexually assaulted some of the body parts he had strewn about the room. He dumped the bodies in the mountains, remembering the spot so he could visit later. After keeping both heads for a time, he tossed them into a ravine. He photographed the whole affair with a Polaroid camera.

His fantasy fulfilled for the time being, Kemper kept picking up hitchhikers without harming them—until September 14. On that day he spotted fifteen-year-old Aiko Koo hitchhiking, so he stopped, enticed her into his car, and took her to a rural road. He strangled the girl into unconsciousness and raped her. When she started coming to before he was finished, he strangled her to death and continued. With Koo's body in his trunk, he paid his mother a visit, then took his "prize" home for dissection. The next day, he had an appointment with a psychiatrist; according to some accounts, while he was inside convincing the doctor that all was well with him, Koo's head sat in his trunk.

Another four-month stretch passed, during which time Kemper bought a .22 caliber pistol. On January 8, 1973, his victim was Cindy Schall, a hitchhiking college student. He killed her with one shot to the head, then took her to his mother's house, put her in a closet, and went to bed. In the morning, after his mother left for work, he took the corpse out of the closet, had sex with it, and dissected it, then washed the blood away in the bathtub, placed the pieces in plastic bags, and threw them off a cliff into the ocean. He buried Schall's head in the yard so that it would be gazing up at his mother's bedroom window, because, he explained, Clarnell always liked to think people "looked up to her."

Less than a month went by before Kemper struck again. This time, he went onto the university campus and picked up two separate hitchhikers, Rosalind Thorpe and Alice Liu. Shooting them both on campus, he drove through the guard station at the campus gates with the bodies sitting upright in the car, then moved them into the trunk when he was safely past. At his mother's house, he decapitated both girls, then carried the heads into his room to sexually assault them.

On March 4, body parts began turning up. Santa Cruz police had recently arrested Herbert Mullin and yet a third Santa Cruz murderer, John Linley Frazier, but when the University of California at Santa Cruz girls disappeared, the authorities knew that a killer still operated in their vicinity. Kemper had kept up his relationship with cops, getting regular reports on how the investigations were proceeding.

He was growing concerned, however. There was a bullet hole in his car and a lot of blood inside it. He bought a new handgun, a .44, and a sheriff's officer who saw the paperwork and remembered Kemper's earlier conviction decided to visit him at his apartment. Kemper handed over the .44 but kept his .22. He didn't know if the officer had looked inside his car, however, or what other dots he might have connected. It was time to bring his murderous streak to an end—but not before he killed his most significant victim.

On Good Friday, April 20, 1973, Kemper went to his mother's house. When she got home from work, they talked, and their discussion became an argument. He let her go to bed, and at around 5:15 a.m. he carried a claw hammer into her room, as he had fantasized about doing many times. He hit her in the head with the hammer, then slashed her throat. Once she was dead he decapitated her, handcuffed her wrists, and put her in the closet. He argued with her head, threw darts at it, and removed the larynx, which he tried to shove down the garbage disposal. The disposal spat it back out. "Even when she was dead, she was still bitching at me," he later said. "I couldn't get her to shut up!" Back in her room, he had sex with her corpse.

He knew that suspicion would fall on him; he had, after all, murdered his own grandparents. But he thought that if there were two victims, his guilt wouldn't be as obvious. Later in the day, he called his mother's friend Sandy Hallett and invited her to dinner. When she arrived, he clubbed, strangled, and decapitated her and left her body in his bed. He slept in his mother's bed, with her corpse lying beside him.

Still unsettled, Kemper drove to Reno, Nevada, rented a different car, and kept going. In Colorado he was pulled over, but he was chagrined to learn it was for speeding, not as part of a nationwide manhunt. Finally he called the Santa Cruz police, directing them to look in his mother's house. At first, knowing "Big Ed," they thought he was joking. It took a second call before they believed him.

Back home, he confessed to all of his murders. His public defender tried an insanity defense, which Kemper abetted by claiming that he had sliced off flesh from some of his victims, cooked it with macaroni, and eaten it—a claim he later recanted, saying it had been intended only to bolster the insanity plea. It was hard to convince a jury that someone as smart and personable as Ed Kemper was insane, and he was found guilty on eight counts of first-degree murder. The judge asked what he thought was appropriate punishment, and Kemper suggested that he be tortured to death. Instead, he was sentenced to life imprisonment, and he remains locked up today.

Ed Kemper's motivations for his crimes were many. He couldn't conceive of a healthy sexual relationship with a woman. He wanted to possess the pretty girls he saw all around him, who his mother said were so much better than he was that he didn't stand a chance. Early in life, he had twisted up his brain's sex-and-death wiring. But he also wanted revenge against his mother, and some believe that if he had simply killed her first, he might have spared others a great deal of suffering.

2 **JAMES MITCHELL** "Mike" DeBardeleben has been mentioned only once on *Criminal Minds*, in the episode "Zoe's Reprise" (415), as one of the subjects of a book by profiler David Rossi, *Deviance: The Secret Desires of Sadistic Serial Killers*. DeBardeleben is definitely an appropriate subject for that book.

Initially, his case was investigated by the Secret Service, because in addition to being a sexual sadist and a serial killer, he was a counterfeiter known as the Mall Passer. He traveled the country using fake bills to make small purchases at malls and get substantial change in real currency. In two years, he had hit thirty-eight states and passed about thirty thousand dollars in funny money. The Treasury Department wanted him badly. It finally got ahead of him, figuring out where he might go next and alerting merchants in the malls he might hit.

In Knoxville, Tennessee, on March 25, 1983, an alert store clerk reported DeBardeleben. The authorities moved in, and the Mall Passer found himself busted.

The suspect clammed up. His ID said one thing, and his car registration said something else altogether. It took the FBI's fingerprint analysis to hang his real name on him: Mike DeBardeleben. Once the Secret Service had that information, they realized they'd arrested him once before, for passing fake hundred-dollar bills in 1976, a rap that earned him two years of federal time.

The car he'd been driving in Knoxville contained drugs, pornography, phony IDs, fake money, and the goods he'd bought with the latter. What they didn't have was his printing equipment, what the Secret Service calls a counterfeiter's "plant." They needed to search his home in Alexandria, Virginia.

All they found, however, were dirty dishes and more small purchases made with bogus bills—no printing press, no plates. Three agents stayed behind when the others left, determined to find something. Greg Mertz picked up DeBardeleben's phone book and flipped through the yellow pages.

There he found that a card had been slipped between two pages in the "Moving and Storage" section. He showed his colleagues, and they canvassed the nearby storage facilities. At one, the manager recognized DeBardeleben's picture and opened up his unit.

Inside, they found much counterfeit money, a single printing plate, bubble lights for posing as law enforcement, drugs and drug paraphernalia, and much more. They also found things that hinted at another pastime they hadn't known about: a bloody chain, women's phone numbers and addresses, panties, a dildo, handcuffs, and lubricant. They also found hundreds of sexually explicit photographs—stills that showed what kind of man they'd captured. Audiotapes made it all real in an even more horrible way.

What DeBardeleben had recorded were torture sessions. His voice could be heard, along with the voices of women in intense agony, begging their captor to stop what he was doing or kill them and be done with it. The victims who survived his attacks reported a man who was obsessed with causing pain, who forced them to perform the most degrading acts imaginable, and who photographed it all and threatened to make the photos public if they told anyone.

With this information, the Secret Service began to track DeBardeleben's movements during the last few years. None of what they found was pleasant.

DeBardeleben was a pure sexual sadist, the kind that is categorized as an anger-excitation rapist. He had murdered at least two women and possibly many more; however, by the time he was sentenced to 375 years in prison on rape, kidnapping, robbery, sodomy, and forgery charges, the prosecutors from other vicinities decided not to bother pursuing convictions on the murders. Not only had DeBardeleben recorded his crimes on audiotape and in photographs, he had also filled notebook after notebook with his own writings, a diary of perversity that stunned all who read it.

Anger-excitation rapists are the most dangerous kind of rapist, because the suffering of their victims is what stimulates them sexually. That is, it's not the act of inflicting pain that they respond to; it's the suffering of their victims from that pain. Edmund Kemper was not a sexual sadist, because his dismemberment of his victims was postmortem. A sexual sadist like DeBardeleben wouldn't bother with that—once the victim is beyond pain, there's no point to it. Former FBI profiler Roy Hazelwood, who has done in-depth studies of sexual sadism, calls sexual sadists "the great white shark of sexual crimes."

DeBardeleben was born on March 20, 1940, in Little Rock, Arkansas. His father was rigid and controlling, and his mother was an alcoholic who punished him frequently and whom DeBardeleben started beating up when he reached his teens. His younger brother eventually committed suicide. His first arrest, on a weapons charge, was at age sixteen. He joined the army but was court-martialed and booted out. He was married five times, and he treated his wives as horribly as he treated his victims, bending them to his will, punishing them, and making them participate in his criminal activities.

DeBardeleben made tapes on which he played both roles, running through a script dictated by his own internal fantasies and acting out the role of the victim, begging for mercy and screaming in pain. He also sometimes dressed in women's clothing when acting out these fantasies.

But it's his writings that are most illuminating. "The wish to inflict pain on others is not the essence of sadism," DeBardeleben wrote. "The central impulse is to have complete mastery over another person, to make him/her a helpless object of our will, to become the absolute ruler over her, to become her god, to do with her as one pleases, to humiliate her, to enslave her are means to this end. And the most radical aim is to make her suffer. Since there is no greater power over another person than that of inflicting pain on her. To force her to undergo suffering without her being able to defend herself. The pleasure in the complete domination of another person is the very essence of the sadistic drive."

Fortunately, the Secret Service agents arrested DeBardeleben when they did, because if he had been able to continue his activities, these would only have gotten worse. Sexual sadists begin developing their fantasies at a young age and typically begin acting them out in early adulthood, but throughout the years they become more violent and bizarre. DeBardeleben had been at it for a while before his 1983 arrest, but he was only in his early forties, and he would not have stopped.

On one occasion he made a tape recording of some of his goals: to create false identities, to buy a house and land on which he could build a structure suited especially for his rapes and murders, and finally, "also of prime importance—top priority—would be an incinerator capable of incinerating at extremely high temperature—total incineration." Had he achieved these goals, there's no telling how many women would have disappeared, never to be seen again.

During their hunt for the unsub in "Zoe's Reprise" (415), members of the BAU mention potential similarities between the victims and the victims of several other sexual predators in addition to DeBardeleben: Jeffrey Dahmer, Robert Berdella, David Berkowitz, Jack the Ripper, Altemio Sanchez, the Hillside Stranglers (cousins Angelo Buono and Kenneth Bianchi), the Mad Butcher of Kingsbury Run (also known as the Cleveland Torso Murderer), and Dennis Rader (the BTK Killer).

The Mad Butcher of Kingsbury Run has never been identified. During the 1930s, he murdered between twelve and forty people in Cleveland, Ohio, dismembering, decapitating, and occasionally cutting his victims in half, as the infamous Black Dahlia Killer did in Los Angeles in 1947. Famed detective Eliot Ness failed to catch the Mad Butcher. One of the strongest suspects was Dr. Francis E. Sweeney, who voluntarily committed himself and remained hospitalized until his death in 1965. After Sweeney took himself off the streets, the bloody murders stopped.

3 **NO U.S. SERIAL** killer and sexual predator has been convicted of killing as many women as Gary Ridgway, the Green River Killer, has. On *Criminal Minds*, he merits four mentions, in the episodes "Unfinished Business" (115), "The Perfect Storm" (203), "About Face" (306), and "Catching Out" (405).

In "About Face," women see their faces printed on posters that say, "Have you seen me?" Shortly after the appearance of the posters, the women are murdered. The first victim is found sexually assaulted and with her face removed, weighted, and dumped in a creek.

Although Gary Ridgway didn't remove his victims' faces or taunt them with posters of themselves, he was an aggressive predator who dumped his victims' bodies in water. Beginning in July 1982, women—most of them prostitutes and teenagers—disappeared from the streets of King County, Washington. Later that month, their bodies started to turn up.

The first was that of Wendy Coffield, sixteen, who was spotted by boys bicycling near the Green River. Coffield was Ridgway's first confirmed victim, although he has claimed that there were at least five victims before her. Coffield was found naked except for shoes and socks. She had been strangled.

Debra Bonner, twenty-two, came next. Like Coffield, she worked as a prostitute. Her body was discovered snagged on a logjam in the river.

On August 1, a third prostitute, Marcia Chapman, thirty-one, vanished. That was followed on August 11 by the disappearance of a fourth prostitute, Cynthia Hinds, seventeen. The next day—the day Debra Bonner's body was found—a sixteen-year-old prostitute named Opal Mills disappeared.

A man rafting on the Green River on August 15 spotted two bodies in the river and called the police. They found Chapman and Hinds, nude and pinned by boulders to the river bottom. Both women had rocks inserted into their vaginas. On the banks nearby the police found Mills.

King County law enforcement officials realized early that they had a serial killer in their midst, and they put together Washington State's biggest task force since the Ted Bundy days of the 1970s.

The next victim, fifteen-year-old Debra Estes, also a prostitute, disappeared in September and wasn't found for six years.

Throughout the next several years, the crimes continued, and more bodies appeared in King County's wooded, remote areas. Most of the victims were teenagers, and most were found nude. Some bodies weren't discovered for a year or more. Generally, Ridgway hid his victims in clusters so he wouldn't forget where he had put them. Every time a dump site was compromised, he chose a new one.

Sometimes Ridgway took pains to disguise his activities. Carol Christensen, twenty-one, was a waitress, not a prostitute. Her body had been posed. She was fully dressed, and he had put two trout on her breasts, a bottle of wine between her legs, and a sausage in her hands. Ridgway later admitted that he was trying to throw off the task force. Experts believed that the killer was making a reference to the Last Supper, but in fact the items were just things Ridgway happened to have on hand. Semen found in Christensen was eventually linked to Ridgway. Throughout the years, he tried tricks such as planting cigarette butts and used chewing gum near the bodies—he neither smoked nor chewed gum. He even took two bodies to Oregon, hoping to persuade the authorities that the killer had moved away from King County.

In 1984, a victim finally escaped Ridgway's clutches. A prostitute named Rebecca Garde Guay was performing oral sex on him when he claimed that she had bitten him, and suddenly he brutally attacked her. He got her in a choke hold, but she broke free and raced to a nearby trailer. She told the police that in order to prove that he wasn't a cop, the man had shown her an employee ID card from the Kenworth Motor Truck Company, where Ridgway had worked for more than thirty years. She described Ridgway and his truck, and when she was shown a photomontage, she identified him.

Ridgway was picked up in February 1985, and a task force detective questioned him. He admitted to the event, claiming that he frequented prostitutes and had become angry when Guay bit him. She decided against pressing charges, and Ridgway was released.

This was his second encounter with the task force. In 1983, a witness described a truck like Ridgway's in connection with the disappearance of prostitute Marie Malvar. Since Ridgway had been seen in the areas where prostitutes worked, he was questioned then. But the witness's description had been vague, and Ridgway denied ever having met Malvar, so the investigators had nowhere to go with the interrogation.

Ridgway easily passed a polygraph test. As a county prosecutor later explained, the Green River Killer's psychopathology was such that he saw nothing wrong with murdering women, so he didn't go into the test with the anxiety that one would normally have when lying.

The detectives questioned him several more times, and once, in 1987, they served a search warrant on his home, his workplace, and several vehicles. They collected ropes, plastic tarps, and paint chips; they analyzed his financial data; and they even took a saliva sample, but they found nothing that tied him directly to any of the bodies. Again, they turned their attention elsewhere.

Meanwhile, the body count kept rising. Ridgway claimed that he would have killed more if it hadn't been for the trouble of dumping the bodies.

His typical method was to cruise areas that prostitutes were known to frequent. If he saw one he liked, and there were no witnesses around, he would invite her into his truck. Sometimes he kept a spare tire in the front seat as an excuse for why they couldn't have sex in the truck and would have to go to his house or some remote wooded location. He would show his identification to make the woman trust him—knowing that he was going to kill her anyway—and he would often let her see a picture of his son in his wallet. He believed that if the woman knew he had a son, she wouldn't think he was going to hurt her.

Whether these women went to his home or to the woods, he would have sex with the woman, usually from behind. After he had achieved orgasm, he would snake his right arm around her neck and strangle her to death. Later in his career he started using ligatures to bind the women so they wouldn't injure him as they struggled.

When a woman scratched him, he'd clip her nails to remove his skin from underneath them. If witnesses saw a woman get into his truck, he often went ahead with the "date" without murdering her, figuring that if the prostitutes saw him around from time to time, they wouldn't be worried when he stopped for them. On those occasions, however, he had to find another victim right away.

Sometimes he had intercourse with the bodies of the women after he killed them, sometimes until the smell of decomposition or the presence of flies made it too distasteful even for him. After he killed them, he disposed of their clothes. Their clothing—like the women themselves—was garbage at that point. He'd had what he wanted from the women, so they were worthless. He occasionally stole their jewelry and left it in the women's bathroom where he worked, so that other women would take it. Seeing new women wearing the jewelry that he had taken from his victims aroused him.

Ridgway, who was white, did not discriminate by race. Most of his victims were white, but many were also Asian or black. The common thread was that most were high-risk victims—their lives as prostitutes regularly put them in dangerous situations.

Ridgway's period of greatest "productivity" was between 1982 and 1984. After 1987, the murders tapered off almost completely. Between 1985 and 1991, more than forty prostitutes were murdered in San Diego, California, under circumstances that made the authorities wonder if the Green River Killer had moved south. Most of those murders have not been solved, but Ridgway never confessed to them, and no evidence links him to those crimes.

Improvements in DNA analysis technology finally led authorities back to Ridgway in 2001. The saliva sample he gave matched the semen that was taken from Christensen and the DNA evidence found on Chapman, Hinds, and Mills. With that evidence in hand, the task force arrested Ridgway, and he started confessing to the other murders.

Gary Leon Ridgway was born on February 18, 1949. There were some early signs that not all was right with the boy. He wet the bed well into his teens. He was sexually attracted to his mother and fantasized about murdering her. When he was sixteen, he stabbed a six-year-old boy, who recovered after surgery for his internal damage. Ridgway was married twice in relatively short order. His second wife claimed that he would sometimes come home late at night inexplicably dirty or wet, and as the marriage progressed he came home later and later. He once put her in a choke hold, and he demanded frequent sex, often outdoors, in locations where it was later determined he had hidden bodies. After his arrest, he declared that if he had just strangled his second wife when he had the chance, it might have saved fifty or more lives.

Ridgway met his third wife in 1985 and married her in 1988, and he was still married when he was arrested. Some have speculated that it was her influence, somehow calming Ridgway, that led to the decrease in victims during those years. He admits that he never stopped soliciting prostitutes, however, and claims to have kept killing through the 1990s.

Although Ridgway was convicted of murdering forty-eight women, he claims there are more victims, as many as sixty. He led investigators to dump sites where previously unknown bodies were found, but for the most part he doesn't remember details about the women he murdered. They were just objects to be used and discarded.

Ridgway adamantly insisted that he was never a rapist, that all the sex he'd had with his victims—including, presumably, post-mortem—had been consensual. And he wasn't a monster, he said, because he didn't torture them. He said he was "good in one thing, and that's killin' prostitutes," an activity that he referred to as his "career." His idea of regret or remorse was to feel sorry that he had been caught. In the end, science nailed him—he's spending the rest of his life in the Washington State Penitentiary in Walla Walla.

4 **GARY RIDGWAY** is far from alone in targeting prostitutes, the number one prey for serial killers. *Criminal Minds* doesn't neglect this common prey; episodes that focus at least in part on the murder of prostitutes include "The Last Word" (209), "Sex, Birth, Death" (211), "Legacy" (222), and the pair of episodes that wraps up the fourth season, "To Hell . . ." (425) and ". . . And Back" (426). While Ridgway plied the wilderness area of King County, Washington, a similar serial killer was working around an entirely different river—the Genesee—in New York State.

The first female corpse to show up in the Genesee River Gorge broke through the ice and was found by a hunting party on March 24, 1988. She was identified as Dorothy Blackburn, a prostitute from nearby Rochester. She had been strangled and badly beaten, with teeth marks around her genital area.

In September 1989, more bodies started turning up, and they came faster than ever in October.

The Rochester police understood that a serial killer was at work, so they went out to the prostitutes in the area and solicited their cooperation. One woman, Jo Ann Van Nostrand, told a story about a strange john she had been with. He called himself Mitch, and he referred to "the Genesee River Strangler" several times in their conversation. He wanted her to lie still and play dead while they had sex. He seemed nervous, which made her nervous, and she showed him the knife she carried. He tried to hire her again after that night, but she avoided him.

Although the hookers were forewarned, they kept disappearing. One woman's body was found with leaves stuffed down her throat. Another woman, who was not a prostitute, turned up badly mutilated, gutted from the breasts to the pubic area, with her labia removed. The police weren't sure how this woman, June Stott, fit into the case, since the victimology was so different and the mutilation so much more severe than they'd seen before.

The Rochester police called in the FBI. By New Year's Day, 1990, there were more missing women. Most of the ones who had turned up were buried, submerged in the river, or otherwise made invisible from above—a skill that made the police believe that their man might have law enforcement experience or a previous record—but they wanted to find the bodies, if they could, so as a last-ditch effort they tried a helicopter search. Despite the uncooperative weather, one last helicopter lifted off for a final sweep of the area in which the first body had turned up.

The police got lucky. Near a bridge they saw a female body flattened on the ice, naked except for a white top. On the bridge was a car, and a man stood close to it, urinating.

The body belonged to a streetwalker named June Cicero. Her genital area had been sawed into, possibly after she was frozen.

The police wanted to talk to the man with his pants unzipped. The helicopter followed his car when he left, and some patrol units joined in. When the man parked at a nursing home, the patrol officers grabbed the driver. He identified himself as Arthur John Shawcross, and he assumed that he'd earned the overwhelming police presence for urinating in the woods. He didn't have a driver's license, and he admitted that he had once been in jail for manslaughter.

Under further questioning, Shawcross told them that the trouble he'd been in before, in Watertown, New York, involved two kids who had died. Since Shawcross turned out to be an almost pathological liar, it was some time before the police got the whole story. He had befriended a young boy who lived across the street and had taken him fishing. The next day the boy disappeared. Shortly thereafter, an eight-year-old girl disappeared; her body turned up, bearing signs of anal rape and with leaves and mud jammed down her throat, under a bridge where Shawcross frequently fished. He ultimately confessed to both crimes and led the police to the boy's body.

Shawcross had been convicted, but he had been a model prisoner, deemed not a threat to society, and released after fifteen years. Parole officers tried to place him in a couple of different cities, but because of the heinous nature of his crimes, the locals resisted. Finally they settled him in Rochester and made it impossible for anyone—even the local police—to access his criminal record.

The Rochester cops were furious. If they had known about the convicted murderer and sex offender in their midst, they would have had a starting point for their investigation much earlier.

Shawcross confessed to the prostitute murders, but he tried to blame them all on events outside his control, and his lawyers used an insanity defense. Shawcross's stories were all over the map. He claimed to have been a super-soldier of some kind in Vietnam and to have suffered post-traumatic stress disorder as a result, but a little checking showed that he had never witnessed, much less taken part in, the wartime atrocities he had described. He said that he had been a bed-wetter and a pyromaniac, the son of an abusive mother, yet other family members denied those claims. It was a fact that he had dropped out of school at nineteen, when he had finally made it to ninth grade, but that only proved that he was not very bright.

In the trial preparation, a test showed that Shawcross had an extra Y chromosome, a condition once called the *criminal karyotype* and believed to cause antisocial, aggressive behavior and low intelligence. Later research disproved this, but some people still cling to it as an excuse for criminal acts (as did fictional murderer Henry Grace, in the *Criminal Minds* episode "Masterpiece" [408]).

Finally, Shawcross was convicted on ten counts of murder (although his body count might be as high as sixteen) and sentenced to ten consecutive twenty-five-years-to-life sentences. He would have been eligible for parole after serving a mere 250 years, but he died of a pulmonary embolism on November 10, 2008.

5 **ROBERT HANSEN** was yet another prostitute killer, albeit one with a more colorful MO. Reminiscent of the deranged brothers in the episode "Open Season" (221), Hansen hunted for sport.

Hansen's early life was marked by terrible acne, a stutter, and domineering parents who forced the naturally left-handed boy to use his right hand, a stress that he claims made his stutter even worse. He had few friends in high school and no girlfriends. He became an occasional shoplifter; this turned into a habit that would persist into his later years.

After finishing high school, Hansen joined the army, then went to work as a drill instructor at a police academy in Iowa. He had been married for a short time when his rage got the best of him and he burned down a school bus garage, supposedly in revenge for all the slights his town had visited upon him. His wife, humiliated, divorced him. Hansen served twenty months of a three-year sentence. A few months after being paroled, he married again.

The Hansens decided to make a new start in life, and in 1967 they moved to Anchorage, Alaska. The final frontier seemed like a good match for a guy who had never fit in anywhere. Hansen became well known as a hunter, setting records with his rifle and his bow. His trophy room filled up with animal heads. After committing insurance fraud and acquiring an easy thirteen thousand dollars, he opened a bakery in town.

But Hansen had another pastime that he didn't tell his wife about. Anchorage's Fourth Avenue was a hotbed of strip clubs and bars in which prostitutes plied their trade, and Hansen often visited them. Quick, impersonal sex didn't turn out to be enough to satisfy his lust, however. At some point, probably around 1971, he turned violent and murdered one of the hookers. He discovered that he liked it.

He committed more murders and began dumping the corpses of the women in a wilderness area. Then another idea came to him—a way to combine his dual passions. He would offer a prostitute a couple of hundred dollars for oral sex—which he claimed he would never ask of his respectable wife—and once the act was under way, he would handcuff the woman, take her someplace and brutally rape her, then fly her into the wilderness. There he would let the woman, usually unclothed, run off. After giving her a head start, he would hunt her down and kill her, leaving the body lost in the wild. Hookers and topless dancers made good prey, since their absences often went unreported.

Hansen was arrested in 1977 for stealing a chain saw, and he was diagnosed with bipolar affective disorder. Although he was ordered to take lithium, the order wasn't enforced, and he stopped taking his meds. The authorities didn't know there was a serial killer working their turf. Hansen wasn't suspected of anything more serious than property theft.

He was finally accused of rape on June 13, 1982. Hansen had pulled his usual routine: hiring a prostitute, cuffing her, and pulling a gun. He took her to his home, where he raped her, bit her breasts, and forced a hammer into her vagina. After immobilizing her, he rested from his travails. When he awoke, he informed her that he was going to fly her into the backcountry for more "fun." If she cooperated, he would bring her back to Anchorage.

The woman was no fool; she realized that because the man had kidnapped her and raped her in his own home, making no effort to conceal his identity, he would never let her live. So while Hansen was loading the plane, the woman saw a chance to escape and ran, still in handcuffs, toward a passing truck. Hansen chased her, but when the truck driver saw her and stopped for her, Hansen turned away.

The police were called, and the woman described the man who had taken her. The cops recognized the description as sounding like local businessman Robert Hansen. They showed her his home and his airplane, and she confirmed both.

When the detectives paid Hansen a visit, he denied everything. "You can't rape a prostitute, can you?" he asked. He said that his wife and two kids were in Europe for the summer, but he'd had dinner with two business associates. His alibi checked out, and the investigation stalled.

During the next year, more bodies of strippers and hookers turned up in the wilderness. Whenever the cause of death could be determined, it was found that the victim had been shot. A single .223 shell casing was found at one of the scenes.

Remembering the complaint against Hansen, the detectives decided to take another look at him. They brought FBI profiler John Douglas up from the lower forty-eight and asked him to profile their suspect. He did so, based on the information that was available, and it was a close match to Hansen, right down to the stutter. He also told them that since the man was both a hunter and a serial killer, he probably kept trophies—not animal heads mounted on a wall, but clothing, jewelry, and the like, which he might give away or stash in the house.

With Douglas's profile in hand, the cops got the district attorney to authorize a grand jury investigation. Then they went back to the men who had buttressed Hansen's alibi and warned them that if they lied they would be looking at serious jeopardy. Both men changed their stories, and Hansen's alibi fell apart.

Hansen was arrested. The authorities took the profile to a judge and were granted a search warrant for Hansen's property; this was the first time a criminal profile had ever been used to support a search-warrant request. In Hansen's house, they found jewelry and identification belonging to some of the victims, as well as a .223 caliber Ruger Mini-14 hunting rifle that was a ballistics match to the shell casing.

Hansen pleaded guilty to the four homicides the police could definitively connect him to, and as part of his plea deal, he showed them seventeen grave sites in the Knik River Valley. Twelve of the sites were ones that the authorities hadn't known about, and human remains were discovered in most of them. Ultimately, the police connected Hansen to twenty-one murders, and they believed that there could be more.

Robert Hansen is serving a 461-year prison sentence at the Spring Creek Correctional Center in Seward, Alaska. His big-game hunting days are far behind him, and his name has been expunged from the record books.

6 **YET ANOTHER PROSTITUTE** murderer who earns a mention on *Criminal Minds* is Joel Rifkin, who is brought up in the episode "Charm and Harm" (120) as an example of a criminal who was also an amateur photographer. Rifkin was busted because of a minor violation—driving a pickup truck with no license plate—in East Meadow, Long Island, on June 28, 1993. Instead of pulling over, he tried to flee, so the patrol officers called for reinforcements and gave chase. His truck missed a turn and smashed into a lamppost, and the driver finally surrendered.

The cops noticed a foul odor coming from beneath a tarp in the truck's bed. Underneath, they found the decomposing, plastic-wrapped body of Tiffany Bresciani, twenty-two years old. Rifkin, thirty-four, explained her presence by saying that she was a prostitute. He had sex with her and then killed her. "Do you think I need a lawyer?" he asked. As it turned out, he did.

Later that day, the authorities searched the house that Rifkin shared with his mother. They found women's clothing and jewelry, purses and wallets, and several photographs of women. He also had books on the as-yet-unsolved Green River Killer and articles about prostitute-murderer Shawcross. In the garage the police found rope and a tarp, plus a chain saw with bits of human flesh stuck in the teeth and a wheelbarrow that contained human blood.

Once Rifkin was in custody, it didn't take long for his tale to emerge. Bresciani, he revealed, was actually his seventeenth murder victim, making him New York's most prolific serial killer. Bludgeoning and strangling his victims, he was then creative in hiding their bodies. His first victim, in 1989, he dismembered, putting her head in a paint can and the rest of her in garbage bags that he spread throughout New Jersey and New York. The next victim he chopped up and put into cans that he filled with fresh concrete, then tossed into the East River.

Dismemberment proved to be too much effort, so after that Rifkin left the bodies whole and simply stashed them inside containers of some sort—oil drums were a favorite. He patronized prostitutes nearly every night, spending almost all of the money he earned on them, but his murders were relatively selective. Rifkin, who was white, victimized white, Asian, Latina, and African American women of various ages.

At the trial, the prosecutor described Rifkin as a sexual sadist who got his satisfaction from causing his victims pain. The jury agreed, and he's now ensconced at the Clinton Correctional Facility, better known as Dannemora, in New York. With a 203-year sentence, he'll be eligible for parole in 2197.

Rifkin, like many other sexual predators, had an abiding interest in photography, and the photographs that were found in his bedroom helped to convict him of his crimes. In the *Criminal Minds* episode "Reckoner" (503), profiler Emily Prentiss says, "Serial killers, especially sexual sadists, often document their kills." Mike DeBardeleben was also brought down partly by his photos of his many rape victims.

The man often thought of as the first of the modern signature killers (murderers whose crimes share some distinctive telltale commonality that can often be used to link them), Harvey Murray Glatman, also had a photography hobby. Known as the Lonely Hearts Killer, Glatman not only used photographs to fuel fantasies that mixed sex, bondage, and violence—which he often found in the pages of detective magazines—he also used photography itself as a way to lure his victims.

After moving to Los Angeles in 1957, Glatman joined a "lonely hearts club" of single people. From that and from the classified ads he ran in the newspapers, he found a ready pool of women who were willing to model for him in suggestive poses. These women didn't get their pictures in the magazines, as Glatman promised, but as Glatman's fantasies became ever more violent, they became the victims of his rapes. Having raped the women, he thought he was left with no choice but to murder them so they couldn't identify him.

Glatman's photo-bug habits tripped him up in the end. He photographed each victim at every stage of her torture and eventual death, and when those pictures were discovered, he broke down. His detailed confession proved to be a kind of entry-level manual for understanding the mind of a sexually sadistic serial killer. He was convicted of three murders and executed on September 18, 1959. A fourth victim, believed to be Glatman's earliest murder, was never identified, and her case remains officially unsolved.

7 **IN THE EPISODE** "Scared to Death" (303), real-life murderer Gary Taylor is used as an example of a serial killer whose

MO changes as his need to control his situation changes. Taylor used weapons as diverse as a wrench, a rifle, and a machete, and he went from sniping at unsuspecting women to using ruses and posing as an FBI agent to earn their trust.

Taylor, born in 1936, was institutionalized as a young man after nonfatal attacks on several women in Royal Oak, Michigan. His MO was to hang around bus stops waiting for likely victims, whom he clubbed over the head with a wrench. From there he took to shooting women who were out after dark, which led to his becoming known as the Royal Oak Sniper or the Phantom Sniper. He admitted to a "compulsion to hurt women," but he was nonetheless granted outpatient status and instructed to take his prescribed medication.

Eventually, of course, he stopped doing that, and then his murders began. While living in Michigan, Taylor abducted two women from Ohio, murdered them, and buried them in his yard. He then moved to Seattle, and his wife reported the two bodies buried in the Michigan yard and claimed that a third was buried there, too, but a third body was never found.

In Seattle Taylor killed another woman and buried her near his home there. The Seattle authorities picked him up, but the authorities in Michigan had not yet entered his name in the national database. Unable to charge Taylor with the Seattle murder and not knowing that he was wanted in Michigan, the police released him, and he vanished again.

After more travel, Taylor surfaced in Texas, where he changed his MO once again: raping his victims but letting them live. On May 20, 1975, he was arrested for a sexual assault in Houston, and he confessed to four homicides. The authorities in California, Texas, and Michigan think he might have been involved in up to twenty murders. He was sentenced to life in prison.

8 **AARON HOTCHNER,** in the episode "100" (509), beats serial killer George Foyet to death with his bare hands after Foyet kills Hotchner's wife, Haley. An investigation concludes that Hotchner was acting in self-defense and defending his four-year-old son, Jack, so no charges are brought against him. In an earlier episode, "Aftermath" (205), profiler Elle Greenaway shoots multiple rape suspect William Lee when the team can't amass the evidence necessary to convict him. She claims self-defense, and with no witnesses to dispute her story, she isn't charged, either, but she leaves the FBI.

Both acts could have been considered vigilantism, when the rules of law and order are bypassed in favor of a more immediate brand of justice. Greenaway actively went after Lee, and even though Hotchner was in the midst of the situation with the man who had kidnapped Haley and Jack (and had already murdered Haley), Hotchner could have arrested Foyet rather than killing him on the spot.

Joe Muller, in the episode "Retaliation" (511), is an ex-cop who helps ex-con Dale Schrader murder three people and evade the FBI. He's pressured into doing this because Schrader has abducted Muller's family and will murder them if Muller doesn't cooperate. Muller is, in fact, an honest man who got caught in a bad situation.

But sometimes good cops just plain go bad, like Deputy Sheriff John Clark Battle, who shoots Penelope Garcia, the team's technical analyst, in the episode "Lucky" (308) and is captured in "Penelope" (309).

Unfortunately, law enforcement officers who dishonor their badges aren't confined to fiction. Lucille Place of Fort Lauderdale, Florida, was concerned when her daughter Susan, who was seventeen, and Susan's sixteen-year-old friend, Georgia Jessup, went to the beach with an obviously older man. He said his name was Jerry Shepherd, and he was twenty-six. Place watched as he loaded the girls into his Datsun, and she wrote down the license plate number—but missing one digit. The date was September 27, 1972. Place never saw her daughter or Georgia alive again.

Because Place had the license plate number wrong, when she reported it to the police it didn't match up with anything. After six months, Lucille realized her mistake. When she added in the missing 2 from a county designation code, the match turned out to be a blue Datsun from Martin County. The car belonged to a jailed

Martin County deputy sheriff named Gerard John Schaefer. Place went to the jail where Schaefer was being held in March 1973, bearing a picture of her daughter, but he denied ever having seen her.

Schaefer was in jail because he had picked up two hitchhiking teenage girls earlier that summer. He warned them that he was a deputy sheriff, which was true, and that hitching a ride was illegal in Martin County, which was false. To keep them safe, he told them, he would drive them home, and the next morning he would personally take them to the beach.

He showed up in the morning, but instead of heading to the beach, he took the kids to a remote part of swampy, bug-infested Hutchinson Island. When the girls protested, he said he wanted to show them an old Spanish fort. He stopped in a wooded area, drew a gun, and told the girls that he meant to sell them into sexual slavery. Then he handcuffed and gagged them, slipped nooses around their necks, and had them balance on the bulbous roots of a tree while the other ends of the ropes were tied to the tree's branches. Should one of the girls slip off the root, she would be hanged.

That was as far as Schaefer got. He checked his watch and told the girls he had to run off for a little while, but he'd be back.

An investigation later showed that he had to go take care of police business. When he returned, in uniform and driving his official vehicle instead of his private car, the girls had escaped. He called his boss, Sheriff Richard Crowder, and confessed to trying to scare two teenagers out of hitchhiking, but perhaps he had let things go a little too far, he said.

Crowder fired Schaefer and then arrested him. The former deputy sheriff made bail and cut a deal, accepting a single charge of aggravated assault. He was sentenced to a year in jail, but with good behavior he could be out in six months.

Between Schaefer's arrest and his trial, while he was out on bail, he met Susan and Georgia. Two other pairs of young women also disappeared during that period. Had Place not had the presence of mind to jot down Schaefer's license plate number, Schaefer might have kept on making young women disappear.

Although Schaefer's childhood was relatively affluent and trauma-free, something in his early days twisted his ideas about sexuality. From the age of twelve, he liked women's panties and would masturbate while wearing them; soon he added the fillip of tying himself to a tree while wearing them, struggling to get free, and hurting himself, which he found incredibly arousing. At the age of fourteen he met his first real girlfriend and sexual partner, a girl who would have sex with him only during elaborate rape scenarios in which he would attack her and tear her clothes. When he tired of the rape games, she broke up with him.

He took to spending a lot of time in the Everglades by himself, hunting and exploring. He also started peeping in windows, especially those of a friend's sister, Leigh Hainline, who was two years older than Schaefer and who had a habit of undressing by a window with the curtains open. She later disappeared after claiming that a childhood friend was getting her a job with the Central Intelligence Agency.

The bones of Susan Place and Georgia Jessup turned up on Hutchinson Island in April 1973. Susan had a bullet hole through her jaw, and evidence at the crime scene indicated that the two girls had been butchered while tied to a tree. With that information, and Place's complaint identifying Schaefer's blue Datsun, the police obtained a search warrant for Schaefer's mother's home, where he lived.

His room was a treasure trove. The investigators found the belongings of seven different young women there, including Susan Place and others who had vanished as far back as 1969. The police discovered purses, clothing, jewelry, an address book, a passport, and two teeth that belonged to a missing woman named Carmen Hallock. In addition to items that had belonged to the missing women, the police found eleven guns and thirteen knives, photographs of yet more women who could not be identified, photos of Schaefer himself dressed in women's underwear, and page after page of Schaefer's perverse writings and drawings, in which he described the torture and murder of "whores" in painstaking detail. Some of his "artwork" consisted of magazine photos of women in perfectly innocent poses, which he cut out and positioned in collages to look as though they were being hanged.

Schaefer had explanations for everything. His writings, he said, had been his psychiatrist's idea; he had complained of disturbing fantasies and the doctor had recommended that he write everything down as a way of defusing them. Even though Schaefer probably would have written them down anyway, the doctor's instruction made most of the writing inadmissible in court, because it fell under doctor-patient privilege.

Schaefer was tried only for the murders of Susan Place and Georgia Jessup, but over the years, he has been suspected of between twenty-eight and thirty-five murders. He once claimed the true number was closer to 110, in several countries. A particular activity he liked to engage in was taking two victims at once.

"Doing doubles is far more difficult than doing singles," Schaefer wrote. "But on the other hand it also puts one in a position to have twice as much fun. There can be some lively discussions about which of the victims will get to be killed first. When you have a pair of teenaged bimbolinas bound hand and foot and ready for a session with the skinning knife, neither one of the little devils wants to be the one to go first. And they don't mind telling you quickly why their best friend should be the one to die."

Because Schaefer was never tried for other murders and is believed to have committed many to which he never confessed, no one knows for sure which of the girls and women who vanished in southern Florida during the late 1960s and early 1970s should be attributed to him. Some bodies have turned up, but others never have. The souvenirs found in Schaefer's room are the only signs that remain of some of the victims.

He did confess, in letters and works of fiction, to certain murders, including that of eight-year-old Wendy Stevenson and nine-year-old Peggy Rahn, both of whom disappeared in 1966, and about whom he wrote, "I assure you these girls were not molested sexually. I found both of them very satisfactory, particularly with sautéed onions and peppers." Since Schaefer was a notorious liar, the veracity of some of his confessions is suspect.

Schaefer was a narcissist of the first order. He considered himself superior to just about everyone he had ever met, including fellow serial killers Ted Bundy (who admitted to having been inspired by Schaefer to try a "double" in 1974) and Henry Lee Lucas's former partner and lover, Ottis Toole, both of whom Schaefer befriended in prison.

Schaefer insisted that his crimes were never sexually motivated, but that's either another lie or a sign of inadequate self-awareness. His writings and drawings clearly show that he was aroused by bondage and hanging, and evidence suggests that he not only sexually assaulted his victims' dead bodies, he also returned after burying them to dig them up and assault them again.

One document that the police found in Schaefer's mother's home was his step-by-step guide to committing the perfect murder, which included this tidbit: "Her panties should be pulled down enough to expose the genitals and clitoral stimulation applied. During the height of her excitement the support would be pulled away and she would dangle by her neck. She may be revived before death if desirable and subjected to further indecencies. After death has occurred the corpse should be violated if not violated already."

Whether Schaefer recognized it or not, his crimes were all about sex. Sexual predators develop elaborate sexual fantasies and are then driven to act them out. Schaefer's writings and art showed what his fantasies were. Had he really carried out his teenage fantasy of women's underwear and self-strangulation to its ultimate extreme, he could only have done so once. By murdering young women—who might have reminded him of himself—in the same way, he was able to experience that particular form of arousal many times.

During two concurrent life sentences in prison, Schaefer developed a reputation as a scammer and a snitch. His narcissism caught up with him when someone slit his throat and stabbed him forty-two times with a prison shank. Various prisoners were suspected of silencing Schaefer for good, including Ottis Toole, but two-time murderer Victor Rivera was convicted, earning an extra fifty-three years in prison in addition to the life-plus-twenty he was already serving.

Sexual Predators: Male Victims

JUST AS MOST SERIAL killers murder within their own race, killers driven by sexual compulsion tend to murder within their own orientation. Heterosexuals like Ed Kemper and Gerard Schaefer kill females, bisexuals like Henry Lee Lucas and Ottis Toole are not so particular—although depending on which version of Lucas's one believes, he might have killed only three people, all female—and male homosexuals kill men.

1 **THE CHAMPION** of male-oriented sexual predators is Chicago's John Wayne Gacy Jr., the Killer Clown. Gacy, one of the most prolific U.S. serial killers, rates passing mentions in a couple of episodes of *Criminal Minds*: "Natural Born Killer" (108) and "The Angel Maker" (402).

Gacy was a man of many facets and seemingly many personalities. He was a successful businessman running a contracting company called PDM Contractors. He was active in local Democratic politics. He was appointed to city office, marched in parades, and was photographed with First Lady Rosalynn Carter. As Pogo the Clown, he made appearances at hospitals and children's parties. He was a family man who threw huge bashes for the neighbors.

But a deep, dark river flowed beneath that outgoing surface, and the disappearance of fifteen-year-old Robert Piest finally exposed it. Piest worked at the Nisson Pharmacy in Des Plaines, Illinois. When his mother, Elizabeth, came to drive him home from work on her birthday, December 11, 1978, he said he needed to talk to a man in the parking lot about a summer job. He went outside and never returned.

Des Plaines Chief of Detectives Joe Kozenczak knew Piest. He didn't think Piest was the kind of kid who would just run off, so he launched an investigation. At the drugstore, he learned that local contractor John Wayne Gacy had been in the store that day. When Gacy denied knowing Piest, Kozenczak said he'd been seen talking to the boy in the parking lot. Gacy amended his tale, admitting that he might have run into Piest out there. Kozenczak sensed that Gacy was lying and got a search warrant for his house.

The first search was superficial. Some clothing that was obviously far too small for the heavyset Gacy turned up, as did a receipt for a roll of film from the drugstore at which Piest worked, in the name of a third party. The film belonged to a friend of Piest's, to whom he had lent his jacket; when she gave the jacket back, the receipt for the film had still been in a pocket. Other items were found that put Gacy in a suspicious light: driver's licenses and a class ring that belonged to other people, marijuana and Valium, gay pornography, handcuffs and other sex toys, a pistol, and more. But it didn't amount to much in terms of evidence.

Without having enough evidence to arrest Gacy, Kozenczak put him under close surveillance and interviewed his friends and neighbors. Gacy filed a lawsuit charging police harassment.

Kozenczak finally got his hands on paperwork showing that Gacy had been sentenced to ten years in jail for sodomizing an adolescent boy in Iowa in 1968. Gacy had served only eighteen months of the sentence. In 1972, there had been another complaint: a teenager had accused Gacy of picking him up in an area where homosexuals hung out, taking him home, and trying to hurt him. Gacy was charged with aggravated battery and reckless conduct. The young man didn't appear in court, and the charges were dropped.

More information surfaced to support charging Gacy in the Piest case. Jeffrey Rignall—whom Gacy had chloroformed and raped, then dropped off in Chicago—had reported his assault and was able to identify his attacker. Rignall waited near a freeway exit that he half remembered from his drugged state during his car ride with Gacy, and he finally spotted his assailant's car. He followed Gacy home and reported his address to the police. The investigators were running down the few leads they had found in Gacy's house, and they identified the class ring as having belonged to John Szyc, a teenager who had disappeared the previous year.

Kozenczak got a more extensive search warrant and returned to Gacy's home. Gacy once again denied having anything to do with Robert Piest's disappearance, but he claimed that he'd had to kill one of his homosexual lovers in self-defense. He said the body was buried under the concrete floor in his garage, and he used spray paint to mark the spot.

Before the authorities dug, they checked out the crawl space under the house, where they found a strange mound with a body underneath. The Cook County Medical Examiner came out and sniffed the air. He smelled death and told them to keep digging. By the time the search was finished, nothing remained of the house but the outside walls and the roof.

In custody, Gacy talked freely. He had raped and killed thirty-three young men between the ages of fourteen and twenty-one, beginning in 1972. Twenty-seven of them were buried under the house; the rest he threw into the Des Plaines River because he ran out of room. Although he was forthcoming at first, his attorney advised him to clam up.

In "Seven Seconds," the BAU team, including Garcia, J.J., Hotchner, Prentiss, and Reid, helps to locate the abductor of a child at a mall.

Gacy's usual approach was to pick up a young man in a gay cruising area in downtown Chicago and ask him over to his house. At other times he invited one of his own employees to come home with him. He offered the young man liquor and dope and brought out some heterosexual pornography. Soon he switched to gay porn. At some point he would offer to show the boy a handcuff or rope trick, and he would use this to confine the boy before the victim realized that what was happening was not just play. Once the victim was immobilized, Gacy would render him unconscious with chloroform and sodomize him. His preferred murder method was to wrap a rope around the victim's neck and twist it with a stick, often while quoting the Bible. He also shoved underwear, socks, or paper towels down the victim's throat to make sure that he didn't vomit and thus leave traces of bodily fluids in Gacy's house.

Once Gacy had put the bodies in the crawl space, he buried them and covered them with lime to aid decomposition. It didn't entirely kill the odor, however, which was often mentioned by his guests.

Gacy's father was an abusive alcoholic. When Gacy was eleven years old, a swing hit his head, forming a blood clot that gave him occasional blackouts until he had it treated at age sixteen. He claimed to have been molested as a boy, first by a teenage girl and later by a male contractor. At seventeen, he had a heart ailment of some kind.

Shortly after Gacy's first marriage, he was given a job managing one of his wife's family's Kentucky Fried Chicken restaurants in Waterloo, Iowa. It was in that job that his homosexuality started to become an issue; he hit on young employees and eventually went to jail for sodomy. His marriage crumbled, and while he was incarcerated, his father died of cirrhosis. After Gacy's parole in 1970, he returned to Chicago and lived with his mother until he could afford to buy his own house.

Gacy's first known murder occurred on January 3, 1972, when he stabbed a young man he had picked up at a bus station.

In June 1972, Gacy married again. His new wife and her two daughters moved into the house with him—never knowing that there was a permanent lodger under the floor.

He killed again in 1975, the same year that PDM Contractors got off the ground. His marriage began to suffer from his odd hours, his seemingly newfound obsession with gay pornography, and his utter lack of interest in sex with his wife. He told her that he preferred sex with boys to sex with women, so they divorced in 1976.

Then he stepped up the pace of his killing. Between April and October of that year, he murdered at least eight young men. Eight more were killed in 1977. There may have been additional murders; he never confessed to any beyond those whose bodies were found, but by 1978 the crawl space was full.

After Gacy was arrested and immediately confessed, his story changed a number of times. He tried to claim insanity. He tried to claim that the victims had suffered accidental deaths while engaging in erotic asphyxia. He insisted that although he had some knowledge of five of the deaths and may have been complicit in two, the real killers were other people. He said that his house was a combination home and business office, with people coming and going all the time. He blamed alcohol and drugs.

In the end, the jury bought none of his stories. It took barely two hours to reach a guilty verdict, and Gacy was sentenced to death.

During his time on death row, Gacy gave interviews, wrote thousands of letters, and created some oil paintings—many with grisly themes, like fellow serial killers (although he hated being lumped in with them, he didn't mind capitalizing on their likenesses). He denied any culpability for his crimes and showed no remorse for his victims. The narcissistic Gacy had an enormous ego and a conviction that the world revolved around him. Society's rules and laws applied only to other people. He used his garrulous personality as a lethal weapon, literally talking his victims into a position where they had no chance to survive.

Shortly after midnight on May 10, 1994, Gacy was executed by lethal injection. His last words were entirely in character: "Kiss my ass."

2 **BOB BERDELLA** is one of the subjects of David Rossi's book *Deviance: The Secret Desires of Sadistic Serial Killers.* The book, of course, isn't real, but Berdella was—real and dangerous, hence his nickname, the Kansas City Butcher.

The police were tipped off to Berdella in the spring of 1988. This was actually the second time that Berdella had come to their attention; he had been questioned earlier in connection with a young man who had disappeared, but that investigation never went anywhere. The tip in 1988 came from Christopher Bryson, who had climbed out of a window of Berdella's Kansas City, Missouri, house and run down the street wearing nothing but a dog collar. When the police caught up to him, Bryson told a terrifying tale of torture. Berdella had picked Bryson up in a neighborhood where male prostitutes worked, brought him home, and then hit him over the head. Once Bryson was unconscious, Berdella bound him, drugged him, and began his "experimentation."

Berdella kept precise notes and a photographic record of every young man he treated in this way—before Bryson, however, none had survived the treatment. Berdella used to invite men to his home only for sex, and they had not been mistreated. But once Berdella decided to torture and kill, there was no turning back.

When the police performed a thorough search of his home, what they found astonished them. The implements of torture that Bryson had described were in plain sight. They also found audiotapes, notebooks and photographs detailing Berdella's abuse of his victims (including Bryson), a human skull, teeth, and a bag full of human vertebrae. Digging in the backyard, they turned up another head, with flesh and hair still attached. Berdella admitted to cutting up bodies with knives and a chain saw, putting the body parts in plastic bags, and leaving them out with his trash. Most of his victims were never found.

There was nothing in Berdella's background to indicate that he would become a sexual sadist and a serial killer. His father's death when Berdella was sixteen was devastating, and he'd had homosexual feelings from a young age. Berdella's explanation—that his first homicide was a mistake, an unanticipated side effect of drugs he had employed to keep his victim compliant—was unconvincing. In the end, he confessed to six murders. There were more people shown in his photographs, as many as twenty, and other men were missing who might have run across Berdella, but he refused to admit to any more victims than the six.

Like other psychopathic sex offenders, Berdella was drawn to manipulation, domination, and control. He wanted full-time, live-in sex slaves (to the point that he experimented with injecting Drano directly into the eyes and the voice boxes of his victims, believing that if they were blind and unable to speak, they would be easier to keep). He claimed to have been partly inspired by the film version of the John Fowles novel *The Collector*, in which the protagonist abducts a woman and keeps her prisoner in his home. That novel also figured prominently in the crimes of serial killers Christopher Wilder and Charles Ng.

Berdella died of a heart attack in prison in 1992, after serving just four years of his life sentence. His death was ruled natural and never investigated.

3 **WESTLEY ALLAN DODD** was another offender who kept records of his crimes, in the form of Polaroid photos and a diary. By the time he murdered his first two boys—brothers Billy and Cole Neer, ten and eleven years old, respectively—in September 1989, he had been exposing himself to and molesting children for fourteen years. But his fantasies of murder had become too powerful to resist. He went to David Douglas Park in Vancouver, Washington, that day with the specific intention of finding a boy to kill.

Instead, he found two. He took them into the woods, molested them, and stabbed them. Billy was discovered, but too late; he died of his wounds. Cole was already dead.

In his diary that night, Dodd, then twenty-eight years old, wrote, "I think I got more of a high out of killing than molesting. . . . I must go find another child."

Dodd, like many pedophiles, was a loner with poor self-esteem. The first children he molested, when he himself was only fourteen, were his own younger cousins. Many molesters prey on children who trust them, as in the case of six-year-old Katie Jacobs, in the episode "Seven Seconds" (305), who is regularly molested by her uncle. Dodd continued to put himself into situations where he would come into contact with children—as a camp counselor and a babysitter, for example.

Periodically arrested, he was always sentenced to light punishment and counseling, which he attended even though he knew he would continue to do the only thing he truly enjoyed.

On October 29, 1989, he took his next victim, four-year-old Lee Iseli, from a public park in Portland, Oregon. Dodd lured the boy with promises of fun and money, then took him home. For hours, he molested Iseli, shooting pictures and recording his experiences in his diary. "He suspects nothing now," Dodd wrote that night. "Will probably wait until morning to kill him. That way his body will be fairly fresh for experiments after work. I'll suffocate him in his sleep when I wake up for work (if I sleep)."

In the morning, he strangled Iseli, then hanged him in a closet and took more pictures. Later, Dodd dumped Iseli's body into Vancouver Lake.

The next boy he grabbed turned out to be his last. At a movie theater, Dodd followed a six-year-old into the bathroom. The boy screamed, and Dodd grabbed him and raced to his car. Some of the theater staff saw him open a yellow Ford Pinto, but as he fumbled with his keys, the boy escaped and ran back inside. The boy's mother's boyfriend raced outside and found the Pinto, which had stalled in the street. The boyfriend detained Dodd until the police arrived.

Once Dodd was in custody, he readily confessed. He claimed he had to kill the Neer brothers once he had molested them, because they would have reported him. In the powerful episode "Profiler, Profiled" (212), Derek Morgan's onetime mentor Carl Buford kills boys for a similar reason: to cover up the fact that he has been abusing children for years.

Sentenced to death, Dodd refused to appeal his case. "I must be executed before I have an opportunity to escape," he said. "If I do escape, I promise you I will kill prison guards if I have to and rape and enjoy every minute of it." Washington law required that the condemned be offered the choice of lethal injection or hanging, and Dodd requested to be hanged, "because that's the way Lee Iseli died."

The state obliged him, and on January 5, 1993, at the age of thirty-one, Dodd became the first person to be legally hanged in the United States since 1965. He admitted to having molested approximately 250 children. The Justice Department reports that the "average" child molester commits 380 acts of molestation in a lifetime. Dodd was well on his way to that mark.

4 **IN THE CRIMINAL MINDS** episode "In Heat" (317), prison guard David Fitzgerald employs the same sort of discipline he uses at work on his son, Steven, trying to force the young man to deny his homosexuality. It doesn't work, and Steven kills a number of gay men around Miami.

In real life, Daniel Conahan's parents might not have tried physical abuse, but when their teenage son admitted to being gay, they weren't happy about it. They sent Daniel to several psychiatrists to try to "cure" him. Daniel didn't appreciate being told that his sexuality was a disease that could be cured.

His homicidal nature probably couldn't be cured, either. Conahan, called the Hog Trail Killer, took gay men out into the woods near Punta Gorda, on Florida's Gulf Coast, promising them money for posing for nude photographs. The path he took them down was a wild hog trail, rarely traveled by human beings. Once they were there, he posed the men in bondage situations, tied to a tree, then he strangled them, and in several cases he cut off their genitals. Some of the men were also raped.

Conahan was arrested after other men reported that he had approached them with similar offers, and one man said that Conahan had actually tied him to a tree and tried to strangle him with a rope but had run out of time and had to leave the job unfinished.

Prosecutors charged Conahan with only one homicide. In his 1999 trial, Conahan pleaded not guilty but was convicted and sentenced to death. He has appealed that sentence while continuing to maintain his innocence; however, his story has changed, to the point of claiming that the victim's death was the result of sex play gone awry. The remains of other men have continued to turn up in the woods of the Gulf Coast, including eight near Fort Myers in 2007. The authorities are investigating Conahan in connection with those new bodies, but we may never know how many people he really killed.

Although the psychoses of sexually motivated serial killers are unique to each individual, the basic thrust behind all of these perpetrators is the same. Somewhere in life they develop a fantasy that conflates sex and death. As time goes on, instead of the fantasy being outgrown, it takes on more force and power, to the point that these damaged individuals are unwilling or unable to deny it. They act out the fantasy as closely as they can.

However, fantasy is perfect in a way that real life never is, so the act they commit is not quite right. Living out the fantasy quells the desire for a while, but even through the cooling-off period, it doesn't leave their minds. The killers ponder it, wondering what they might have done differently to make the act more like the imagination. And so they try it again, but once again it isn't quite true to how they've constructed it mentally.

At the same time, usually with the use of trophies they've kept from each murder—photographs, diaries, personal possessions, body parts—they relive the best parts of it in their heads, once again achieving sexual release. But reliving it only feeds the fantasy, so they keep at it, over and over, until they are captured or killed—or, in a very few cases, like Ed Kemper's, until they murder the person at whom the rage aspect of their fantasy is truly directed, and they give themselves up.

Also key to these fantasies is that the killers are without empathy. They not only can't understand how other people feel, they don't care to find out. To them, other people are useful only as props for their fantasies, and their deaths aren't tragedies but are necessary elements of those fantasies. The only serial killers who factor the feelings of others into their mental equations at all are the sexual sadists, whose pleasure comes from the suffering they inflict.

It's crucial to profilers to be able to figure out as much about each killer's fantasy life as they can, because that's the key to determining what sort of person committed the murders. Profiling can never lead to a specific individual; it can only narrow the scope of a search. The solution to the fantasy riddle is in the killer's individual signature.

For instance, Daniel Conahan's signature was tying nude men to trees and strangling them. He achieved sexual gratification through these acts, and sometimes through the rape of the men and the removal of their genitals. These things aren't necessary aspects of murder—he could just as easily have clubbed them over the head or shot them—but they were necessary to his fantasy.

Conahan was born in 1954; when his fellow Floridian Gerard Schaefer was tying women to trees in remote areas and murdering them, he was a young man, and it would not be at all surprising to learn that Conahan, still struggling with his sexual identity, paid close attention to the news reports of Schaefer's crimes.

Schaefer's victimology was different from Conahan's, because his sexual preference was for women. But the way he treated the girls who made the news was almost too similar to Conahan's method to be coincidental. Conahan's fantasies took shape at an early age, and as is the case with most sexual predators, his fantasies determined the ultimate shape of his murders.

Killers on the Road

THERE ARE SERIAL KILLERS who stay home and become closely associated with a specific location or region: Son of Sam, the Green River Killer, the Atlanta Child Murderer, and the Boston Strangler come to mind.

Then there are those who take their act on the road, like Henry Lee Lucas and Mike DeBardeleben. This chapter takes a closer look at the traveling road shows of serial-killer history, beginning with the poster boy for the breed—in fact, the person most Americans probably think of when they think of serial killers at all.

1 **TED BUNDY'S** name is mentioned in ten episodes of *Criminal Minds*. It first arises in the fourth episode of *Criminal Minds*, "Plain Sight" (104). It's brought up again in "Unfinished Business"

(115), "Charm and Harm" (120), "The Boogeyman (206), "The Last Word" (209), "The Big Game" (214), "Penelope" (309), "Limelight" (313), "Omnivore" (418), and "The Slave of Duty" (510). With more mentions on the series than any other criminal, Bundy is the guy you're talking about when you're talking serial killers.

In many ways, Bundy's case offers us an archetypal serial killer to study, with a clearly observable signature and pattern of behavior. After his final arrest and conviction, people who knew him would say that they had never seen any signs of the monster-to-be within the Ted Bundy they had known. If they'd been familiar with the makings of a serial killer, they might have had a different interpretation.

Bundy was born Theodore Robert Cowell on November 24, 1946, to a mother who was a temporary resident at a home for unwed mothers in Burlington, Vermont. His father—although Bundy wouldn't know it for decades—was probably a war veteran who seduced his mother. Louise Cowell went far from home to have her baby, and upon their return (she kept the baby), her family engaged in a charade, claiming that she and Ted were brother and sister and that Ted's grandparents were his parents. His grandfather was a cruel, intolerant man with a taste for mild pornography, which Ted sampled early. His mother's sister woke up one night to find herself in bed surrounded by kitchen knives. Her three-year-old nephew stood beside her, grinning.

When Ted was four, he and his "sister" (mother) moved to Tacoma, Washington, to live with his mother's uncle Jack, a college professor who lived a cultured lifestyle to which Ted spent the rest of his life aspiring. After a year, Louise married Johnnie Culpepper Bundy, a cook at the veteran's hospital, who gave Ted his last name. Johnnie's marginal lifestyle, however, was one that Ted—even at that early age—wanted no part of.

By the time Ted was in his teens, he had begun shoplifting, which later evolved into petty theft and burglary. He also developed a taste for peeping into women's windows. In high school, he was nearly friendless, incapable of mixing socially with the other kids. He could speak up in the controlled situation of the classroom but felt lost in the halls. And although he was a good-looking, athletic kid, he wasn't skilled at team sports. Using stolen equipment, he became an avid skier.

These factors would all play into Ted Bundy's psychosis: identity confusion from being lied to about his birth and parentage, the shame he felt at being born out of wedlock, his lack of respect for law and authority, the melding of sex with lawbreaking and pornography, the loner-outsider persona, and his desperate yearning for a social status he could never quite achieve. These things, combined with the sociopathic lack of empathy and remorse so common among his serial-killing peers, led Bundy down a terrible path.

He graduated from high school and went to college, first at the University of Puget Sound and then at the University of Washington (UW) in Seattle, settling in the city's University District. There he fell in love with a wealthy coed from California, a pretty girl with long brown hair parted in the middle (this detail would become significant later on). He was starting to come into his own, becoming active in Republican politics; when most people his age were involved in the antiwar movement and growing their hair long, Bundy was a staunchly proestablishment, law-and-order guy. He grew into a handsome, charming young man who dressed and spoke well.

On one occasion, he saved a drowning child; on another, he ran down a purse snatcher, returned the purse to the victim, and held the culprit for the police. He worked at the Seattle Crisis Center, answering phones, helping people who were suicidal or suffering from extreme situations like rape. One of his coworkers, who became a friend, was Ann Rule, who would later become a best-selling true-crime writer.

The summer after Bundy's sophomore year at UW, he went to Palo Alto, California, to be close to his upper-middle-class sweetheart. But the relationship foundered over the summer. Like a fish out of water, Bundy was awkward and ill at ease. His girlfriend lost interest in him and broke off their relationship. Back in Washington, crushed and dispirited, he gave up on school, set off on a trip around the country, then returned to Washington

In "Catching Out," the BAU team, including Hotchner, Prentiss, and Reid, presents a profile to local law enforcement officials to help find a serial killer who jumps trains and targets people living near the railway.

and took a couple of low-paying jobs. He redoubled his burglary efforts and began moving up in Republican politics.

Bundy met another woman who became his girlfriend. Under the pseudonym Elizabeth Kendall, she would later write a book about her life with the most notorious U.S. serial killer. While Bundy was involved with her, he made another trip to the Bay Area and rekindled his relationship with his former flame. Once the former girlfriend had become firmly committed and they were talking about marriage, he returned to Seattle and didn't get in touch with her for a month. When she finally called him, he blew her off—revenge for dumping him earlier. He played a similar game with Elizabeth, going so far as to get a marriage license, then dramatically tearing it up.

During this period, it's believed, he began killing. He never confessed to his murders, and they might have started earlier than anybody knows.

His first confirmed attack came in 1972, when he followed a woman to her front door. While she was trying to unlock it, Bundy hit her with a club. She screamed, and he ran off, terrified. In January 1974, he pulled off a more successful assault, breaking into a woman's apartment while she slept, striking her skull with a metal rod, and shoving a medical instrument into her vagina. The attack left her in a coma.

Then his terror escalated. On January 31, 1974, Lynda Ann Healy was abducted from the house she shared near the university. Healy was a pretty twenty-one-year-old with long brown hair parted in the middle.

Bundy's pattern established itself early. His victims were attractive young women. Most had long hair parted in the middle. He developed a very effective ruse: he made himself a cast, put it usually on his arm but sometimes on a leg, and pretended to need help with a task that involved putting something in his car, such as groceries or books that he had dropped. Samantha Malcolm, in the *Criminal Minds* episode "The Uncanny Valley" (512), uses a similar technique to good effect, convincing a woman to help her load a wheelchair into her van; the helpful woman is subdued with a Taser and kidnapped for her trouble.

Once Bundy got the young woman to lean into his car, he would push her inside, sometimes hitting her with the cast to knock her out. He then handcuffed his victim, took her someplace private—a wooded area or his own home—and raped and murdered her. Sometimes he kept the body around the house for several days. In some cases he shampooed his victim's hair and put makeup on her before dumping her in the woods. He often had sex with the corpses, even visiting them after dumping them to repeat the act. He kept some of the heads for a time as trophies. Although he took most of his victims from Seattle's university community, he also traveled as far as Corvallis, Oregon, hoping to make it hard for the authorities to link his crimes.

In the summer of 1974, Bundy met Carole Ann Boone, whom he would eventually marry and who, while he was on death row, would bear a daughter she claimed was his. That was still a long way off, however, and many corpses later.

The Washington murders stopped abruptly that summer, after ten victims. Bundy had been accepted into the University of Utah's law school.

By October, he was busy in Utah, brutalizing, raping, and killing women who resembled his lost love. Deciding that he needed to spread out his activities more, he took to traveling to Colorado for victims. In August 1975, he was arrested and charged with kidnapping in Utah and murder in Colorado.

Two escapes later, he was on the run and wound up in Tallahassee, Florida. As before, he got a room in a college community, near Florida State University.

Bundy was rapidly devolving. Up to this point his murders had been signature crimes, each recognizable as his work, from the victimology to the MO to the body dumps. In Florida, he didn't bother trying to fit in to society. He lived on credit cards, drank a lot, and stopped keeping up with his formerly immaculate grooming. On January 15, 1978, he dressed in dark clothing and a knit watch cap, wrapped a log in a piece of cloth, and broke into the Chi Omega sorority house. There he went on a horrific rampage, killing two sorority sisters outright: he beat one with the log, raped her, bit a nipple and her buttocks, sodomized her with a hairspray can, and strangled her; he beat the other so hard that her skull was crushed and her brain exposed. Two other women he attacked lived but were badly injured.

The same night, Bundy broke into the nearby apartment of another student and attacked her while she was sound asleep in bed. She survived, but with permanent injuries that ended her hope of a career as a dancer.

For the next several weeks Bundy roamed around Florida, degenerating further. He drank, he drove, he drank some more. On February 9, he talked a twelve-year-old girl into leaving her school playground. She was found the first week of April, dumped in an abandoned hog shed, with her throat slit and severe damage to her pelvic area.

On February 12, Bundy was arrested for the last time. He loudly proclaimed his innocence, but hair and fiber evidence, his semen found at various crime scenes, and bite-mark evidence from the sorority massacre were more convincing to a jury.

During the trial for the twelve-year-old's death, Carole Ann Boone (Bundy's friend from Washington who married him), was a witness for the defense. Bundy and Boone startled observers by exchanging their vows during her questioning; since he was serving as his own counsel and she was under oath, it was considered legal. He had already been sentenced, in the Chi Omega case, to two death penalties. Shortly after his very public nuptials, he received a third death sentence.

On January 24, 1989, Bundy's life came to an end in a Florida electric chair. He had killed at least thirty-six women, but many estimates put the number much higher, perhaps as many as a hundred. He killed them in Washington, Oregon, Idaho, Utah, Colorado, and Florida—at least, these are the states that we know of. His good looks and occasionally charming personality, his ruse of injured helplessness, and his winning ways with women— until he blitzed, bound, abused, and murdered them—all combined to make him a kind of folk hero to serial-killer fans. He received many proposals and propositions during his time on death row, and Boone believed in his innocence to the end.

2 **IN THE *CRIMINAL MINDS*** episode "Catching Out" (405), Armando Salinas rides the rails up and down central California, murdering people in homes that are within easy walking distance of the tracks. In that episode, it's explained that there are two categories of traveling killers: the itinerant homeless and those with an occupation that allows them to travel.

One of the former type was Angel Maturino Resendiz, who plied his trade in Texas, not California, and became known as the Railroad Killer. Because he was a Mexican national who was in the United States illegally and had no fixed address, he was hard to track down. When he jumped onto a freight train, even he didn't know where he was going, so how could the authorities get ahead of him?

Angel Leoncio Reyes Recendiz was born on August 1, 1960, in Mexico. Even before his confirmed homicides began, he had an arrest record that began at the age of sixteen. The first time, he was picked up trying to cross the border at Brownsville, Texas. In later years, he was arrested several times; once he was sentenced to twenty years in prison for auto theft and assault, but he was paroled and deported back to Mexico after just six years. By the time his fingerprints were found on a vehicle stolen from Dr. Claudia Benton, whom he had raped and bludgeoned with a statue, those prints were on file in the system and the authorities knew who their man was. But knowing and being able to find were two different things.

The Benton murder took place on December 16, 1998. Nine earlier murders have been attributed to Resendiz; many took place in railroad yards and close to the train tracks. His signature really established itself with his eighth murder, that of eighty-seven-year-old Leafie Mason. All of his later murders took place in his victims' homes, close to the tracks. He used objects he found in the homes, and he sometimes stayed in those houses for a while. When he left, he took jewelry and other easily disposable items. He sent much of that jewelry to his wife in Mexico.

After the Benton killing, there were seven more confirmed or suspected murders in Texas, Florida, Kentucky, California, and Illinois. Resendiz claims to have also killed seven people in Mexico. Since he frequented the area of Ciudad Juárez, the Mexican police suspect that he might have had a hand in the more than four hundred unsolved murders of women in that city. In 1999, after the murders of Pastor Norman Sirnic and his wife, Karen, Resendiz was briefly apprehended by border agents, who, when their computers didn't indicate that he was wanted for any crimes, took him to the border and released him back into Mexico.

Resendiz was finally brought in when Texas Ranger Drew Carter convinced Resendiz's sister, who was living in the United States, that he could promise Resendiz a fair shake in U.S. courts. She got word to her brother in Juárez, and he agreed to turn himself in. He walked across the international bridge between Juárez and El Paso on July 13, 1999, shaking Carter's hand at the midpoint and surrendering.

For the Claudia Benton assault and murder, Resendiz was sentenced to death, and he was executed on June 27, 2006. Some believe that far more murders can be attributed to him, but unless he was right in his claim to be immortal, a true angel, the world will never know.

3 **LONG-HAUL TRUCKER** Bruce Mendenhall is mentioned in the episode "Catching Out" (405) as an example of a killer with an occupation that allows him to travel. Mendenhall's case is still unfolding; at the time of this writing, he was on trial for murder. On January 14, 2010, he was found guilty of soliciting the murders of three witnesses against him in the murder trial and was sentenced to thirty years in prison. Sometimes called the I-40 Killer, Mendenhall is believed to be responsible for an undetermined number of murders—no fewer than six, possibly ten or more—that he committed while he was driving his rig across the nation's highways.

Mendenhall, fifty-six, was arrested on July 12, 2007, when an alert Nashville, Tennessee, cop noticed blood on the door of his truck. Inside the rig he found a bag of bloody clothes. The truck was an apparent match to one that had shown up on a surveillance video three weeks earlier from the night that Sara Nicole Hulbert's body had been found at the same truck stop.

Later investigation found the truck's cab to be "awash in blood," according to an Indiana prosecutor who added to Mendenhall's legal problems by charging him with a murder in that state as well. The blood of at least ten different people was discovered in Mendenhall's cab. Some of it has been definitively linked to victims he is suspected of killing. After his arrest, Mendenhall confessed to six murders, but not to Hulbert's. The investigators suspect his involvement in many more, possibly going back as far as 1992. Tennessee is seeking the death penalty for him for the murders of three women in that state, including Hulbert.

Because so many murdered women were showing up along I-40, the FBI launched the Highway Serial Killer Initiative in April 2009. The initiative played a part in the episode "Solitary Man" (517). Using a computer database and studying the details of these crimes, the bureau hopes to get a better handle on killers like Mendenhall who travel hundreds of miles a day, crossing state lines on a regular basis and confounding the typical laws of jurisdiction. The database currently contains more than five hundred victims and two hundred killers. So far, the FBI's work has resulted in the arrests of ten suspects believed to be responsible for at least thirty homicides.

4 **LIKE MARK GREGORY** in the episode "Charm and Harm" (120), Christopher Bernard Wilder was sought by the authorities, but because he was on the move, taking victims as he went, they couldn't catch up to him.

Wilder was born on March 13, 1945, in Sydney, Australia, to a U.S. naval officer and an Australian woman. His first brush with the law was in Australia in the early 1960s, when he pleaded guilty to taking part in a gang rape. He was put on probation and ordered to undergo therapy, which included electroshock therapy. He formed a connection between electric shock and sex that became part of his signature and remained so for the rest of his life. Fictional killer Jeremy Andrus, in the episode "Limelight" (313), has a similar fondness for electrical torture.

After emigrating to the United States at twenty-three, Wilder made a fortune in Florida real estate. He also developed hobbies such as auto racing and photography. The latter he combined with his interest in rape, inviting women to be models for him and then sexually assaulting them.

In February 1984, Wilder graduated to murder. His first two victims were pretty, young women who had participated in the Miss Florida contest and wanted to be models. Both knew Wilder, and he was reportedly seen in their company before their disappearances. Their common experience gave him the nickname the Beauty

Queen Killer. When Wilder read in the newspaper that the police were closing in on a suspect—who sounded quite a bit like him—he decided it was time to hit the road. He had just turned thirty-nine, and his road trip would end badly.

His next victim was another Floridian, and after he dumped her body he grabbed a victim whom he took across state lines into Georgia. In a motel room he raped her, tortured her with electric shock, and glued her eyes shut. After she locked herself in the bathroom, screaming and pounding on the walls, Wilder fled.

Wilder then struck in Texas, Oklahoma, Colorado, Utah, Nevada, and California, raping, torturing, and killing. In California he abducted sixteen-year-old Tina Marie Risico, and after raping her he kept her alive and used her to lure additional victims into his trap. With her coerced help, he abducted another sixteen-year-old, Dawnette Wilt, in Gary, Indiana. Wilder was able to rape and torture her en route because he had Risico driving for him. He kept Wilt with him as they traveled through Ohio, Pennsylvania, and New York, where he finally killed her. Then Wilder, with Risico still with him, abducted another woman, shot her, and took her car. In Boston, Wilder took Risico to the airport and gave her money for a plane ticket home.

Wilder tried to grab one more victim on April 13, but she got away. He then drove into New Hampshire, where a pair of state troopers recognized the man the entire country was looking for. Wilder went for his gun and a scuffle ensued, during which he was shot in the heart. "Suicide by cop" is a common end to killing sprees, and it was also the ultimate end of spree killer Mark Gregory in the *Criminal Minds* episode.

When police searched Wilder's car, they found his gun, duct tape, and other tools of abduction, along with the special rig he had created to electrically shock his victims and his prized copy of John Fowles's novel *The Collector*, which was mentioned in chapter 3. Wilder's therapists reported that the killer had "practically memorized" the book.

After his death, Wilder was tentatively tied to two murders in Australia back in 1965 and to two in Florida that had taken place before his final spree.

5

Team Killers

ANY CRIMINAL PROFILER can be wrong at any time—human nature is too mutable to always follow any strict guidelines, and that's why profilers insist that their practice is an art, not a science. But the profilers of the FBI's Behavioral Analysis Unit, at least as depicted on *Criminal Minds*, are rarely wrong, and when they are, they usually figure out their error quickly.

The series begins with a difficult case, in the episode titled "Extreme Aggressor" (101). While the team is trying to find the killer known as the Seattle Strangler, the facts of the case lead the profilers in what seem to be two separate directions. In reality, there are two unsubs, which accounts for the confusion in the initial analysis. Timothy Vogel and Richard Slessman met in prison, where Vogel was a guard and Slessman was an inmate.

Vogel, powerful and dominant, protected the weaker Slessman, who came to believe that he owed Vogel his life.

Team killers are too well known in real life. The crimes of Lawrence Bittaker and Roy Norris, for instance, are brought up again in "A Real Rain" (117) and "Lo-Fi" (320) as examples of this terrible strategy.

1 **BITTAKER HAD BEEN SENT** to the California Men's Colony at San Luis Obispo for assault with a deadly weapon, and Norris was there for rape. Many single people despair of ever finding the "right" person; Bittaker and Norris knew that with their particular shared interests, they were a match made—well, not in heaven, but a match just the same.

Lawrence Sigmund Bittaker was born in Pittsburgh on September 27, 1940, and adopted shortly thereafter by George Bittaker and his wife. The family moved often, and at age sixteen Lawrence dropped out of school in California and was arrested for auto theft, a hit-and-run accident, and evading arrest. He served a couple of years in the California Youth Authority, was paroled, and was almost immediately arrested again—this time in Louisiana, for violating the Interstate Motor Vehicle Theft Act.

This was how Bittaker's life progressed—incarcerated more often than not. As of this writing, he is sixty-nine years old and has spent forty-two years in jail. He was diagnosed by prison psychiatrists as "borderline psychotic," "basically paranoid," and having "poor control of impulse behavior." Despite these diagnoses and the opinions of experts that he would never stop committing crimes, every institution that held him sooner or later let him out.

Comparatively speaking, Roy Lewis Norris had had a stable childhood. Born on February 2, 1948, he lived with his parents in Greeley, Colorado, until he dropped out of school at seventeen and joined the navy. He served four months in Vietnam without seeing combat and was then stationed in San Diego, where he started attacking women. The navy discharged him because of his "psychological problems," and the state put him in Atascadero

In "Lo-Fi," the BAU team must investigate whether a killing spree in New York City is the work of a single serial killer or a that of a team.

State Mental Hospital and labeled him a mentally disordered sex offender. After five years Norris was released; he returned to his old habits and was sent away for rape once again—this time to San Luis Obispo, where his path would intersect Bittaker's.

Norris claimed that Bittaker saved his life twice. Thus, according to the "prisoner's code," he owed Bittaker, and would do anything the older man asked of him. They began to formulate a plan. They would have some "fun" when they got out: kidnapping, raping, and torturing at least one girl of each of the teen years, thirteen through nineteen. After seeing how long they could keep the girls alive and screaming, they would kill them, because they decided that Norris's mistake had been letting his victims survive to testify against him. Bittaker had already killed once, in what started as a simple shoplifting incident. He put some meat down his pants and left a supermarket; when an employee confronted him, Bittaker stabbed the employee to death.

Once again, mental health experts warned that Bittaker was a psychopath and a continuing danger to society. Once again, he was released from prison. In November 1978, he moved in with his mother in Los Angeles and waited for Norris to be released.

When Norris got out in early 1979, the two retired to a hotel in downtown Los Angeles to refine their plan. Their first move was to acquire a 1977 GMC cargo van with no windows in back and a sliding door. Naming it "Murder Mack," they outfitted it for rape and abduction and began cruising the Pacific Coast Highway. The investigators later found around five hundred photos the pair took of teenage girls they spoke to during their time on the streets. The two predators also drove Southern California's more isolated reaches, looking for the right spot to have their "fun." Finally, they found both things they were looking for: the place and the girl.

The morning of June 24, 1979, they worked on the bed they were constructing in the back of Murder Mack; the bed would have a space underneath in which to hide a body. After they finished that task, they started cruising, drinking beer, smoking dope, and flirting with girls. Soon they spotted one they could both agree on. Cindy Schaeffer, sixteen, was walking home from a church youth group meeting. Bittaker and Norris offered her a ride. She declined. They swung into a driveway ahead of her and offered more forcefully. Norris grabbed her and heaved her into the van through the sliding door, and they raced away. With Bittaker at the wheel, Norris wrestled with their captive, covering her mouth with duct tape and binding her wrists and ankles.

On a dirt road in the San Gabriel Mountains, the psychopaths took turns raping Schaeffer. When they finished, Norris tried to kill her. He failed, and Bittaker took a crack at it. Finally they teamed up and strangled her with a wire coat hanger, then wrapped her body in a plastic shower curtain and hurled it into a canyon.

The adventure had been almost everything they'd hoped for, but it left them wanting more, so they tried again on July 8, abducting and repeatedly raping Andrea Hall, an eighteen-year-old hitchhiker. This time they took Polaroid pictures. Bittaker sent Norris to fetch more beer, and while his partner was gone, Bittaker murdered Hall, driving an ice pick into each ear and then strangling her when the stabbings failed to kill her. Once again, the body was tossed off a cliff.

Their next assault involved two girls at once: Jackie Gilliam, fifteen, and thirteen-year-old Leah Lamp. Bittaker and Norris kept the girls alive for two days of torture and documented the ordeal with pictures and audiotapes. When they threw the girls over the side of the canyon wall, Bittaker's ice pick was still jammed into Jackie's head.

A few weeks later, the pair maced Shirley Sanders and raped her in the Murder Mack, but she escaped. Although she reported the attack, she couldn't identify her attackers.

The killers were anxious, but no official scrutiny came their way. On Halloween night they grabbed Lynette Ledford, their second sixteen-year-old. Instead of taking her to the mountains, they raped and tortured her in the back of the van. While Norris drove, Bittaker went to work with vise-grip pliers, a tape recorder going the whole time. Eventually, Norris took a turn. They strangled Ledford with a coat hanger and dumped her in a random yard.

This corpse—the first of Bittaker and Norris's victims to be found—startled a metropolitan area that was still reeling from the Hillside Stranglers case. One of the two stranglers, Angelo Buono, had just been arrested on October 22.

Ledford was the beginning of the end for the psychopathic killers. It's not uncommon for organized killers to become less organized as their crimes continue, because their tenuous psychological state progressively degenerates. Had the men continued with their plan of picking up at least one girl of each teen year, taking all of their victims to remote locations and hiding the bodies, they might have been able to finish what they started. But they abandoned a routine that had been working for them because they were unable to delay their gratification.

The Los Angeles Police Department's job was made easier by the fact that Norris couldn't keep his mouth shut. He had bragged about the murders to another prison buddy, who thought that Norris was blue-skying him until he heard about Ledford. This onetime friend told his lawyer, and the two of them alerted the cops. The police showed Shirley Sanders (the victim who had gotten away) photos of Norris and Bittaker, and she identified them as her rapists.

While the authorities were constructing their case, Norris was seen selling marijuana. He was picked up for dealing, and Bittaker was arrested for the kidnap and rape of Sanders. In custody, Norris blamed Bittaker for everything and showed the police where the bodies were hidden. Bittaker's ice pick was still stuck in Jackie Gilliam's skull. Norris couldn't find Andrea Hall or Cindy Schaeffer, and those bodies have never turned up.

The audio recordings made clear that Norris was every bit as engaged in the crimes as Bittaker was, but the state needed Norris to testify. In return for his confession and his testimony against Bittaker, Norris was promised a life sentence with the possibility of parole. He received a sentence of forty-five years to life, with the possibility of parole after thirty years. He is eligible for release in 2010.

Bittaker tried to blame everything on Norris. The jury didn't buy it, and in March 1981 he was sentenced to death. He remains on death row in San Quentin, where he's a celebrity in the world of serial-killer fandom. He signs his responses to his fan mail "Pliers" and gives interviews, and for a while he sold artwork and souvenirs to the outside world. Noted FBI profiler John Douglas has referred to Bittaker as "among the vilest human beings I have ever come across." One would be hard-pressed to disagree.

2   **LAWRENCE BITTAKER** committed his first murder when he was stopped for shoplifting. For Leonard Lake and Charles Ng—who, along with Bittaker and Norris, are mentioned in the episode "Lo-Fi" (320)—the crime of shoplifting had somewhat different consequences.

On June 2, 1985, a hardware store clerk in south San Francisco saw an Asian man hide a bench vise under his jacket and leave the store, so he called the police. When an officer responded, the clerk showed him that the vise was sitting in the open trunk of a Honda; the Asian man had put it there and then ran away. A burly man intervened, telling the cop that he had paid for the vise, so there was no problem. But the cop, looking in the trunk, saw a .22 revolver and a silencer, so he had more questions. The man had a picture ID that didn't seem to match his appearance, and the Honda belonged to someone else altogether.

The officer took the big bearded man in and found paperwork among his possessions that belonged to yet another man. The burly man told the interrogators that the Asian man's name was Charles Chitat Ng, his name was Leonard Lake, and he was wanted by the FBI. Then he swallowed a cyanide capsule that he had hidden under his shirt collar and went into a coma from which he never awoke. Four days later he died.

In the car, the authorities found property belonging to still more people who weren't Ng or Lake. Some of it led to Lake's ex-wife, Claralyn Balasz, who led them to Lake and Ng's hideaway, a cabin in the Sierra Nevada foothills of Calaveras County. What they found could have been a set for a horror movie.

The walls were covered with bullet holes and blood. Inside a locked bunker was a torture chamber that included a workshop full of power tools, many of them coated with dried blood; a hidden bedroom; and a second, even more hidden room that the police termed a "hostage cell." In addition, they found a huge array of weapons, books on chemicals and explosives, and photographs of nude and seminude young girls (taken at the juvenile hall where Balasz worked). In the main part of the cabin they found Lake's diary, which detailed a series of abductions, rapes, tortures, and murders as well as Lake and Ng's goal of building a series of similar remote camps that they would outfit with weapons and female sex slaves. The latter they planned to use to repopulate the world after a nuclear holocaust.

Outside, the police found a powerful incinerator and a long trench that had been treated with lye. In the trench and around the property, the police found personal effects and enough belongings to suggest that at least twenty-five people had been brought to the cabin, tortured, and killed. There were videotapes that showed some of the victims being abused.

Ng, an ex-marine like Lake, was the son of a wealthy Hong Kong businessman. He had plenty of money and now had a head start of several days. Ng had been drummed out of the marine corps for theft, but Lake had been allowed to finish a tour in Vietnam despite being hospitalized for "exhibiting incipient psychotic reactions" and having had another tour cut short for medical reasons. It's uncertain exactly how Ng and Lake met, but they wound up living on the remote mountain ranch with Balasz and then using that ranch to try to amass their army of sex slaves. Like Christopher Wilder and Bob Berdella, Lake was partially inspired by John Fowles's novel *The Collector*. He called his plan Operation Miranda, after the imprisoned woman in the novel.

On July 6, shoplifting entered their story again. Ng was picked up in Calgary, in Alberta, Canada, after stuffing groceries into his backpack. A scuffle ensued in which he drew a pistol and shot one of the security guards, then he was overpowered and taken into custody. He was tried and sentenced to four and a half years for shoplifting and assault. The battle to extradite him to the United States, which Canada doesn't typically do because it doesn't agree with the U.S. practice of using the death penalty, took six years. Canada finally complied, and on February 11, 1999, Ng was convicted of eleven murders. He was sentenced to death but remains on death row in San Quentin.

It's often said that in killing teams, there's usually one partner who is dominant and one who's submissive. In this case, burly Leonard Lake was definitely the dominant one, the one who had the idea of maintaining a bunker full of sex slaves. Ng went along willingly, and he participated fully in the brutal and vicious acts the pair committed. He's every bit as guilty as Lake was, but apparently he was less willing to end his life with a cyanide pill. Instead, he has already been responsible for the most expensive legal proceedings in California's history, and he has not stopped his appeals.

3 **BITTAKER AND NORRIS** launched into their murders so closely on the heels of the Hillside Stranglers that it made terrified Los Angeles residents wonder if the police had locked up the right people. In fact, they had—Angelo Buono and Kenneth Bianchi had killed at least ten women entirely on their own and didn't need help from Bittaker and Norris to do it. Their crimes earned them their joint nickname and references in two episodes of *Criminal Minds*, "Children of the Dark" (304) and "Zoe's Reprise" (415).

Kenneth Alessio Bianchi was born on May 22, 1951, in Rochester, New York. His mother was an alcoholic prostitute who gave him up for adoption immediately after his birth. As if his destiny were already set, when he was a very young boy his adoptive mother recognized that he was lazy, irresponsible, and a constant liar. He was a bedwetter until late in childhood. After high school he married young, but his marriage didn't last. After a series of menial jobs, he was hired as a security guard, a profession that gave him plenty of opportunity to engage in a hobby of petty theft. He was bright but never lived up to his potential in any area of life.

In 1977 Bianchi drifted to Los Angeles, where his older cousin, Angelo Buono Jr., lived. Bianchi was no prize, but Buono was even worse. Also born in Rochester, on October 5, 1934, by age fourteen he was bragging to friends about his rapes. He hated women, but he married several in order to have sex with them and get them pregnant. In each marriage he fathered more children, seemingly all for the purposes of abusing them physically and sexually. His idol was rapist Caryl Chessman, and he later adopted one of Chessman's favorite techniques: posing as a police officer. Even before Buono started killing, he was very familiar with the inside of a jail cell.

Bianchi and Buono were awful individuals, but when they got together they were even worse.

When Bianchi arrived in Los Angeles, Buono seemed like quite the successful ladies' man. Somehow, in spite of his personality, Buono was surrounded by a bevy of underage girls. The cousins came up with the idea of using the threat of physical violence to coerce girls to work for them as prostitutes. It worked for a while with two girls, until one found somebody bigger than Buono and the other ran away.

Bianchi and Buono tried abducting more girls, and they bought a "trick list" from a prostitute that turned out to be phony. When they found out it was a fake, they raped and strangled the hooker who had sold it to them. This was their first murder, but it was far from their last. The victim's naked body showed up near Forest Lawn Cemetery on October 17, 1977. Two more prostitutes, one of them only fifteen, met their ends at the cousins' hands in the next few weeks.

The next five victims were found during Thanksgiving week, and the cousins had shifted their focus; they were no longer killing prostitutes, or people whom they had previously known. The first two victims, also raped and strangled, were twelve- and four-teen-year-old girls who were last seen getting off their school bus and who had no connection to the cousins' lifestyle. The third proved to be a woman who had been missing since early November. The fourth and the fifth showed signs of torture. Another teenage prostitute's body turned up after that, and then a final victim was found in the trunk of her own car after it had been rolled off a cliff.

In 1978, Bianchi moved to Bellingham, Washington, to be with his girlfriend and their infant son. While he was there, working as a security guard, he tried his hand at solo murder. He strangled two women and was arrested almost immediately. The police there put two and two together, and, knowing that Bianchi had lived in Los Angeles, they contacted the Hillside Stranglers task force.

The various agencies that were involved amassed the evidence, and after Bianchi's attempt at an insanity defense failed, he took a plea deal: confess and testify against Buono, and he would get life with a possibility of parole, served in California instead of Washington. He reneged on the testimony, contradicting himself, and is currently serving his life sentence in Washington. Buono was sentenced to life in California, but he died of a heart attack on September 21, 2002.

4 JUST AS DES PLAINES, Illinois, is terrorized by a sniper in "L.D.S.K." (106), which is FBI parlance for "long-distance serial killer," so was the Greater Washington, D.C., area in the autumn of 2002.

The Beltway Snipers actually used a different MO in their first documented attacks. On September 5, 2002, Paul LaRuffa closed his restaurant in Clinton, Maryland, and carried his laptop computer and a bank deposit to his car. While he sat behind the wheel, someone shot him six times but failed to kill him. Someone he described as "a kid" ran up to the car and snatched the laptop and the deposit bags. The bags and the laptop case were discovered six weeks later. Clothing found nearby held the DNA of Lee Boyd Malvo, a seventeen-year-old. Had the items been found right away, the Beltway Snipers might never have become national news, and eleven other people might have lived.

Ten days later, also in Clinton, Muhammad Rashid, the proprietor of Three Roads Liquor, was attacked while locking up his store. Someone later identified as Malvo shot him in the stomach. Rashid survived.

On September 21, twelve hours away, in Montgomery, Alabama, Claudine Parker and Kellie Adams were closing the Zelda Road ABC Liquor Store when they were both shot. Parker died from her wounds, but Adams survived, badly injured. The Beltway Snipers had killed their first victim. A police car arrived while two men, later identified as Malvo and his companion, John Allen Muhammad, forty-one, were rummaging through the women's purses. The police chased Muhammad and Malvo, but they escaped.

On September 23, Hong Im Ballenger, who managed a store called Beauty Depot in Baton Rouge, Louisiana, was shot in the head while walking to her car after closing the store. Malvo was observed grabbing Ballenger's purse. She died from her gunshot wound.

So far, these had seemingly been random robbery-murders, widely scattered and with no reason to link them beyond the common MO. On October 2, that all changed, and the nation became aware of the Beltway Snipers at last.

On that autumn evening, at 5:20 p.m., a shot smashed the window of a Michaels Craft Store in Aspen Hill, Maryland. No one was hurt in that shooting, but at 6:30 p.m., James Martin, a government program analyst, was shot and killed in the parking lot of a supermarket in nearby Wheaton.

The next morning, four people in the area were shot and killed, each outside: at a gas station, mowing a lawn, sitting on a bench. After that bloody morning, the snipers rested, but they went out again after dark, killing one more victim. Each of the day's murders was accomplished with a single shot from some distance away.

The next day, the shooters struck outside another Michaels Craft Store, this one at the Spotsylvania Mall outside Fredericksburg, Virginia. The snipers shot Caroline Seawell in the parking lot; she survived. The authorities had already connected the Maryland sniper attacks and determined that the bullet fragments were all from high-intensity .223 caliber bullets. The same was true of the Virginia attack.

After lying low for a couple of days, Muhammad and Malvo attacked again on October 7, shooting thirteen-year-old Iran Brown as he arrived at his middle school. Brown survived and was able to testify at Muhammad's trial.

This time, the snipers left a message near the scene—the tarot card Death with "Call me God" written on the front and "For you mr. Police. Code: 'Call me God'. Do not release to the press" on the back.

The law enforcement response was massive. Coming just one year after 9/11 and the subsequent anthrax attacks, the shootings were considered to be the possible work of a terrorist cell. More than four hundred agents from the FBI; the Bureau of Alcohol, Tobacco, and Firearms; and the Secret Service; as well as police officers from every jurisdiction where the shootings took place all worked under the command of the Montgomery County Police Department and its chief, Charles Moose, who later wrote a book about the weeks of terror.

By October 22, the Beltway Snipers had shot five more people, including FBI analyst Linda Franklin, who was killed in Falls Church, Virginia. Only one of the five victims survived.

In the woods near one shooting site, the authorities found evidence galore: a shell casing, a candy wrapper with DNA from Muhammad and Malvo on it, and a plastic bag that contained a long handwritten note demanding a payoff of ten million dollars to stop the killing.

Phone calls had started coming in from someone who knew the words written on the tarot card. One of those calls, which the FBI referred to as an "investigative tease," led to the break that the authorities needed. This call referred to the shootings in Montgomery, Alabama. The FBI learned that a fingerprint was found on an arms catalog that had been dropped at the scene. That fingerprint had not yet been analyzed, but the bureau matched it to Malvo, who had been arrested previously in the state of Washington. That arrest report also contained a reference to John Muhammad.

Investigators swarmed the Muhammad home in Tacoma, Washington, and found a tree stump that had been used for target practice. The .223 caliber bullets embedded in the stump were all too familiar.

The FBI discovered that Muhammad owned a Chevrolet Caprice, a former police car with almost 150,000 miles on it. The car's description and license plate number were broadcast, and the car was spotted in a rest stop off I-70 near Myersville, Maryland. Law enforcement officials flooded the area and apprehended Muhammad and Malvo, asleep in the car.

Inside the vehicle, they found a Bushmaster .223 caliber semiautomatic rifle, a bipod, and other items connecting the men to the slayings. The car had been modified so that someone could enter the trunk from the rear seat, and a hole had been cut near the license plate so that the rifle's barrel could poke through without being seen. The Caprice had become a mobile sniper station, just like the vehicle in "L.D.S.K."

The reign of terror had come to an end, but big questions remained. Who were these people, and why had they done it? Muhammad and Malvo had questionable pasts. Muhammad was a Gulf War veteran, trained in the military as a mechanic, a truck driver, and a metalworker. He had earned the Expert Rifleman's Badge, the highest level of marksmanship for basic soldiers. During his military career, he had joined the Nation of Islam. He had been born John Allen Williams in Baton Rouge, Louisiana, but had changed his name in April 2001 to John Allen Muhammad.

His second wife, Mildred Williams, had been granted a restraining order against him after he abducted their three children and threatened her with bodily harm. She claimed that he could make anything into a weapon and that she feared for her life. Ultimately, she believed the murders were all about her—that Muhammad intended to kill her and make it appear that she was another random victim of the spree. She had moved to the Beltway area to be far away from Tacoma, where Muhammad lived, but she believed that he knew where she had gone.

Muhammad met Malvo in Antigua, where he dated the boy's mother. Although there was never any legal or blood relationship between the two men, Malvo became close to Muhammad and referred to the older man as his father. He and his mother were Jamaican citizens, in the United States illegally.

The real motive for the attacks has never been definitively stated. Malvo, when not citing Islamic jihad or the movie *The Matrix*, said it was all part of a campaign to terrorize the nation while recruiting an army of boys and young men who would accompany them to Canada for training and then be sent back into the United States to carry out the same type of random attacks.

Initially, Malvo took credit for all the murders, then admitted that he had done so only because it was harder to sentence a teenager to death. In fact, he was not sentenced to death; he received several consecutive life sentences without the possibility of parole. After the sentencing, Malvo revealed that the pair had committed four earlier shootings that killed two people between March and August 2002.

John Allen Muhammad was executed by lethal injection on November 10, 2009.

5 **APRIL 19 AND 20** are dates with a considerable amount of bloodshed attached to them. Adolf Hitler was born on April 20, 1889. On April 19, 1993, the siege at the Branch Davidian Compound in Waco, Texas, ended in a cataclysmic fire, and at least seventy-four lives were lost. On that date two years later, 168 people died in Timothy McVeigh's bombing of the Alfred P. Murrah Federal Building in Oklahoma City. And on April 20, 1999—in celebration of the 110th anniversary of Hitler's birth, but probably with those other occasions in mind—Eric Harris, eighteen, and Dylan Klebold, seventeen, brought firearms and explosives into Columbine High School in Littleton, Colorado, where both were students, and opened fire on their classmates, the staff, and the police.

For an hour, beginning at 11:10 a.m., Harris and Klebold terrorized the school, firing semiautomatic weapons and shotguns and throwing pipe bombs and Molotov cocktails. They brought larger bombs to school as well; their original plan was to detonate two large bombs that would blow up the cafeteria and the library and then to shoot students as they fled the building. When those bombs didn't detonate, Harris and Klebold instead entered the school building and did their killing up close.

Before finally killing themselves shortly after noon, they had murdered twelve students and one teacher and injured twenty-one other students. Three more students were hurt trying to escape the slaughter.

Harris and Klebold were deeply disturbed young men, both of whom had been in trouble with the law. They planned their attack for a year before they carried it out, posting bits and pieces of their plan online and keeping detailed journals of their preparations. They were part of a clique that was known as the Trenchcoat Mafia because of the members' habit of wearing black trench coats to school. Although they were often bullied and tormented by the school's jocks, and speculation has pointed to that (as well as to the influence of video games and heavy metal music) as a factor, the exact cause of or motive for the tragic assault will never be fully understood, since both students committed suicide at the scene.

Aaron Hotchner mentions the Columbine Killers in the episode "The Perfect Storm" (203) while discussing murder teams.

Killing Couples

SARAH JEAN DAWES, in the episode "Riding the Lightning" (114), is on death row, scheduled to be executed for murdering at least twelve teenage girls with her husband, Jacob. The argument is made that there are no genuine serial-killer couples, and she is eventually shown to be innocent of the crimes to which she admitted.

It's true that serial-killer couples are rare, especially in the United States. But they're not unheard of, the man almost always "in charge" and the woman abused and isolated. The most famous North American example, and the pair most like Sarah Jean and Jacob, is probably the Canadian rape-and-murder team of Paul Bernardo and Karla Homolka.

1 PAUL KENNETH BERNARDO was born on August 27, 1964, in Toronto, Ontario, into a severely dysfunctional family. His mother,

Marilyn, was married at the time, but Bernardo's father was not her husband. The husband, Kenneth Bernardo, was abusive toward his wife and was later charged with child molestation and with sexually abusing the daughter whom he and Marilyn had had together. Marilyn became depressed, withdrawn, and morbidly obese.

At sixteen, Bernardo was devastated to learn the real circumstances of his birth. His relations with his parents, which had been tenuous at best, grew worse. When he went away to college, he began beating and humiliating the women he dated, purposely seeking out women who appeared to be the submissive type.

In May 1987, his career as the Scarborough Rapist began; he was named for the Toronto suburb in which he lived and operated. By the time he met Karla Homolka in October, he had raped twice and attempted a third rape.

Homolka, by contrast, seemed well adjusted. She was beautiful, blond, popular, and smart. An animal lover who worked at a veterinary clinic, she was seventeen when she met Bernardo at a pet convention in Toronto. Within two hours, they were in a hotel room having sex. Homolka was submissive, allowed herself to be bound during sex, and gave Bernardo everything he wanted in that area.

It wasn't long before she knew that he was the Scarborough Rapist, and she not only condoned his activity but encouraged it. On at least one occasion she recorded Bernardo's assault with a video camera. Eventually a composite drawing of the rapist was released, and so many people noted Bernardo's resemblance to it that the police picked him up and questioned him. He convinced them of his innocence, and they let him go. By then, a darker phase of his life was about to begin.

One thing had always bothered Bernardo about his new girlfriend: the fact that she wasn't a virgin when they met. But her fifteen-year-old sister, Tammy, was, so Bernardo wanted Tammy as a replacement virgin. As usual, Homolka not only agreed but assisted. She stole animal anesthetic from the veterinary lab where she worked, and at dinner at the Homolka family's home, a few days before Christmas in 1990, she spiked her sister's drinks with a powerful sedative. After the rest of the family had gone to bed,

In "Riding the Lightning," after interviewing a married couple sitting on death row for serial murder, the team races against time to prove the wife's innocence.

Homolka held a rag soaked with anesthetic over Tammy's face, and while Bernardo raped Tammy, her older sister videotaped the whole thing.

Tammy had eaten a big meal, however, so she vomited and then choked to death. Bernardo and Homolka quickly dressed her, hid their drugs and video gear, and called an ambulance.

With Tammy dead, Bernardo still felt cheated. Determined to make it up to him, Homolka settled on a wedding gift for her husband-to-be: a teenager, a friend of Homolka's, who looked quite a bit like Tammy. When the time came, Homolka knocked the girl out with the animal sedatives, then sexually assaulted her for Bernardo's viewing enjoyment. She took over the camera and recorded Bernardo deflowering the girl and anally raping her. In the morning, the girl awoke, sore but unaware of what had been done to her.

They let that victim live, but having killed once, they were quite willing to do so again. One night Bernardo came upon fourteen-year-old Leslie Mahaffey, who was locked out of her parents' house after missing her curfew. Bernardo blindfolded her and took her home, where he and Homolka both sexually molested her, then killed her. To dispose of the evidence—except what they had recorded on videotape—they cut her into pieces, encased them in cement, and threw it all into Lake Gibson.

The pieces of Mahaffey were found two weeks later, on June 29, 1991, the day Bernardo and Homolka wed.

On April 16, 1992, Homolka approached fifteen-year-old Kristen French in a church parking lot and persuaded her to come over to her car, which Bernardo then forced her into at knifepoint. They kept her for three days, sexually assaulting, beating, and torturing her, and capturing the whole ordeal on video before they finally killed her.

Other women are believed to have been raped and/or murdered by Bernardo and Homolka, but those allegations have never been proven. The pair's run came to an end when Bernardo brutally beat Homolka and her parents called the cops.

Seeing the writing on the wall, Homolka blamed everything on Bernardo. She made a deal that would give her two twelve-year sentences, served concurrently, with parole eligibility after three years for good behavior. All she had to do was tell the truth about the crimes. After her trial and sentencing, the videotapes surfaced. When they were shown at Bernardo's trial, the prosecutors realized that they had made a terrible mistake with Homolka's plea bargain— she was not the innocent victim she had pretended to be.

Bernardo was convicted of kidnapping, rape, and murder on September 1, 1995, and remains in prison, whereas Homolka was released from prison on July 4, 2005. She remarried, changed her name to Leanne Teale, and has a son.

2 **YEARS BEFORE** Bernardo and Homolka, the Sunset Strip Murders rocked a Los Angeles that was still staggering from the Hillside Stranglers and Bittaker and Norris.

On June 12, 1980, the bodies of two teenage girls showed up near the Ventura Freeway. Both had been shot, and there was evidence of necrophilia. The bodies were identified as Cynthia Chandler, sixteen, and her stepsister, Gina Chandler, fifteen; both were frequent runaways who'd seen their share of trouble. Two more bodies, both of prostitutes, were discovered on June 23. One woman's head was missing. Both hookers had been shot, and those bullets were a ballistics match to the Chandler girls'.

The head was found four days later, ensconced in a wooden box in an alley. The cut marks on the neck matched those on the decapitated corpse from the June 23 murders.

By the time a fifth victim appeared, on June 30, the media had attached the name the Sunset Strip Murders to the killings. This victim was also a young woman, shot three times, and her stomach was slit open.

In an unexpected twist, the sixth and final victim in this series was a man, who was discovered rotting inside his sealed van on August 9. His head had been cut off and he'd been stabbed and slashed multiple times, in addition to being shot. Shell casings found in the van matched those of the previous murders.

Two days later, Carol Bundy (no relation to Ted) broke down and told her coworkers that she had killed some people. Someone called the police, and Bundy was picked up. She turned over evidence, including panties belonging to some of the victims, and a photo album showing her boyfriend, Douglas Clark, sexually abusing an eleven-year-old girl. Bundy said that she had killed the man, a country bar singer named Jack Murray, but that Clark had killed the women and had helped her to decapitate Murray.

Bundy described an existence not unlike Karla Homolka's. Clark didn't just want a girlfriend, he wanted a sex slave, and Bundy willingly played that role. When Clark was bored with her, he would bring prostitutes home. One day he came home covered in blood. He told her about having murdered the Chandler girls, whom he had picked up, molested, and then killed. After they were dead, he had sex with the bodies and then dumped them.

His tale excited Bundy, and she let him know it. That night, when the TV news reported that a man was dead in the trunk of a car, Clark took credit for that killing as well.

When Clark went hunting again, Bundy joined him. They picked up a hooker, and Clark shot her in the head while she was performing oral sex on him. Bundy's excitement at watching this could hardly be contained. After dumping the body and dropping Bundy off, Clark found another hooker. This one bit him—an involuntary reaction when he shot her—and in his anger he cut off her head. Seeing yet another hooker nearby, he shot and dumped her, then took the severed head home to Bundy to use as a sex toy.

Clark went out without Bundy on August 1, taking with him instead the eleven-year-old girl with whom he had been photographed. He picked up a hooker and had sex with her while the girl watched, then dropped the girl off at her home and shot the hooker. After raping the corpse, he dumped her, too.

Bundy turned to country singer Jack Murray, an occasional lover, for comfort, and revealed some of her recent activities. When Murray threatened to tell the cops, she silenced him.

At least, that was Bundy's version of things. In Clark's version, the same basic acts took place, but he hadn't done any of the killing. Bundy, he said, imagined herself to be Ted Bundy's wife, and she had enticed Murray into her delusion. Bundy and Murray had done all of the murders and then blamed Clark.

Finally, the bodies of the other hookers Clark had shot were located, and in one of them, ballistics comparisons proved that the bullet came from the same gun that had been used in some of the other murders. This and other evidence were enough to earn Clark six death sentences, and he's still on San Quentin's death row. Bundy died of heart failure in prison in 2003.

3 **HOWEVER PERVERSE** these North American couples were, they had a pair of British counterparts whose depravity makes them look like amateurs by comparison. From 1967 to 1987, Fred and Rosemary West of Gloucester, England, raped, tortured, and murdered at least ten women and girls (although Fred later put the figure at closer to thirty). In addition to casual acquaintances, their victims included Fred's first wife and his three daughters from that marriage. The wife and two of the daughters were murdered (one of the daughters was cut into pieces and buried in the yard). The third daughter was repeatedly raped by Fred and his friends and was later impregnated by Fred.

Rosemary engaged in prostitution in their home and occasionally brought in other women to work with her; some of those coworkers also became victims. Among Fred and Rosemary's eight children, at least one was fathered by Rosemary's clients rather than her husband; at the same time, Fred fathered children with other women. Fred hanged himself rather than face trial, and Rosemary received a life sentence for each of their ten proven victims.

We don't know the specifics of all the crimes committed by the fictional Dawes couple in "Riding the Lightning" (114), but we can safely say that there have been sexually motivated serial-killer couples, and Fred and Rosemary West set the bar high for the rest.

4 **ANOTHER** murderous couple on *Criminal Minds* was Amber and Tony Canardo, in the episode "The Perfect Storm" (203). In a switch on the usual pattern, Amber calls the shots— and one of the murders investigated was committed by Amber and another man before Tony even entered the scene. This couple is reminiscent of a real-life couple, Alvin and Judith Neelley, who roamed the southeastern United States from 1979 to 1982.

Judith Ann Adams met Alvin Neelley when she was fifteen and he was twenty-seven. He was married, but he soon ended that in order to be with Adams. She fit easily into his low-rent criminal lifestyle, and they traveled about the southern states robbing gas stations and convenience stores and cashing stolen checks. In 1980, they were arrested. Neelley went to prison, and Adams was sent to the Youth Development Center in Rome, Georgia, where she made never-substantiated claims that the staff sexually abused her. Adams was pregnant by then and gave birth to twins while in custody.

By 1982, both were out and ready for more action. After a couple of strikes against the homes of people who Adams swore were responsible for her abuse, on September 25 they kidnapped thirteen-year-old Lisa Millican from a Rome mall and held her at various motel rooms in the area. For three days, they kept Millican handcuffed to a bed and raped her in front of the infant twins. Then Adams took the girl to a remote Alabama locale and injected her six times with drain cleaner, which was meant to kill her without leaving any trace. Adams was wrong on both counts—the drain cleaner didn't kill Lisa, but it did leave traces. Finally, Adams shot her and shoved the body over a cliff.

On September 30, Adams was cruising for a victim and finally came across John Hancock and his developmentally disabled fiancée, Janice Chatman. Adams invited them to a party with her; they agreed and got into her car to go for a ride. Eventually they met up with Neelley. Adams took Hancock into the woods and shot him in the back; she thought that she had killed him, but he survived. Adams and Neelley turned their attention to Chatman; they raped her repeatedly in a motel room, then shot her and dumped the body.

Adams and Neelley were arrested in Tennessee. Although Adams tried to blame all of their crimes on Neelley, it quickly became apparent to all—including the jury and the judge—that Adams was the instigator. She craved power over others, and Neelley said that if he hadn't gone along with her whims, he would have been one of her victims. Various accounts say that Neelley blamed her for between eight and fifteen sexually motivated murders, but no bodies except those of Millican and Chatman were ever positively connected to the couple.

In an Alabama trial (during which Adams gave birth to another child), eighteen-year-old Adams was sentenced to death for the kidnapping and murder of Lisa Millican. In order to avoid a trial in Georgia, she pleaded guilty to the kidnap, rape, and murder of Janice Chatman. Neelley was convicted of those crimes as well and died in custody while serving a life sentence.

During his last days in office as Alabama's governor, Fob James—in what was to become a controversial decision—commuted Adams's sentence to life in prison, where she remains today. She is one of the longest-serving female prisoners in the country.

The Family That Preys Together

IT ISN'T JUST COUPLES—or cousins, as in the case of the Hillside Stranglers—who kill together. Sometimes it's an entire family affair, as represented in a couple of *Criminal Minds* episodes.

In "Bloodline" (413), a mother and a father and their son prey on families; they're trying to find a young girl who'll be a suitable wife for the son, who's about to turn ten. The family is an offshoot of a Romany tribe, and at the episode's end we learn that there are other families who are also involved in these activities. And in "Haunted" (502), viewers are introduced to Bill Jarvis, who used to abduct and kill young boys while forcing his own young son to participate in their imprisonment.

Although these situations are fictional, they are unfortunately not that far removed from the reality of some family situations.

1 **LIKE MANY KILLERS,** Joseph Kallinger was adopted at an early age. Born Joseph Lee Brenner III on December 11, 1936, he was adopted at the age of eighteen months by Anna and Stephen Kallinger. The adoption was more a means of getting another pair of hands for their shoe repair business than a display of love or concern. The Kallingers should never have been parents, and that was one family tradition that Joseph passed along.

His adoptive parents' idea of child rearing involved regular beatings and other forms of torture, including locking their son in a closet, making him consume excrement, forcing him to kneel on rocks, and burning him. At the age of six he was hospitalized for a hernia operation necessitated by the beatings; his parents told him that the procedure was meant to ensure that his "bird" (the household's euphemism for *penis*) would stay small and not work. By the age of eleven, Kallinger's idea of sexuality was so distorted that he became aroused by cutting and stabbing pictures of naked men and women.

When he was fifteen, he redirected his sexual interests toward schoolmate Hilda Bergman, over the objections of his parents. The same year, he received what he called a message from God, which directed him to heal and save people through their feet. Stephen Kallinger had taught Joseph the shoemaking business, and Joseph believed that there were people everywhere whose poorly constructed shoes had damaged their brains. Kallinger's idea of "saving" people was, to no surprise, on the twisted side.

He and Hilda married at age seventeen. They had two children together before she left him, claiming physical abuse, for another man when Kallinger was twenty. Hospitalized for a possible brain lesion, Kallinger was diagnosed with a psychopathological nervous disorder. After he got out, he married again. Soon he set fire to his home, an act that would become almost habitual.

With his second wife, he had four children, whom he began to abuse just as he had been abused. In 1972, he branded his oldest daughter with a hot iron after she tried to run away from home. Three of his children went to the police and accused Kallinger of abuse. Kallinger was found guilty and sentenced to four years'

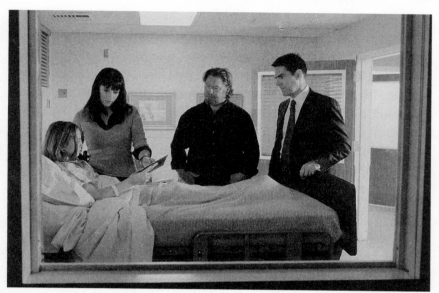

In "Bloodline," Agent Prentiss talks with a girl who was abducted, but then released, by a strange family.

probation with mandatory psychiatric treatment. His son Joey, evaluated as "seriously disturbed," spent time in a reformatory—a chip off the old block.

By the middle of 1974, when Kallinger was living next door to his mother in Philadelphia, he was regularly hallucinating. Those messages from God were still coming in, and he told his thirteen-year-old son Michael that they instructed him to murder young boys and sever their genitals. Michael's response, reportedly, was an enthusiastic "Glad to do it, Dad!"

Eleven days later, a Puerto Rican youth was murdered, and according to some reports, his genitals had been cut off. Kallinger had finally graduated to murder and had made his son his assistant.

Kallinger's next victim would be his son Joey. Two weeks after Kallinger took out a huge life insurance policy on his sons, Joey "ran away from home." His body was found under the rubble of a collapsed building, so crushed that the cause of death could not be determined. The insurance company, suspecting foul play, never paid out the claim.

On November 22, 1974, Kallinger and Michael broke into a home in Lindenwold, New Jersey. The house was empty, so they tried another house and forced their way in. Joan Carty was home. Kallinger tied her to a bed and raped her.

Father and son went out again on December 3, crashing a bridge game in Pennsylvania. They found four women there, and after stripping them and posing them suggestively, stole twenty thousand dollars in jewelry and cash. Flushed with that success, the Kallingers invaded a home in a Baltimore suburb, where they forced a woman to fellate Kallinger at gunpoint.

The beginning of the end for the Kallinger pair came on January 8, 1975. Posing as an insurance salesman, Kallinger, once again accompanied by Michael, forced his way into a home in Leonia, New Jersey. Armed with a pistol and a knife, he and Michael tied up the three residents. During the next several hours, as more people came home they were each seized and bound. Some were forced to strip and were tied up with electrical cords cut from lamps and appliances. Duct tape was put over their eyes and their mouths.

Maria Fasching was the eighth person to arrive. Upon learning what the situation was, she began to reproach Kallinger for his behavior. Kallinger slit her throat, and she drowned in her own blood. Another of the house's residents, with legs bound, managed to get outside and cry for help. Some neighbors saw her and called the police. When the cops arrived, the intruders were gone.

Kallinger decided to use a city bus as their getaway vehicle. On the way to the bus stop, they discarded their weapons, and Kallinger dumped his bloody shirt. These items were quickly found.

The police put these clues together with the reports of similar home invasions in the region and saw a pattern. They had a physical description of their unsubs now, including the fact that the man and the boy shared a strange odor. Tracking down a laundry mark in the shirt that Kallinger had discarded gave them the next piece they needed. They learned that the shirt belonged to a Joseph Kallinger, who did indeed smell strange, thanks to chemicals used in his shoe repair business. The Philadelphia police remembered looking into Joey's death, and they didn't trust Kallinger.

They arrested Joseph and Michael Kallinger on January 17, 1975. Joseph, in his defense, told about his messages from God and his mission to save people whose badly made shoes had destroyed their lives. If he could create special plates for their shoes, he said, it would align their souls in the right way to prepare them for God's coming—which was scheduled for 1978, he claimed.

In spite of an attempt at an insanity defense, Kallinger was found competent to stand trial. He had, after all, run a business and a crowded home and taken care of his aged mother. His crimes had been planned and carried out. The jury found him guilty in less than an hour. The judge saw no reason for mercy, telling him that "to corrupt your own son is vile and depraved." A second trial was held in New Jersey, for the Maria Fasching murder and other crimes committed in that state, and Kallinger was again found guilty.

Michael was sent to a reformatory, having been deemed to be under his father's control at the time of the crimes, and was eventually released into the custody of foster parents. He changed his name and moved away from the area. Joseph Kallinger's behavior grew erratic, even for him. He stabbed and tried to strangle another inmate, went on a hunger strike, and said that he wanted to slaughter every person on Earth and become God. These activities resulted in his transfer from prison to the Fairview Psychiatric Hospital for the Criminally Insane. He remained there until March 26, 1996, when he died of a seizure.

Compared to Joseph Kallinger, even the fictional Bill Jarvis comes across as relatively well balanced.

2 **THE UNSUB IN THE EPISODE** "Jones" (218) is a woman—a rarity in the world of *Criminal Minds* and in the ranks of multiple murderers in general (though not unheard of, as I'll detail in the next chapter). While the types of female killers are being discussed in the show, one of the people mentioned is Sante Kimes, who, it's said, was cold and calculating and preyed on men for money.

Kimes, born Sante Louise Singhrs on July 24, 1934, spent most of her life on the far side of the law. After the family moved from Oklahoma to Los Angeles, her father abandoned his wife and children, and Sante's mother turned to the streets, making her living as a prostitute. Sante started out small, with shoplifting, petty theft, and forgery. After high school, she married and divorced twice, bearing a son whom she left to be raised by his father.

After adding prostitution and auto theft to her repertoire, she fell in with Kenneth Kimes, a con man who had already put together a sizable ten-million-dollar bankroll. They had a son, Kenny, and the family worked its way across the country, amassing more wealth. Sante was beautiful, sometimes mistaken for Elizabeth Taylor, and one of her more audacious cons with her husband involved slipping uninvited into a White House reception during the Nixon administration, to create the illusion of contacts in high places.

Sante did her first serious prison stint for slavery. She had imported young women from Mexico with promises of jobs, then kept them locked in her houses to serve as cleaning ladies. Some got out and risked deportation to go to the police. Kenneth cut a deal and got a three-year suspended sentence and a fine, but Sante got five years and served three. When she got out, she was determined never to go to prison again, and she had decided that the way to do it was to never leave witnesses.

In 1990, she might have put that philosophy into practice. A family lawyer burned down one of the Kimeses' homes for the insurance money and then blabbed about it. When he agreed to talk to federal investigators, Kenneth and Sante took him on a vacation to Costa Rica, from which he never returned.

When Sante's son, Kenny, was old enough to go to college, Sante stopped sleeping with her husband and started sleeping with Kenny, living off-campus with him in Santa Barbara. Kenneth died and Sante had him cremated, but she didn't report his death so that she could keep spending his fortune. He had never updated his will to include her—and there is some question about the legality of their marriage, since there is a suspicion that Sante had simply forged the license.

She lured one of Kenneth's real estate cronies into her scams, but when he objected to having his name forged on a $280,000 mortgage document and threatened to go to the authorities, he disappeared. His body turned up in a Dumpster near the Los Angeles airport. Sante and Kenny took off in a limo, scamming their way across the country.

In Florida they learned of a wealthy New York socialite named Irene Silverman, who ran a sort of Manhattan bed-and-breakfast for the rich and fabulous. Kenny showed up at her door, dropped the name of a friend of Silverman's, and flashed a big wad of cash. He was in. A few days later, Sante arrived, posing as his assistant. On July 4, 1998, with the household staff off for the holiday, Kenny strangled Silverman and crammed her body into a suitcase. He and Sante dumped it at a New Jersey construction site, then called a friend in Las Vegas who had done odd jobs for them and invited him to come and run Silverman's Manhattan operation for them.

But their friend had already been turned by the feds, and he reported the call. When he arrived to meet with Sante and Kenny, g-men moved in and arrested the pair. After a showy trial, Sante was convicted of 58 separate crimes and sentenced to 120 years in prison. Kenny, convicted of 60 crimes, got 125 years. Another murder trial followed, at which Kenny confessed and implicated his mother. Each wound up with an additional life sentence tacked on to their existing sentences. Sante is serving out her life term in New York, and Kenny is serving his in California. Keeping a continent between a murderous mother and son seems like a good idea.

3 **SOMETIMES BROTHERS MURDER,** together or—more rarely—separately. Ronald and Reginald Kray, mentioned in "Lo-Fi" (320), were twins, born ten minutes apart on October 24, 1933.

They grew up to be the undisputed crime bosses of London's East End during the 1950s and 1960s. As celebrity nightclub owners they fraternized with Frank Sinatra, Judy Garland, George Raft, and other actors. They committed at least two murders themselves, of gangland figures George Cornell and Jack "the Hat" McVitie, and were most likely responsible for several other murders that had been committed on their instructions. Ronnie died in prison on March 17, 1995, whereas Reggie was released on compassionate grounds in August 2000, shortly before his death from cancer.

Henry Grace, also known as Professor Rothschild in the episode "Masterpiece" (408), seeks revenge on the BAU because it caught his brother, William, a serial killer. In real life, motives aren't always so noble.

Consider Larry and Danny Ranes. Their father was a gas station attendant—an alcoholic who beat his four children and his wife, humiliated his boys, and finally abandoned the family when Larry, the youngest boy, was nine. Both boys were in trouble early and often, fighting with each other and eventually taking their rage out on others.

On June 4, 1964, Larry Ranes, nineteen, admitted to an acquaintance that he had killed people. He planned to confess to a priest and then kill himself. The acquaintance alerted the police, and when they arrived, Larry readily admitted to murdering a man who had given him a ride on a lonely country road. Larry had robbed him and locked him in his own trunk, and when the man started banging on the hood, trying to alert people to his presence, Larry had pulled over and shot him in the head.

Once Larry had started confessing he kept going, admitting to killing a couple of gas station attendants in Michigan and Kentucky and another man who had given him a ride in Death Valley, California. In prison, Larry, who said he hated his name and everything it represented, changed his name to Monk Steppenwolf.

Danny Ranes wouldn't begin to kill until after Larry had already confessed to murder and been sentenced to life in prison. Danny's first homicide was in March 1972, when he was twenty-eight. He grabbed, bound, and raped a woman outside a shopping center, leaving her seventeen-month-old son wandering around by himself. Danny, who worked at a gas station himself at that time, enlisted a young partner named Brent Koster in more abductions, rapes, and murders. Eventually Koster turned on Danny, implicating him and testifying against him. Danny received five life sentences for his crimes, but the Supreme Court later set three aside on appeal. He continues to insist upon his innocence, despite Koster's testimony and his multiple convictions.

In "Children of the Dark" (304), profiler Spencer Reid points out that it's not unusual for unsubs to be related, and he uses as an example that "the Carr brothers perpetrated the Wichita Massacre."

The Wichita Massacre occurred on the snowy night of December 14, 2000. Five friends in their twenties (three men and two women) were in their beds, when two armed men—the Carr brothers, Reginald, twenty-two, and Jonathan, twenty—invaded the house sometime after eleven o'clock, killing the victims' dog. The brothers made their victims undress, forced the women to perform oral and manual sex on each other, made the men have sex (or try to) with the women, and raped the women themselves. They took them one at a time to an ATM machine and made them withdraw cash for the brothers.

Finally, they squeezed the men into the trunk of a car, put the women in the backseat, and drove them to an empty, snow-blanketed soccer field. There the victims were made to kneel while the Carr brothers shot them. One woman, whose identity has never been made public because of the nature of the crimes perpetrated against her, survived when her hair clip deflected the bullet that would have killed her. Naked, she ran through snow and subfreezing weather for more than a mile before finding help.

The next day, as word of the horrific massacre spread throughout the city, some neighbors reported seeing a truck that looked like one stolen from one of the victims parked outside an apartment building, and a new TV set was being carried from the truck into the Carrs' apartment. The police surrounded the building, and Reginald surrendered. Jonathan was caught running from a girlfriend's house after her mother turned him in.

The Carr brothers' crime spree had actually begun on December 8, when they committed an armed robbery against one victim and shot another, mortally wounding her, when she tried to escape in her car.

Although the brothers tried to finger each other in court, they were both convicted of multiple counts of kidnapping, rape, theft, and murder.

Their upbringing came into focus during the penalty part of the trial. The boys had been raised by a distant, emotionally aloof mother who sometimes beat them with electrical cords. Their father was violent as well, and he sexually abused their sister. After he abandoned the family, their mother had boyfriends who sexually abused both boys. The brothers were in frequent trouble in school, when they bothered attending.

Despite these factors, both men were sentenced to death. When the Kansas Supreme Court ruled that the state's death-penalty statute was unconstitutional, executions were halted in that state, and as a result both Carrs remain in prison.

4 **ANOTHER TYPE** of family-oriented crime sometimes comes into play on *Criminal Minds*. "Family annihilators" are people who murder whole families at once—a crime made all the more horrible when it's committed by a member of that family. Recurring villain George Foyet is described as a family annihilator. In the episode "Children of the Dark" (304), the same one that mentions the Carr brothers, reference is made to family annihilator John List.

On November 9, 1971, forty-six-year-old John Emil List waited until his children left for school and then put out a note for the milkman, canceling delivery. While his wife, Helen, ate her toast in the kitchen of their nineteen-room mansion in Westfield, New Jersey, List shot her in the jaw. Leaving her dead on the floor, he went up to his mother's third-floor apartment, burst in, and shot her just above the left eye. Her knees broke when she fell. List shoved her onto a carpet runner and pulled her into a storage closet.

Back downstairs, he dragged his wife forty feet into the ball-room. There he opened up Boy Scout sleeping bags on the floor, two side by side and a third perpendicular to them. He dumped Helen on the third one and tried to clean up the blood.

His plan was to wait for the kids to come home from school, but his daughter, Patricia, sixteen, phoned from school and said she was sick. List picked her up, then hurried to enter the house ahead of her. When Patty entered, he shot her in the back of the head. He dragged her by her feet into the ballroom and deposited her on part of the other two sleeping bags.

With time to spare, he left the house, did some banking, and mailed a batch of letters. Later in the day, he picked up his son Frederick, thirteen, from an after-school job. When they got home, List shot Fred before he had even taken his coat off. Fred was put in the ballroom with his mother and his sister.

John Jr., fifteen, came home from soccer practice earlier than expected and caught List unprepared. They struggled, but List managed to kill the boy, shooting him ten times. List put him on the sleeping bags, straightened everybody out, draped towels over their faces, and then knelt and prayed over his family. John List was a very devout man.

All that done, he sat down and wrote out a detailed confession, addressed to his church's pastor, and put it in an envelope with other documents. He had already informed the children's schools that they would be gone for a while, on a family trip to North Carolina. He ate dinner and slept in the billiards room. In the morning, he switched on all the lights in the house, turned on music that would play throughout the house on an intercom and cranked it up, and left.

Patty had told her drama coach that she was worried about her father and that if the coach heard anything about a family vacation, it would mean that her father had killed her. That night, her coach drove past the house, but seeing it all lit up, he decided that everything must be okay.

Nobody entered the house for nearly a month. On December 7, a neighbor noticed that the lights were burning out and that the place seemed abandoned. The neighbor called the police, and List, whose body was not present, was immediately the prime suspect, but he was nowhere to be found.

List had adopted the name Robert Clark and moved to Colorado, where he had remarried and started a new life. When his second marriage started to fray and his new life seemed to be disintegrating in much the way that his old one had, he turned to a neighbor for comfort. That neighbor was an avid reader of the tabloids, and in 1987 she saw a story about those long-ago murders in New Jersey, complete with a photo and a description of the missing man. She knew it had to be the man she knew as Clark, but she didn't report him. When *America's Most Wanted* ran a segment on the crime in 1989, she was again reminded of Clark, who had moved to Virginia with his second wife. The neighbor called the show, and soon some FBI agents had List in custody.

His life had fallen apart, List claimed in his letter to his pastor. His wife refused to attend church with him anymore, his professional life was collapsing, he was deeply in debt, and his daughter didn't respect him. He couldn't think of any other way out. At his trial he claimed that by killing his mother, his wife, and his three children, he was sending them to heaven, but he couldn't kill himself because that would doom him to hell. On November 5 of that year—just four days before the murders—he had even sat them all down and asked them how they would want their remains handled in the event that they died.

It wasn't much of a defense, and the jury found him guilty on all counts and sentenced him to five consecutive life terms. List died of complications from pneumonia on March 21, 2008.

5 **THE EPISODE** "Children of the Dark" (304) also makes reference to another family annihilator: Mark Barton. Barton was different from John List in two ways: he didn't confine his killing to his immediate family, and he murdered his family over a much greater span of time.

Barton, born in Germany to an air force family on April 2, 1955, was raised in South Carolina. He attended Clemson University and the University of South Carolina, earning a degree in chemistry in spite of an ongoing drug habit that he resorted to crime to feed. In Atlanta, Georgia, after graduation, he seemed to be settling down. He married Debra Spivey, and they had two children, Matthew and Mychelle.

But his life wasn't as stable as it seemed. The family moved to Arkansas for Barton's job. He became paranoid and distrustful of his wife, and he lost his job when his performance slacked. He sabotaged company data on his way out the door and served a brief stint in jail as a result.

Back in Georgia, Barton found a new job and a new girlfriend, Leigh Ann Vandiver, about whom his wife knew. In 1993, while on a family camping trip to Alabama, Debra Spivey and her mother, Eloise, were bludgeoned to death. Barton was a suspect, but since there wasn't enough evidence to prosecute him, he was never charged.

In 1995, he and Leigh Ann were married. Again he started acting strange, suffering deep depressions and paranoid delusions. He lost a big settlement from his wife's death through day trading and ended up owing money instead of making it. After losing $105,000 in a single month, he decided the time had come to act.

He woke early on July 27, 1999, and bludgeoned Leigh Ann to death in her bed. The next night, he did the same to Matthew and Mychelle. He covered them with blankets and left notes on their bodies, and on July 29 he went to the downtown offices of the company he worked for, the All-Tech Investment Group. He chatted with his coworkers for a while, then said, "I hope this doesn't ruin your trading day," pulled out two pistols, and started shooting. After killing four people in one building, he calmly walked through the police lines into another building and opened fire again, killing five more. Then he passed through the police yet again and vanished.

The police eventually searched for Barton at his home and found the bodies of his family members. In a note Barton left behind, he denied responsibility for the deaths of his first wife and her mother.

An intensive manhunt ensued. Five hours later, Barton threatened a young girl. She ran away from him and called for help, and once more the police were on his trail. When his van was spotted, the police followed him into a gas station in Acworth, Georgia. Surrounded, Barton ducked back into the van and shot himself, elevating that day's total to thirteen dead at his hands. We will probably never know if he also murdered his first wife and his mother-in-law. But the real question that will always remain is this: Did his second wife know whether he had killed his first wife?

6 **ALTHOUGH THIS FINAL** pair has yet to merit a mention on *Criminal Minds*, it seems remiss to close out a chapter on families killing together, and family annihilators, without at least a passing reference to a pair of brothers who famously teamed up to murder their parents.

On the night of August 20, 1989, film and music executive Jose Menendez and his wife, Kitty, were dozing in the family room of their Beverly Hills mansion, with the James Bond flick *The Spy Who Loved Me* playing on their TV. Two men came into the room bearing 12-gauge shotguns. One fired two shots at Jose, then held the barrel to Jose's head and finished him off. The commotion woke Kitty, who tried to run. A shotgun blast savaged her leg and knocked her down. She tried to get up, but the blasts kept coming. Before it was over, Kitty had been shot ten times at close range. Finally, each victim's kneecaps were maimed, gangland style, presumably to make the whole event look like an organized-crime hit.

A few weeks earlier, Kitty had confessed to her sons' psychotherapist—who was treating them as part of their sentence for some burglaries they'd been convicted of—that she feared her two sons were psychopaths.

Before the year was out, the sons, Lyle and Erik, had spent more than a million dollars of their inheritance. Erik, eighteen, confessed the double homicide to the brothers' psychotherapist, who initially kept quiet about it even though Lyle, twenty-one, threatened him, thereby technically releasing the therapist from the bond of doctor-patient privilege. The doctor's girlfriend overheard one of their sessions, however, and she went to the police, fearing for her boyfriend's safety. When the police arrived with arrest warrants, the doctor told them everything.

The Menendez brothers had been worried that their father would cut them out of his will. They'd been in trouble for various crimes, and relations were tense. They claimed—although there was no independent verification—that their parents had abused and molested them all their lives. Erik was in Israel when Lyle was arrested, but when Erik flew back to Los Angeles, the detectives met him at the airport.

Their first trials ended with hung juries, but the brothers were tried again, found guilty of first-degree murder with special circumstances and conspiracy to commit murder, and sentenced to life in prison, where they remain to this day.

The Fairer Sex

SO FAR WE'VE BEEN discussing male criminals almost exclusively, except for those women who act as part of a couple or a family. The reason for this is simple: most serial killers and mass murderers are men. Women tend to murder people they know, family members or acquaintances, and they're more likely to choose poison over other weapons. *Most* is not the same as *all*, however, and the balance depicted on *Criminal Minds* is pretty close to the balance in real life.

One of the show's notable exceptions is Megan Kane, the high-priced call girl in the episode "Pleasure Is My Business" (416). Megan is not exactly the fictional cliché of the hooker with a heart of gold, but she does focus her murderous impulses on men who avoid—as her father avoided—their parental responsibilities.

Referenced in that episode, as well as in another with a female unsub, "Jones" (218), is a hooker whose heart was anything but gold—and who, in her professional life, was anything but high-priced.

1 **TWO YOUNG MEN** looking for scrap metal along I-95 in Volusia County, Florida, made an entirely different sort of discovery on December 13, 1989. They came across a male body, wrapped in a carpet runner. The victim, shot three times in the chest with a .22, was identified as Richard Mallory of Clearwater, who was last seen thirteen days earlier. Mallory owned an electronics repair business, but he didn't have any regular employees, so when he vanished, no one paid much attention. He had a habit of vanishing anyway, taking off on liquor-and-sex binges for days at a time. He had a fondness for booze, pornography, strippers, and hookers. The police had few clues, and the case went cold in a hurry.

Six months later, another corpse turned up. This one, a nude man identified as David Spears, had been missing for a couple of weeks after vanishing during a drive to Orlando.

A few days later, the authorities found yet another dead man, shot nine times with a .22. Eventually identified as Charles Carskaddon, he was a rodeo worker.

On July 4, 1990, a car with two women in it ran off the road near Orange Springs, Florida. A witness reported that the two women got out, screaming and cursing at each other, and asked the witness not to call the police. They tried to get the car going again, but the damage was considerable, and they soon abandoned it and set off on foot. The sheriff's deputies were able to identify the car as belonging to Peter Siems, who had been missing since June 7. His body has never been found.

Troy Burress disappeared on July 30 and turned up five days later. He had been killed by two bullets from a .22.

Dick Humphreys, a retired air force officer and a onetime police chief, celebrated his thirty-fifth wedding anniversary on September 10, vanished on September 11, and was found on September 12. He had been shot seven times with a .22.

More than a month passed before the nude body of Walter Gino Antonio, a trucker and a reserve police officer, was found. He had been shot four times with a .22.

Although these murders took place in different jurisdictions over many months, the similarities did not go unnoticed. Steve Binegar of the Marion County Sheriff's Criminal Investigation Division figured that the men would not have picked up hitchhikers, so the killer had to be someone they would have seen as nonthreatening. He suspected the two women who had been driving Peter Siems's stolen car, and he had the media run sketches of them.

By mid-December, many people had reported what appeared to be the same two women to police, although the names varied considerably. One of them was probably Tyria or Ty Moore; the other was Lee, or Lee Blahovec, or Susan Blahovec. They were a couple, and Lee, or Susan, was a prostitute. The authorities in Harbor Oaks, Florida, knew Blahovec as Cammie Marsh Green. She also used the aliases Sandra Kretsch and Lori Grody. Cammie Marsh Green had pawned items that had belonged to David Spears and Richard Mallory, and a palm print found in Peter Siems's car matched Lori Grody. All of these names were aliases used by Aileen Wuornos.

Wuornos's story had a hard beginning. Born Aileen Carol Pittman on February 29, 1956, she, like many serial killers, was given up by her birth mother. Her maternal grandparents, Lauri and Britta Wuornos, adopted Aileen and her older brother, Keith, in 1960. She never met her father, a psychopathic child molester who had spent time in mental hospitals and later hanged himself in prison. Wuornos said that her grandfather and adoptive father, Lauri, physically and sexually abused her from a young age and that her grandmother and adoptive mother, Britta, was an abusive alcoholic.

Wuornos didn't know that they weren't her birth parents until she was twelve. By the time she was fourteen, Wuornos had had multiple sexual partners, including her brother, according to her claims, and was pregnant. She went to a home for unwed mothers and gave birth to a boy, whom she put up for adoption.

That year, Britta Wuornos died. Within the next few years, Aileen ran away from home and took up prostitution to support

In "Doubt," after shutting down a college campus, the BAU team creates a detailed profile of their unsub, but when the killings on campus continue after they take a suspect into custody, the agents begin to doubt themselves.

herself. Soon her brother, Keith, died of throat cancer, and Lauri committed suicide. Wuornos's life looked as if it might turn around when a wealthy sixty-nine-year-old man married her, but she was already out of control, and the marriage was quickly annulled.

With her face severely scarred from burns she had suffered in a childhood accident, Wuornos could never have been the kind of high-end call girl seen in "Pleasure Is My Business." Instead, she plied her trade at cheap motels and low-end bars. She abused drugs and alcohol, and in addition to hooking, she relied on theft, forgery, and armed robbery to make ends meet. In 1986, she met Tyria Moore in a gay bar in Daytona, and they fell in love. Their relationship was troubled, but although the romance died off, they remained friends and traveling companions.

After Wuornos was arrested she confessed to the murders but insisted that Moore was innocent. Wuornos had killed the men, she said, because they had threatened her. She'd been raped several times on the job, and she'd gotten tired of it. After that, whenever a man started to rape or threaten her, she responded with violence. All of the killings had been done in self-defense, she insisted. But the more times she told the story, the more it changed; each time she cast herself in a better light, as the victim rather than the perpetrator of the crimes.

Wuornos was tried and convicted of Richard Mallory's murder even though she continued to claim self-defense throughout the trial. She received her first death sentence for that one. To the charges of the murders of David Spears, Troy Burress, and Dick Humphreys, she pleaded no contest, and she pleaded guilty to the murders of Charles Carskaddon and Walter Gino Antonio, earning six death sentences altogether.

No charges were ever brought in the Peter Siems case. After the Mallory trial was over, evidence emerged that Mallory had served ten years in prison for violent sexual attacks. A new trial for Wuornos was denied, despite this new twist that might have convinced jurors that her first murder had, in fact, been self-defense. She had recanted her claims of self-defense in the other cases.

Eventually Wuornos chose to fire her attorneys and cease her appeals. "I'm one who seriously hates human life and would kill again," she wrote to Florida's Supreme Court. She was allowed to choose her method of execution and picked lethal injection over the electric chair. Her last words, on October 9, 2002, were, "I'd just like to say I'm sailing with the Rock and I'll be back like Independence Day with Jesus, June 6, like the movie, big mothership and all. I'll be back."

2   **MORE TYPICAL** of female serial killers was Dorothea Puente, who ran a boardinghouse in Sacramento, California—an occupation she took up after the law shut down her brothel. When the rent she collected wasn't enough to maintain the lifestyle to which she aspired, she took to killing her boarders, many of whom were elderly and disabled, and then she continued to cash their Social Security checks.

Puente buried seven bodies in her yard, but officials believe that she killed at least nine people. Her crimes were revealed when an investigation into a missing tenant turned up bodies buried in the yard. She was sentenced to life in prison without parole on December 10, 1993, when she was sixty-four years old.

3 **THE QUEEN** of female killers—and perhaps the most prolific serial killer in history, of either sex—was Countess Erzsébet Báthory of Transylvania. Known as Elizabeth Báthory in the United States, she is believed to have tortured and killed at least 650 girls and young women between 1585 and 1610, with the help of four servants.

Her victims were originally servant girls, but when that crop began to run out, she turned to lesser aristocrats. After the testimony of the participating servants and some survivors, Báthory was convicted of eighty murders and believed to be responsible for at least three hundred.

The figure of 650 comes from her own diaries, in which she kept track of her victims. She was imprisoned for life, walled up in her own rooms, where she died on an unknown date in 1613 or 1614. Given the nature of her crimes, Báthory was clearly a sexually sadistic serial killer of the highest order, and her station in life allowed her to live out her wildest fantasies.

4 **FEMALE KILLER** Chloe Kelcher, in the episode "The Angel Maker" (402), is said to suffer from hybristophilia, a state in which one becomes sexually aroused by the knowledge that a partner has committed a violent act. Perhaps the most infamous hybristophiliac of modern times is Veronica Lynn Compton.

In June 1980, Veronica Compton, then twenty-three, was a writer and a would-be actress with a serial-killer obsession. She contacted Kenneth Bianchi while he was in prison awaiting trial as one of the Hillside Stranglers, and she described to him a play she was writing called *The Mutilated Cutter*, about a female serial killer. She wanted a real serial killer's take on the material.

Their correspondence reveals that Compton had an unhealthy fascination with rape, mutilation, murder, and necrophilia—just Bianchi's kind of pen pal. They rapidly developed a romantic relationship, and Bianchi suggested a desperate defense ploy to which Compton readily agreed. She visited him in prison, and he gave her a book with part of a rubber glove pressed between the pages. Inside the glove was some of his semen. She flew to Bellingham, Washington, where he had been arrested for a pair of murders, with the plan of murdering another woman and planting Bianchi's semen on the corpse. This would, Bianchi hoped, make the police believe that they had the wrong man in custody and that the real rapist-murderer was still on the loose.

In a fictional variation on this idea, Anna Begley, a student in the episode "Doubt" (301), attacks and stabs a girl, copying the MO of the already-arrested Nathan Tubbs, in order to win Tubbs's release.

Compton managed to lure a woman to a motel room, but when she tried to strangle her victim, the woman overpowered her and ran away, then reported the attack to the police. Compton escaped and returned to California, but she made a scene when she landed at the San Francisco airport that brought her to the attention of the authorities.

Although Compton had failed in her murder attempt, she wrote a letter to Bellingham officials anyway, claiming that the attack proved that the killer was still at large. With the victim's description, the California postmark on the letter, and pictures from the airport scene, the police were able to quickly identify Compton and arrest her. In jail in Washington for attempted murder, she was no longer any use to Bianchi, but he continued writing to her until it was more than obvious that she had lost interest in him.

A new serial killer had earned her fascination, and she began corresponding with him: Sunset Strip Murderer Doug Clark, formerly romantically linked to Carol Bundy. Compton soon took Bundy's place in Clark's heart, and the two shared an intense romance through the U.S. mail. As a valentine, Clark sent Compton a photo of himself posed with a headless female corpse. Romance flared in Compton's heart, and she wrote to him, "I take out my straight razor and with one quick stroke I slit the veins in the crook of your arm. Your blood spurts out and spits atop my swelled breasts. Then later that night we cuddle in each other's arms before the fireplace and dress each others wounds with kisses and loving caresses."

Compton escaped from prison in 1988, but was recaptured. She was finally released in 2003. After her release, she married a college professor she had met and seduced in prison. She wrote and self-published a book in 2002 called *Eating the Ashes*, about her experiences in the penal system.

9

The Helpless Ones

AS HEINOUS AS THE ABDUCTIONS, rapes, and murders of adults are, there's something particularly chilling when the same crimes are committed against children, the most helpless among us. A man or a woman who is victimized at least has a fighting chance of surviving and, having survived, of overcoming the mental and emotional trauma. But a child victim, even if he or she survives, faces an entire life scarred by the experience.

On *Criminal Minds*, as in real life, children can be both victims and perpetrators of crimes. In the episode "What Fresh Hell?" (112), eleven-year-old Billie Copeland is the victim of stranger abduction, and this serves as the focal point for a discussion of various child victims.

1 ONE OF THE CHILDREN mentioned in "What Fresh Hell?" is Polly Hannah Klaas, who is also referred to in the episode "Seven

Seconds" (305). Twelve-year-old Polly was having a slumber party on October 1, 1993, when a man entered her bedroom with a knife. Insisting that he was "just doing this for the money," he tied up the three girls, put pillowcases over their heads, and left with Polly. One of the girls freed herself and woke Polly's mother, Eve Nichol. Nichol was separated from her second husband at the time, and she and Polly lived with Polly's half-sister in Petaluma, California. Nichol dialed 911 immediately, kicking off a search that would include terrible missteps.

Although Polly's father, Marc Klaas, was an immediate suspect, the story the girls told seemed to eliminate him, since Polly would certainly have recognized him. The Petaluma police broadcast a description of Polly's abductor, but not every police officer in the area received the report.

Responding to a trespassing report near Santa Rosa, twenty-five miles away, the sheriff's deputies encountered a man standing by a Ford Pinto stuck off the road. He was sweating profusely, despite the late hour and the cool night. The police checked for outstanding warrants, and the man came up clean. However, a full background check would have shown that he was wanted for violating parole on a previous crime and that he had a long history of violent assaults against women and girls, along with robbery, burglary, and kidnapping. That would have allowed them to search his car, which might have saved Polly's life. Instead, the police freed the stuck Pinto and let Richard Allen Davis drive away.

Within days, the details of Polly's abduction and her abductor were everywhere: printed on posters, spread through computer networks, faxed around the country, and shown on *America's Most Wanted*. Actress Winona Ryder, who grew up in Petaluma, offered a reward of two hundred thousand dollars. The Polly Klaas Center was established to coordinate the efforts and accept telephone tips. Nichol and Klaas were definitively ruled out as suspects through polygraph tests.

On October 19, Davis was picked up for drunk driving. The arresting officers didn't note his resemblance to the sketches of

Polly's abductor that had been so widely circulated, and he was released once again.

The Polly Klaas Foundation achieved tax-exempt status, and Bill Rhodes, the print-shop owner who had started it, was named its president. Although the hunt for Polly was still on, the foundation expanded its mission to the search for missing children everywhere. Rhodes turned out to be a registered sex offender who had preyed on young girls, using a knife to subdue them. He then became an instant suspect, since the perpetrators of such crimes often like to involve themselves in the investigations. The police checked out his alibi and cleared him, but he was removed from the foundation.

On November 28, the owner of the rural land on which Davis had been trespassing when his Pinto got stuck found some strange items on the property, including a sweatshirt, red tights, a condom wrapper and a loose condom, and binding tape. Police looked at the old trespassing complaint and finally matched Davis with a palm print found in Polly's room. They picked Davis up, and after a few days in custody he confessed to Polly's murder, then led the investigators to where her body had been exposed to the elements for the last two months. He had strangled her with a piece of cloth after the run-in with sheriff's deputies over the stuck Pinto. He denied having molested her, but his story was full of inconsistencies, and there was no scientific way to tell after so much time had passed.

Davis, a loser who had spent his life in and out of prison, was convicted of first-degree murder with special circumstances. His reaction to the verdict was to display both middle fingers to the courtroom. When he was allowed to speak at his sentencing hearing, he used the opportunity to claim that Polly told him that her father had sexually molested her. The judge said that this outburst made it very easy to sentence Davis to death, which he did. As of this writing, although the California Supreme Court recently upheld the sentence, Davis remains on death row at San Quentin.

Marc Klaas (who later created the group KlaasKids) and the original Polly Klaas Foundation have become tireless advocates for missing children and have helped many families reunite.

In "The Boogeyman," Dr. Reid and Morgan examine a tight-knit community in Texas to determine who has been victimizing local children.

2 **ANOTHER YOUNG** victim mentioned in the episodes "What Fresh Hell?" (112) and "Seven Seconds" (305) is Danielle Van Dam. Danielle was seven years old on February 1, 2002, when she was taken from her home in the upscale San Diego suburb of Sabre Springs. Her mother, Brenda, had gone out to a bar with friends, leaving her father, Damon, at home with the girl and her two brothers. Damon put Danielle to bed around 10:30 p.m. When Brenda returned home at 2 a.m. with her friends, she shut Danielle's door but didn't look in on her. The friends stayed for about an hour, then left. In the morning, Danielle was gone. Her parents searched the house, growing increasingly frantic, then called the police.

The case quickly turned into a media sensation—it was a Polly Klaas–style disappearance, but in an age even more saturated with twenty-four-hour news channels and the Internet. Brenda and Damon held news conferences and appeared on national TV shows like *Today* and *Larry King Live*, expressing their hopes that their daughter's abductor would bring her home safely.

It didn't take long for the Van Dams' personal lives to be made an issue in the case: they were swingers and were open about their lifestyle. Brenda was bisexual, and she had watched her husband having sex with her friends. While their private lives didn't seem to make a difference, when a suspect was arrested and the case finally brought to court, these factors were raised as a way to claim that the accused wasn't the only person with access to Danielle; the friends—two women and two men with whom Brenda had been out drinking and dancing—might have done something to the girl.

In the end, that was all a distraction. One of the people in the bar that night was David Westerfield, a neighbor who lived two doors down from the Van Dams. Westerfield drove his RV out into the California desert that weekend, and a tow truck operator reported having towed it from deep sand near the Mexican border. When Westerfield returned home with his RV, he had it thoroughly cleaned. He also dropped off laundry at a dry cleaning shop that weekend: comforters, pillowcases, and a jacket. Testing would later reveal Danielle's blood on the jacket as well as inside the RV. The police rapidly made Westerfield a suspect and put him under surveillance. They found child pornography in his home, but it was the DNA evidence from the jacket and the RV that led them to place him under arrest. He denied abducting Danielle, and he had no criminal record.

Five days later, on February 27, Danielle's body was found in a remote desert spot, twenty-five miles from San Diego. She had been dumped almost immediately after her disappearance, with no attempt made to cover her up. The authorities were unable to determine the cause of death because her body was badly decomposed.

At his trial, Westerfield, who had failed a polygraph test, continued to proclaim his innocence. In addition to offering the DNA and fiber evidence and the massive amounts of pornography found in his home, the prosecution showed that Westerfield had fondled his own niece when she was seven years old. (In an echo of this case, the victim in "Seven Seconds," six-year-old Katie Jacobs, is abducted from a shopping mall by her uncle, who has been molesting her.)

The jury convicted Westerfield of kidnapping and murder, and he was sentenced to death. After the trial was over, a rumor spread that he had been about to make a deal for life in prison in return for showing the location of Danielle's body, but just before the details were hammered home, her body was located. Like Richard Allen Davis, Westerfield is currently awaiting execution at San Quentin.

3 **DR. SPENCER REID** looks into an old case that stimulates dreams about half-recalled memories of his own childhood, in the two-part "The Instincts" (406) and "Memoriam" (407). When Reid was a boy, he had known the victim, six-year-old Riley Jenkins, and the mystery's solution reaches deep into Reid's own life, helping to explain his parents' divorce.

During the initial investigation, Riley's parents were suspected, and they stopped cooperating with the police—just like, it's explained in the episode, the parents of JonBenét Ramsey.

JonBenét's murder is one of the most infamous unsolved crimes of the twentieth century, and it's also brought up in the episode "Children of the Dark" (304). JonBenét's mother, Patsy, was a former beauty queen, and her father, John, ran his own computer company. The family was affluent and had moved from Atlanta, Georgia, to Boulder, Colorado, when JonBenét was nine months old. They lived in a large, expensive home at which they entertained frequently. Only six years old, JonBenét had already participated in and won many beauty pageants. The winter of 1996, Patsy had just overcome ovarian cancer, and John was selected as Boulder's "businessman of the year." It should have been a charmed time for the Ramsey family.

But the morning after Christmas 1996, Patsy was on her way downstairs when she found a note on the staircase demanding a $118,000 ransom for JonBenét's safe return (John Ramsey had received a holiday bonus of just that amount). If the ransom wasn't paid, the note warned, JonBenét would die. Patsy dashed to JonBenét's room, but the girl was gone. She called the police, and the couple almost immediately started working on raising the ransom payment.

The Boulder police didn't do themselves or the case any favors. They didn't immediately search or seal the house or perform a full investigation of the crime scene. Neighbors and friends came and went at will. Hours after the police had arrived, a detective suggested to a family friend, Fleet White, that he and John search the house for anything unusual. In the basement, eight hours after the police had been called, John and Fleet found JonBenét covered with a white blanket, dead. There was duct tape over her mouth. Her wrists were bound with white cord, and more of the same cord was wrapped around her throat, where it had been used, along with a paintbrush handle, to garrote her. She had been strangled, and her skull was fractured. There was inconclusive but likely evidence of sexual assault, and although DNA evidence was recovered from her underwear, it has never been matched to anyone.

Because the little girl had never left the house, and John Ramsey had found her, the parents, and to a lesser extent JonBenét's brother, Burke, were immediately suspected. The media coverage played up this angle, stretching the facts on occasion to make it appear more likely that the Ramseys were involved.

JonBenét was buried in Atlanta on New Year's Eve 1996. After the Ramseys returned to Boulder, the stories about them grew ever more heated. Videos of JonBenét participating in pageants hit the airwaves, and the Ramseys were accused of sexualizing and exploiting their six-year-old and perhaps even sexually abusing her during her lifetime. Seeing the suspicion with which the police viewed them, the Ramseys did indeed cease cooperating.

Various bits of evidence—a boot print, a palm print, a pubic hair, and more—were found that indicated that an intruder had come into the house and murdered JonBenét. However, there was no sign of forced entry. Experts suggest that the killer probably knew the family, knew about John's bonus, and felt comfortable enough in the house to assault and kill JonBenét there instead of taking her away. The murderer brought in the duct tape and the white cord, so he always intended to abduct, if not kill, the child.

The years have passed, with accusations, suspicions, and lawsuits, but with no solid suspects and very little movement in the case. A convicted sex offender named John Mark Carr confessed to JonBenét's murder in 2006, but it didn't take long to determine that he didn't know the facts of the case and wasn't even in Boulder that fateful Christmas.

Patsy Ramsey died on June 24, 2006, after her ovarian cancer recurred. She went to her grave never knowing who killed her daughter—unless, as many continue to insist, she was involved. Some evidence suggests otherwise, however, and she was never charged. Although the Boulder police have kept the case open and return to it from time to time, there's every likelihood that this case will never be solved and that JonBenét's murderer will never be brought to justice.

4 **BILLIE COPELAND,** the eleven-year-old victim in "What Fresh Hell?" (112), is abducted by a stranger using the "lost dog" trick: asking a child to help search for a lost dog in order to lure the child away from adult supervision. A similar ruse was used on July 15, 2002, to abduct five-year-old Samantha Bree Runnion, who is mentioned in that episode, from outside her home in Stanton, California. A stranger approached Samantha and a friend, who were playing outside, and asked if they had seen his lost Chihuahua. When Samantha moved closer to the man, he grabbed her and wrestled her into his car. She kicked and screamed and called out to her friend to tell her grandmother, and then she was gone.

Samantha's friend remembered enough details about the kidnapper and his car to allow police sketch artists to come up with a reasonable likeness. The drawing was promptly displayed on posters and in the media, but it was too late for Samantha. The next day, her battered, sexually molested nude body was found beside a rural road in nearby Riverside County. Her killer had spent several hours with her before crushing her abdomen and strangling her.

Alejandro Avila was arrested three days later, after having been singled out by a telephone tip. He had been to Samantha's apartment building before, because his ex-girlfriend and her daughter lived there. Avila had been accused of molesting the daughter and another friend when they were young girls, but he had been acquitted. With the Danielle Van Dam trial making headlines not far away in San Diego, there was furor over Avila's arrest, with local and national officials, including President George W. Bush, declaring Avila "Samantha's killer" before he had even gone to trial.

The physical evidence was overwhelming. His tire tracks were found near Samantha's body, her DNA was inside his car, and his DNA was under Samantha's fingernails. This and other evidence from the abduction scene and the murder scene was presented to the jury, which convicted him of kidnapping, murder, and lewd acts upon a child.

Avila was sentenced to death on July 22, 2005. In Samantha's memory, her mother, Erin Runnion, and Erin's partner, Ken Donnelly, established the Joyful Child Foundation to advocate for the protection of children from abduction and sexual abuse.

5 WHEN A CHILD DISAPPEARS, one of the first responses of law enforcement today is to issue an AMBER Alert. (AMBER stands for America's Missing: Broadcast Emergency Reponse, but in some states the alerts go by other names, commemorating local abduction victims.) AMBER Alerts have shown up on *Criminal Minds* in the episodes "The Instincts" (406) and "A Shade of Gray" (421).

When an AMBER Alert is issued, it is broadcast on commercial radio, network TV, and cable TV stations; on the national Emergency Alert system; on electronic highway signs; and over the Internet and cell phones to people who have signed up to receive alerts. The system is voluntary but elicits a great deal of cooperation among law enforcement and other branches of local and state government, private industry, and individuals.

The original source of the acronym and the name was the case of Amber Hagerman, a nine-year-old girl who was snatched while riding her bicycle in Arlington, Texas, on January 13, 1996.

A witness saw a man grab her from the bike and throw her into the front seat of a pickup truck.

Four days later, a man walking his dog found Amber's corpse in a creek bed. Her throat had been slit, but she had been kept alive for two days before being killed. Her murderer has never been discovered, but the knowledge that her legacy continues to help other families helps Amber's loved ones cope with their loss.

6 **NOT EVERY** violent crime against children is committed by an adult. Some attacks on children are committed by other children—a tragedy that can ruin or end two young lives instead of just one. *Criminal Minds* acknowledges this sad pattern. The serial killer of young children in "The Boogeyman" (206) is a child himself. And in "A Shade of Gray" (421), the killer of seven-year-old Kyle Murphy is Kyle's older brother.

"A Shade of Gray" first aired in April 2009, so it couldn't have been inspired by the case of Andrew Conley, who was arrested in December 2009 for killing his little brother. But Conley admitted to being inspired by TV—specifically the cable series *Dexter*, about a serial killer. After Conley, seventeen, allegedly strangled his ten-year-old brother, Conner, to death, he said the act made him feel just like Dexter.

Conley says that he was wrestling with his brother and then began choking him. This went on for about twenty minutes, until he saw blood leaking from the younger boy's nose and mouth. Pulling a plastic bag over Conner's head, Conley affixed it with electrical tape, then dragged the body into the basement and finally to his car, striking Conner's head on the ground several times en route. He put the body in the trunk of his car, then drove to his girlfriend's house to give her a ring.

The girlfriend later told the investigators that Conley seemed happier than he had been in a while. Conley dumped Conner's body in a park. He confessed to the police and told them where to find Conner, admitting that he had fantasized for years about killing someone.

.   .   .

A few weeks earlier, on October 21, 2009, according to her confession, fifteen-year-old Alyssa Bustamante allegedly stabbed to death a nine-year-old neighbor, Elizabeth Olten, in Missouri. Bustamante, whose online profile listed "killing people" and "cutting" as hobbies, had been institutionalized for a suicide attempt in 2007. Days before the murder, Bustamante dug two holes in the ground in a wooded area; then she killed Olten with no provocation, she said, because she wanted to know what it felt like.

Conley and Bustamante will both be tried as adults, a process that owes much to a young man named Willie Bosket.

One of the most vicious young offenders in U.S. history, Willie Bosket is already in prison, where he will spend the rest of his life. But for Bosket, prison doesn't necessarily mean an end to violent crime.

Bosket was fifteen when he killed for the first time, on March 19, 1978, but he already had an extensive criminal history. He once attempted to rob a snoozing New York City subway passenger, but the man woke up. Bosket pulled a .22, sold to him by his mother's boyfriend, and shot the man through the eye and in the temple, killing him instantly. Within days, the boy was robbing again, in and around the transit system, and on March 27 he killed again.

It didn't take long, given this record, for the police to pick Bosket up. The boy was intelligent but disrespectful and foul-mouthed, even in court. At fifteen, he claimed to have committed more than two thousand crimes, many of them stabbings. His father had gone to prison for robbery and murder, and now it was his turn. He entered a guilty plea and received a sentence of five years in a Division of Youth facility. He would be out by the age of twenty-one.

In response to Bosket's case, the New York legislature passed the Juvenile Offender Act of 1978, allowing kids as young as thirteen who commit murder to be tried as adults.

Bosket broke out of his facility, and although he was recaptured within hours, he had turned sixteen before his breakout, which made his escape a felony. He was sentenced to four years in a state prison. After his release at twenty-one, he was accused of another robbery, and while in court he was involved in a scuffle that ended with him being convicted of assault, resisting arrest, and contempt of court—another felony count.

In prison again, convinced that he would never be released, Bosket assaulted some guards and set fire to his cell, which resulted in a third felony conviction. Because of the "three strikes" law, Bosket was right: he was in prison for life. Once he realized that, he became even more belligerent and dangerous: he stabbed a guard, clubbed another guard with a lead pipe, continually set fire to his cell, and even mailed a death threat to President Ronald Reagan. By 1989 he had been confined to a special dungeon cell in upstate New York, with a Plexiglas wall behind the bars, so he can't throw things or strike at the guards. Several video cameras keep him under surveillance at all times.

For his crimes in prison he has earned multiple life sentences, ensuring that he'll never leave custody. Yet determined to live despite his circumstances, Bosket said, "If they bring back the death penalty, I won't kill. I'll just maim. I want to live every day I can just to make them regret what they've done to me."

7 **THE YOUNG KILLERS** in "Hopeless" (504) are older than Conley, Bustamante, and Bosket when they committed their murders. But the final homicides of the group killers in the episode are set off by the press and police giving credit for the crimes to a flash-mob riot, in which young people of various ages tear apart Washington, D.C.'s, Dupont Circle. Flash-mob riots are still a new thing, and, one hopes, not a growing trend. A flash mob is a group of people who have been summoned by cell phone and social messaging sites to congregate in one place. In most cases (despite the name *mob*), their purpose is peaceful—more participatory performance art than violent chaos. But in some cases, these events turn bad.

A flash-mob riot in Philadelphia on May 30, 2009, caused thousands of dollars of loss to a looted store, damage to businesses and vehicles, assaults on individuals, and criminal charges filed for assault, theft, and rioting. More than a hundred teens and young adults turned out for the flash mob, in which a fifty-three-year-old man, riding his bike home from work, was grabbed, thrown over the hood of a car, and beaten. The victim, who is now on disability, has been having seizures ever since the incident.

At the University of Tennessee in Chattanooga, the police were called when a flash mob of about a thousand stormed the university library in April 2009 after having been messaged to attend a party there. The students dispersed after the police emerged from the library and sprayed the crowd with pepper spray.

Young people have always been drawn to violence, and in too many cases they are victimized by it. Some statistics show that the number of young violent offenders is growing even as overall violent crime in the United States is shrinking. This is a trend that everyone should hope will quickly be reversed.

Angels and Heroes

THE PHRASE "Angels of Death" comes up occasionally on *Criminal Minds*, notably in the episodes "Penelope" (309) and "A Higher Power" (315). Angels of Death murder people who are suffering in some way; the unsub in "A Higher Power" kills people who lost their loved ones in a tragic fire. A similar concept, "Hero Homicide," arises in "L.D.S.K." (106) and in "Doubt" (301). Hero Homicide occurs when someone puts people at risk in order to save them and be granted hero status for doing so. It's a common form of murder for health-care practitioners, for instance, who sometimes endanger patients so that they can be credited with saving their lives; if the patients die anyway, the practitioners can tell themselves that the patients' pain was so great that they did their victims a favor.

Some of history's most prolific serial killers fit into these two categories. Angels of Death can be hard to catch, and because their victims are at risk anyway, the deaths are often not recognized as murders. Some, like Dr. Jack Kevorkian—used as an example in the episode "Children of the Dark" (304)—publicize their activities. Kevorkian has made a career and a cause of physician-assisted suicide, claiming that patients have the right to die if they so choose. He says that he's responsible for helping to end the lives of at least 130 patients. In 1999 he was sentenced to a prison term of ten to twenty-five years for second-degree murder. He was paroled in 2007 for good behavior. Kevorkian continues to draw crowds with his lectures and to make the case for the right to die.

Kevorkian's patients actually do want to die, and in most cases they carry out the final steps of their procedures themselves, with his coaching and assistance. Most Angels of Death are far less discriminating.

1 **IN "LIMELIGHT"** (313), FBI agent Jill Morris declares that the unsub she's after "may be the most prolific serial killer since Charles Cullen." Cullen's exact body count is uncertain, like the counts of some other murderers in competition for that particular dishonor, but in any listing of the worst U.S. killers, he's definitely in the running.

Cullen was born on February 22, 1960, in West Orange, New Jersey. He was the youngest of eight children; his father, Edmond, was fifty-eight years old when Charles came along. Edmond died when Charles was seven months old, and during his youth two of Charles's siblings also died. His mother perished in an auto accident while he was in high school.

After high school, Cullen enlisted in the navy. An officer once found him at a submarine's control panel for nuclear missiles, dressed in a green surgical gown, a mask, and gloves that he had taken from a supply cabinet. He was disciplined for the transgression—and he could not have fired the missiles—but he never explained why

In "Children of the Dark," Hotchner and the team suspect that two unsubs may be working together in a series of brutal home invasions and murders taking place in a Denver suburb.

he was so attired. Cullen was socially awkward and a constant target of ridicule by his shipmates.

After the submarine incident, Cullen transferred to a supply ship and was discharged after a suicide attempt. He went back to New Jersey and in 1987 graduated from nursing school, married, and got his first nursing job, at St. Barnabas Medical Center in Livingston, New Jersey. He stayed at that job for four years, a record in a career in which he raced through nine jobs in the next eleven years.

His second nursing job, at Warren Hospital in Philipsburg, New Jersey, put him in the cardiac and intensive care units—where it's not uncommon for patients to die. Cullen preferred the graveyard shift, when he was largely unsupervised and had alone time with many patients and ready access to potentially dangerous drugs.

He and his wife had two daughters, but she filed for divorce in 1993, claiming that he wouldn't talk to her or have sex with her and that he beat their Yorkshire terriers and spiked people's drinks with lighter fluid. He lost custody of the children and moved into a basement apartment. Around this time he began harassing another nurse at the hospital, trying to date her and even give her an engagement ring. Finally he broke into her home while she and her six-year-old son were sleeping, and Cullen was arrested. The day after his arrest, he tried to commit suicide again.

Later that year, Cullen was accused of murder for the first time. It would not be the last.

On August 30, 1993, he gave a ninety-one-year-old breast cancer patient an injection that had not been ordered by her doctor. She complained, but no one at the hospital took action, and she was released. She died the next day. Her son claimed that Cullen had killed her, but the autopsy missed the evidence: although screening for a hundred different toxins, it didn't include the potentially deadly heart medicine digoxin—one of Cullen's favorites. A polygraph test was inconclusive, and the prosecutor didn't pursue the case. The hospital took no disciplinary steps on the murder accusation or the stalking and trespassing charges, and Cullen left his job voluntarily at the end of that year.

Throughout the next decade, he worked at several more hospitals, leaving behind a trail of unexplained deaths. On December 12, 2003, he was finally arrested and charged with one murder and one attempted murder. Cullen not only chose not to contest the charges against him, he also upped the ante by telling the investigators that in sixteen years he had poisoned thirty or forty patients—he had lost count—at ten different hospitals in New Jersey and Pennsylvania.

The investigators had to study hundreds of cases, and they will never be certain how many people Cullen killed. Various institutions along the way had suspected him, but when he hopped to a new job, no warnings or negative evaluations followed him. Despite his homicides, his attempts at suicide, and his psychiatric hospitalizations, he was always rehired and able to kill again.

Cullen's initial explanation was that he had killed to end the suffering of his patients. That didn't meet the smell test, because some victims were recovering just fine without his "help." He had also put insulin into stored intravenous bags; he didn't know if that had claimed any victims, but he had no way of knowing what patients would get which bags, so he wasn't particular about whom he hurt. Finally, he said, "I couldn't stop myself. I just couldn't stop."

The pattern of Cullen's crimes through the years indicates that he struck when things were going badly in his personal life: when his wife divorced him, when he got into trouble for stalking his fellow nurse, when he filed for bankruptcy in 1998. Powerless against the pressures of life, he sought the power of life and death over others.

Cullen offered hospitals advice on how to protect patients from people like himself, but it was couched in a self-aggrandizing way. The implication was that the hospitals were ultimately responsible for letting him get away with his crimes; the murders weren't his fault because they could have been prevented.

Forced to appear in court against his wishes, Cullen sat silently and was unapologetic when he received eleven consecutive life sentences in New Jersey. Made to show up for trial a week later in Pennsylvania, he interrupted a sentencing hearing by repeating, "Your honor, you need to step down" over and over. The judge had been quoted in a newspaper saying that he would make Cullen attend the hearing, and apparently Cullen took offense at that.

Cullen continued his chant even after the court officers had gagged him with cloth and duct tape. The families and loved ones of the victims tried to speak, but even muffled, Cullen was audible, disturbing their last chance to have their say. The judge, ignoring Cullen's complaint as best he could, sentenced Cullen to six more life sentences. He'll be in prison in New Jersey for the rest of his life.

2 **COMPARED TO DR. HAROLD SHIPMAN'S** murder score, Charles Cullen's was amateur.

Harold Frederick Shipman was born in Nottingham, England, on January 14, 1946, and graduated from medical school in 1970.

By the time he was arrested in 1998, he had, according to a massive British government investigation called the Shipman Inquiry, killed at least 250 of his patients, and possibly twice that number. On January 31, 2000, despite insisting on his innocence, Shipman was convicted of fifteen murders and sentenced to life imprisonment. That sentence didn't last long, because he hanged himself in his cell on January 13, 2004, without ever satisfactorily answering the question of why he had killed so many.

3 **ANGELS OF DEATH** and Homicide Heroes are not always male. During a two-month period in 1982, at a pediatrics clinic in Kerrville, Texas, seven children suffered seizures while under the clinic's care. The clinic's director, Dr. Katherine Holland, didn't find this suspicious, but the clinic staffers knew that something was wrong. Then a one-year-old infant died on the way to the hospital—a child who had not even been very sick to begin with.

In the days after that incident, a licensed vocational nurse named Genene Jones told Dr. Holland that she had found a bottle of a powerful muscle relaxant that had been missing for three weeks. The cap was missing, and the rubber top had been punctured. Later, Holland found that what looked like medicine in the bottle was really saline water—someone had used up the bottle's real contents. When another bottle was found to be missing, Dr. Holland fired Jones.

Damage had already been done to Dr. Holland's practice, however, and to her personal life. Her husband wanted a divorce. A Kerr County grand jury held hearings about the suspicious rash of seizures at the clinic.

A separate grand jury convened in San Antonio in February 1983 to study forty-seven suspicious deaths of children at the Bexar County Medical Center Hospital—where Genene Jones had worked before joining the staff at Dr. Holland's clinic.

Jones liked to feel needed and important. She made judgment calls that were better left to doctors, and she harangued new nurses into turning to her when they had problems. She was fascinated with doctors and saw them as powerful beings. She had a hero complex, wanting to bring children to the brink of death so she could save them.

As her seniority at Bexar had grown, she'd been able to pick her own shifts, so she was able to arrange for most of the critically ill children in the hospital to be under her care. Her odd behavior was noted: Jones once grabbed a dead infant from the arms of a family member and ran down the hospital corridor; on another occasion she used a syringe to squirt fluid on a dead child in the shape of a cross, then repeated the gesture on herself.

The hospital decided to replace its licensed vocational nurses with registered nurses, and Jones resigned, so no further action was taken. It is believed that at the two facilities she killed between eleven and forty-seven children. The staff at Bexar destroyed thousands of documents that were under subpoena by the grand jury, so the full extent of Jones's crimes is uncertain.

Kerr County charged Jones with one count of murder and brought charges of causing injury to the other seven children there. San Antonio brought a charge of attempted murder. Jones was sentenced to 159 years in prison, but because of a law intended to reduce prison overcrowding, she'll be automatically paroled in 2017.

4 **GENENE JONES** is mentioned in "The Uncanny Valley" (512), along with another Angel of Death, Amy Archer-Gilligan. Archer-Gilligan did not directly inspire any episodes of *Criminal Minds*, but she is believed to have been an inspiration for the famous play *Arsenic and Old Lace*. In 1907, Archer-Gilligan, called Sister Amy by her patients, opened a nursing home for the elderly in Connecticut. Her business model was to extract a payment of a thousand dollars, in advance, for lifetime care.

Once she had the money, she made sure that "lifetime" was brief indeed. Between 1911 and 1918, forty-eight people under her care died, including her two husbands, who each died within a year of marrying her. When someone finally got suspicious, some of the bodies were exhumed, and high levels of arsenic were found. She was charged with only six murders and convicted of just one. She got a life sentence, which she served in a mental institution.

5 **A DOCTOR** is a murder suspect in "L.D.S.K." (106). He's arrogant and conceited, and Jason Gideon thinks the BAU is dealing with a Homicide Hero—someone who, like Genene Jones, puts people in danger so he can save them. The doctor, in this case, turns out not to be the killer. But Spencer Reid compares him to a similar type of killer, Richard Angelo, a nurse at Good Samaritan Hospital in West Islip, New York. Angelo had a history of wanting to do good works, as an Eagle Scout and a volunteer firefighter.

At the hospital, Angelo's plan was to inject elderly patients with muscle-paralyzing drugs that would lead to respiratory failure. Then, when the Code Blue sounded, he would rush to the scene and save the patients.

Angelo's problem was that he wasn't very good at the saving part. As a result, the patients kept dying. When one patient caught him making an unknown, unordered injection, he used his call button to summon help before he succumbed. After a search of Angelo's locker and home revealed stores of the problem drugs, the police arrested him and exhumed the bodies of some possible victims.

Angelo, who was believed to have committed at least twenty-five murders, was convicted on December 14, 1989, of two counts of depraved-indifference murder, one count of second-degree manslaughter, and associated crimes. He was sentenced to sixty-one years to life.

6 **INDIRECTLY RELATED** to Angels of Death is the problem of Munchausen syndrome by proxy. Munchausen syndrome is a disorder in which a person reports imaginary illnesses out of a craving for the care and sympathy with which the ill are treated. Unlike hypochondria, in which a person's delusion of having an illness is based on an underlying emotional conflict, Munchausen syndrome is characterized by the feigning of an illness out of a pathological desire to undergo diagnostic tests, hospitalization, surgery, and other medical procedures.

Munchausen syndrome by proxy, however, adds a sinister twist: the perpetrator acts as if *someone else* is sick—usually a child, a spouse, or a person under his or her care. The perpetrator's drive to indirectly "benefit" from medical care lavished upon the victim is so great that cases have been seen in which, for example, a parent actually harms a child (such as by poisoning), falsifies the child's medical history, or tampers with the child's medical specimens in order to create a situation that appears to require medical attention.

While most cases of Munchausen syndrome by proxy don't make headline news, perhaps because of the vulnerable nature of the victims and the intimate relationship they have with their victimizers, a notable exception is the case of Julie J. Gregory. Gregory wrote a book called *Sickened* that details her victimization at the hands of her mother, who fed her books of matches, pills that caused blinding headaches, and more. Gregory spent what seemed like much of her childhood in doctors' offices and hospitals, and underwent a needless heart catheterization. If not for the resistance of one doctor, Gregory's mother would have succeeded in forcing Gregory to undergo open-heart surgery.

In the episode "Risky Business" (513), Will Summers is an emergency medical technician (EMT) who poisoned his wife gradually, sending her to the hospital many times before her eventual death. Now he's persuaded his own son, and other teenagers, to play a dangerous "choking game." As an EMT, he knows he'll be sent out on calls and can revive the participants. He has done so many times with his son, but in other cases it has been too late for the victims.

Killers with a Cause

THE KILLER IN THE EPISODE "Doubt" (301) is a campus security guard. With murdered girls turning up on campus, it's easy for him to attract more victims, since he's someone they turn to for protection. Although the BAU team has a profile, Derek Morgan reminds them that Richard Jewell fit the profile of the bomber at the 1996 summer Olympics in Atlanta, but he was innocent, and the accusation ruined his life. When a defense attorney in the episode "Tabula Rasa" (319) also points out that the BAU's profile led to Richard Jewell, Aaron Hotchner counters that when you look at the real Olympic bomber, Eric Rudolph, the profile was dead-on.

1 **RICHARD JEWELL** was a college security guard. While working as a guard at the 1996 Summer Olympic Games in Atlanta,

Jewell found a backpack containing three pipe bombs. He alerted the authorities and helped them to clear the area. The bombs exploded, killing one person and wounding more than a hundred. Another victim, a Turkish television cameraman, died of a heart attack while running to cover the blast.

Without Jewell's discovery and a warning phone call from the real bomber, the number of dead and injured could have been considerably higher. At first Jewell was called a hero, but as the days passed, he went from hero to suspect. It was theorized that he had planted the bombs he "found," and the whole plot stemmed from his desperate need to be seen as heroic. He was crucified in the media and was sued, and his entire life was put under a public magnifying glass. Virtually everyone he had ever known was interrogated, and he found himself under surveillance.

In October 1996, he was officially cleared by the investigating U.S. attorney, and in August 1997, U.S. Attorney General Janet Reno formally apologized. On April 13, 2005, an Army veteran named Eric Rudolph pleaded guilty to planting the bombs. Jewell died on August 29, 2007, at the age of forty-four, suffering from heart disease, kidney disease, and other ailments.

The real bomber, Rudolph, wasn't finished.

Two bombs exploded at an abortion clinic in Sandy Springs, Georgia, an Atlanta suburb, on the morning of January 16, 1997. The first, placed on the building's rear porch, damaged an empty examination room. The second explosion, about ninety minutes later, was near the parking lot, and seven people were injured in the blast. Bombers often plant two devices, the first intended to cause some damage and the second to kill or injure emergency responders on the scene.

On February 21, a bomb exploded at the Otherside Lounge, a lesbian nightclub in Atlanta, and injured five people. The police found a second explosive device and defused it.

Investigators were looking into similarities among the three bombings when a letter showed up at some Atlanta news media outlets from a group calling itself the Army of God. The letter included details about the bombings that caused the investigators to believe that the writers were involved. It also railed against "sodomites" and abortion clinics and concluded with the phrase "Death to the New World Order."

The next bomb, at a clinic that provided abortion services in Birmingham, Alabama, exploded on January 29, 1998. An off-duty police officer working as a clinic guard was killed, and a clinic nurse was badly injured.

This time a witness saw a man get into a pickup truck and drive away. The truck, it turned out, belonged to Eric Rudolph.

Eric Robert Rudolph was born in Florida on September 19, 1966, but after his father died in 1981, his mother moved the family to rural North Carolina. They lived in a cabin in the mountains, with a wood-burning stove, a generator in case of power failures, and a distiller so they wouldn't have to drink fluoridated water. Rudolph's mother held a variety of fringe beliefs that were passed on to her children: she was paranoid about Social Security numbers, didn't trust the government, partly homeschooled her kids, and taught her children the racist beliefs of the Christian Identity movement, which claims that Anglo-Saxons are the "true" Israelites of the Bible and that Jews are the offspring of Satan.

When Rudolph was in a public school, he turned in a paper on the Holocaust in which he "proved" that it never happened. He grew up hating gays, blacks, and Jews and admired Nazi general Erwin Rommel. He was also a devoted user, and eventually cultivator and seller, of marijuana, reportedly earning sixty thousand dollars a year from it.

Two days after the Birmingham bombing, Rudolph essentially vanished. The authorities believed that he shouldered a backpack and headed into the hills around his North Carolina home. They swarmed into the area, launching one of the largest manhunts in U.S. history. While on the run, Rudolph became a folk hero to many in the fringe movements of the extreme right. In absentia, federal grand juries handed down twenty-three counts against Rudolph in the bombing incidents.

A rookie police officer spotted a suspicious looking man in an alley behind a grocery store in Murphy, North Carolina, on May

In "Amplification," when a new strain of weaponized anthrax is released into the public, Dr. Reid and the team work with members of the Centers for Disease Control and the Department of Homeland Security to catch the unsub.

31, 2003. Suspecting that a burglary was in progress, the officer drew his gun and ordered the man to come out and lie down on the ground. The man complied, and the manhunt came to an end. Rudolph had been captured at last.

Survivalist and military training had kept Rudolph alive through cold winters in the North Carolina mountains. His defense team seemed anxious to keep him a free man, but in April 2005, he agreed to a plea deal. As part of the deal, he directed the authorities to a stash of more than 250 pounds of dynamite he had buried in the mountains, and he admitted guilt in all of the crimes with which he was charged. In exchange, he would receive four consecutive life sentences instead of the death penalty. The way he put it, he "decided to deprive the government of its goal of sentencing me to death." He claimed it was a "purely tactical choice" on his part and did not indicate any guilt.

Rudolph wrote further that he believes that abortion is murder and that force is therefore justified in trying to stop it. He considers homosexuality "aberrant sexual behavior," permissible in the privacy of one's home but not in public, and any attempt to present it as something legitimate and normal should be met with force. He saw the Olympic games as an example of "global socialism," and he hoped to shut them down.

In other words, in his statement Rudolph doesn't admit to doing anything wrong (although he has apologized for the Olympic bombing and claims to have felt remorse at the time); he merely details and excuses his actions on the basis of his extremist political beliefs.

The Army of God organization continues to support Rudolph, hosting a Web site where his writings can be found and soliciting funds for him to use in prison. He's spending the rest of his days in a supermax facility in Florence, Colorado, where the only continuing damage he can do to society is as a propagandist and an inspiration to those who share his views.

2 **A DIFFERENT** Olympic attack is referenced in "The Tribe" (116), in which the killers are members of a cult who strike in a pack. BAU profiler Elle Greenaway mentions the 1972 Munich Olympics, in which members of Black September, a faction of the Palestine Liberation Organization, broke into the housing for the Israeli Olympic team, killed an athlete and a coach, and took nine more hostage. The terrorists demanded the release of 234 Palestinians from Israeli prisons. They also wanted two German terrorist leaders, Andreas Baader and Ulrike Meinhof, released and given safe passage out of West Germany.

Israel refused to negotiate with the terrorists, but West Germany, hoping to avoid a bloodbath at the games it was hosting, tried to stall the Palestinians. The terrorists kept pushing back the deadline for when they would start killing, knowing that the longer the drama played out, the more people watching on TV around the world would be exposed to their cause.

The Palestinians demanded a flight to Cairo, so the West German authorities developed a plan to take out the terrorists at the airport. While the terrorists and their hostages helicoptered in from the Olympic Village, the police got into place. Five police sharpshooters would try to hit the terrorists on the tarmac, but in case that failed, there were to be more police positioned on the airplane, disguised as crew. At the last minute, the backup plan was called off, so everything was up to the sharpshooters.

However, the sharpshooters—none of whom had sniper training—were expecting five terrorists, and there were eight. The shooters got into position, and two terrorists crossed the tarmac to check the plane. Unexpectedly finding it empty, they hurried back to the helicopters.

As the other six terrorists came out of the helicopters, the Germans opened fire. Three Palestinians went down right away. Finally, after more than an hour, armored personnel carriers moved on the helicopters, and as they did, the terrorists killed their hostages. Five terrorists were killed in the firefight, along with one West German police officer. The remaining Palestinians were captured, but they were released later when more terrorists hijacked an airliner and demanded their release.

The West German rescue plan had been flawed from the start, and the resulting tragedy almost brought the games to an end. The decision was made to continue the games, and after a memorial service on September 6, 1972, the games went on as scheduled.

3   ANOTHER REFERENCE in "The Tribe" (116), as well as in "The Crossing" (318), in which Stockholm syndrome is discussed, is to Patty Hearst and the Symbionese Liberation Army (SLA). Patricia Campbell Hearst came from a wealthy family; she was the granddaughter of newspaper magnate William Randolph Hearst.

Hearst was attending the University of California at Berkeley when, on February 4, 1974, members of the SLA kidnapped her from the apartment she shared with her fiancé. The SLA demanded the release of two convicted killers, members of the group, from prison. Officials refused. The kidnappers changed their demand,

and the Hearst family met the new one, providing two million dollars in food aid to the poor. Then the group wanted more.

Meanwhile, Patty had been tied up and kept in a closet. In addition to experiencing food, sleep, and sensory deprivation, she was repeatedly raped and ranted at. All she knew was what her tormentors told her, and she had to do whatever they said in order to stay alive. The next time she appeared in public, she was calling herself Tania and helping the SLA to rob a bank. Two bystanders were shot, though not by her.

On May 16, SLA member Bill Harris was detained for shoplifting at a Los Angeles sporting goods store. In this incident, "Tania" unloaded a whole clip from an M-1 carbine, then got another rifle and continued shooting. She and her friends got away, but the next day the police surrounded the SLA hideaway, and after a massive shootout the place went up in flames. Six SLA members were killed, but Hearst, Bill Harris, and Bill's wife, Emily, were holed up in a motel near Disneyland, watching the whole thing on TV.

After more bank robberies and some bombings, Hearst was arrested in San Francisco on September 18, 1975. Convicted of bank robbery and use of a firearm during the commission of a felony, she was sentenced to seven years in prison.

The theory at the time was that Hearst's transformation into Tania was the result of Stockholm syndrome, the phenomenon in which captives come to identify with their captors. Hearst later said that that's not what happened, that she was coerced into committing the crimes. An FBI agent who interviewed her after her arrest, however, said that she was a classic case of Stockholm syndrome.

In 1979, after Hearst had served two years of her sentence, President Jimmy Carter commuted her sentence.

4 **EVERY AMERICAN** who is alive today knows about Osama bin Laden and al-Qaeda, the Islamist group that attacked the United States on the morning of September 11, 2001. One *Criminal Minds* episode, "Lessons Learned" (210), deals explicitly with al-Qaeda when Jason Gideon, Spencer Reid, and Emily Prentiss travel to the U.S. detainment facility at Guantanamo Bay, Cuba, to interrogate a prisoner who has knowledge of a terrorist plot in Virginia.

Al-Qaeda has its roots in the opposition to the Soviet invasion and occupation of Afghanistan from 1979 to 1989. The mujahedeen (Muslim freedom fighters)—both native Afghanis and Arabs who came to join the struggle—fought the Soviets, and they were financed by the CIA, which was working with the Pakistani intelligence service, and Saudi Arabia. One of the Arabs who came to join the Afghanis was a Saudi Arabian named Osama bin Laden, who built roads (with the resources of his family's construction company), collected financial contributions from wealthy Saudis and other gulf-state Arabs, and organized the Arab volunteers who flooded in to join the fight.

Bin Laden was born into a very wealthy family in Riyadh, Saudi Arabia, in the year 1377 in the Islamic calendar, which corresponds to July 1957 to July 1958 (his exact birth date is unknown, despite various rumors on the Internet). His father, Mohamed, was a poor man in Yemen who started a construction company and rose to become the main building contractor for the Saudi royal family. Mohamed had fifty-four children (twenty-five sons and twenty-nine daughters) by twenty-two wives. Osama was somewhere between the seventeenth and twenty-first son. He was the only son of the marriage of his father and his mother, a Syrian-born woman whom Mohamed divorced soon after the birth of their son—and for whom he then arranged a marriage to another man. Osama continued to live with his mother, who had four children with her next husband.

In 1968, the year after his father's death in a small-plane crash, bin Laden was enrolled in an exclusive school in Jedda, Saudi Arabia. At his school, instead of wearing traditional Arab dress, the students wore uniforms similar to those of British schoolboys (white shirts, ties, and blazers in the winter months). Having lost his father (and despite having a stepfather), bin Laden might have been susceptible to the Syrian-born (like his mother) physical-education teacher, who offered an informal Islamic study group after school.

The teacher used soccer to entice the boys to join, then he told them that before playing each time they would read a verse from the Koran. Gradually he increased the study of the Koran and eliminated the playing of soccer. The teacher was a member of the Muslim Brotherhood, a religious and political movement formed in opposition to British rule in Egypt. After the British abandoned the region, the group remained active, opposing the rule of President Gamal Abdel Nasser in Egypt and secular rule in any Muslim country. Despite being suppressed by Nasser, the Muslim Brotherhood flourished underground and continued advocating for rule by sharia, or Islamic law.

It was in this study group that bin Laden was exposed to the concept of violent jihad, or holy war against non-Muslims, and other forms of extreme political and religious activism. Bin Laden became committed to the group and its fervent cause of politically transforming the entire Muslim world.

In Afghanistan, bin Laden finally got to put some of his ideas into action. The Soviet invasion was exactly the sort of colonial-style takeover by "infidels" that he opposed. His role was as an organizer and a financier, and he worked with Saudi officials (and, indirectly, the CIA) to raise funds for the cause. When the Soviets withdrew early in 1989, this was evidence to bin Laden that Islamic fundamentalists could defeat a major superpower. Ultimately, he believed, the Soviets' defeat in Afghanistan helped to break up the Soviet Union. Bin Laden would soon transfer this belief and this goal to the United States.

Bin Laden's network coalesced into the organization called al-Qaeda, which means "the Base" in Arabic. After the Soviets withdrew, he returned to Saudi Arabia to work for his family's construction company, but he was already more radicalized than most of the family, and he made no secret of his views. In 1990, when the Saudi government permitted U.S. troops to be stationed there after Iraq's invasion of Kuwait, bin Laden was outraged by the idea of a non-Muslim presence in his homeland, which he viewed as a desecration. He offered his mujahedeen to fight the Iraqis, but his offer was rebuffed by the Saudi king, and the U.S. military arrived in Saudi Arabia. Bin Laden was expelled from his country the next year as a result of his antigovernment activities and diatribes. He took his fortune and moved to Sudan, where he owned a farm on which he raised horses and trained jihadis. A couple of years later Saudi Arabia revoked his citizenship.

In 1993, al-Qaeda's first violent action inside the United States took place: the bombing of New York's World Trade Center. Six people died and hundreds more were wounded by a truck bomb that exploded in an underground garage. Six people were arrested, tried, and convicted on terrorism charges.

Bin Laden didn't restrict his ire to U.S. soil, however. In October 1993, his jihadis teamed with Somalis to kill eighteen U.S. soldiers in Somalia. An al-Qaeda truck bombing in Riyadh in 1995 claimed five American lives and killed two Indians.

Bin Laden left Sudan in 1996, when that country, bowing to pressure from the U.S. and Saudi governments, expelled him. His next home was Afghanistan. Many have called the pressure on Sudan a mistake—at least there people knew where he was. In Afghanistan, he slipped off the radar. But he was far from inactive. That year, a U.S. Air Force barracks in Saudi Arabia was bombed, and nineteen U.S. servicemen were killed.

Bin Laden issued a fatwa (an Islamic legal decree) in early 1998 declaring war on the "Jews and Crusaders" of the United States: "The ruling to kill the Americans and their allies—civilians and military—is an individual duty for every Muslim who can do it in any country in which it is possible to do it," he stated.

Truck bombs exploded on August 7, 1998, outside the U.S. embassies in Nairobi, Kenya, and Dar es Salaam, Tanzania, killing 224 people, 12 of them Americans. The United States responded with cruise missile attacks against terrorist camps in Afghanistan and a pharmaceutical plant in Sudan.

The next direct attack against U.S. interests came on October 12, 2000, when al-Qaeda suicide bombers blew up a small boat beside the USS *Cole*, a destroyer moored in a harbor in Yemen, killing seventeen U.S. sailors.

Then came September 11, 2001, when nineteen al-Qaeda suicide bombers flew two airplanes into the World Trade Center's Twin Towers and a third airplane into the Pentagon; a fourth plane was intended to strike the U.S. Capitol but was downed by passengers in a field in Pennsylvania before it could reach its target. Nearly three thousand people were killed on this day, which made it the world's worst terrorist attack to date. *Bin Laden* and *al-Qaeda* became household names. A month later a multilateral military action, led by the United States, was launched in Afghanistan against al-Qaeda and its Taliban hosts. Bin Laden narrowly escaped capture and death at Tora Bora and remains on the loose today.

Subsequent al-Qaeda attempts against the United States include the failed airliner bombings of Richard Reid, who carried explosives in his shoe, and Umar Farouk Abdulmutallab, who carried them in his underwear. Quick-acting civilians foiled both plots. There are also alleged al-Qaeda connections to 2009's Fort Hood shooting.

The last *Criminal Minds* episode of the third season, "Lo-Fi" (320), and the first episode of the fourth season, "Mayhem" (401), involve the planning and execution of a terrorist attack in New York City, during which Special Agent Aaron Hotchner unknowingly helps to place an ambulance loaded with explosives near a hospital in which an unspecified but very important person is being treated. On January 18, 2010, well over a year after the episode first aired, a Taliban suicide bomber drove an explosives-packed ambulance close to Afghani president Hamid Karzai's presidential palace and detonated it.

On July 7, 2005, Muslim suicide bombers exploded four bombs in London, killing fifty-six and injuring about seven hundred. This attack is mentioned in the episode "Mayhem." The same episode refers to Dr. Azahari Husin, a Malaysian terrorist and an engineer who is believed to have built the bombs used in devastating terrorist attacks in Bali and Indonesia. Associated with the terrorist group Jemaah Islamiyah, Husin was killed in a police raid on November 9, 2005.

Al-Qaeda remains the focus of a great deal of controversy and uncertainty. Rather than a rigidly controlled organization, it appears to be a loose network of many groups, some of which, like al-Qaeda in Iraq or al-Qaeda in the Arabian Peninsula, use the name but don't necessarily share any operational structure with other branches or have a direct connection to bin Laden. Even if bin Laden were to die or be captured, his role at this point might be largely symbolic; new al-Qaeda leaders are rising up all the time. Since the struggle of the West is against Islamist jihadism as a whole rather than against a specific group or people, many believe that the best way to approach the effort is through a combination of intelligence and law enforcement tactics. Others consider it war and prefer a military-oriented response. The usual U.S. approach has been to combine the two, using every tool possible.

Despite al-Qaeda's many attacks around the world and the impact that those attacks have had on the civilian populations of the targeted countries, the overall goal that Osama bin Laden espouses—to remove Western countries from the Middle East and reestablish the caliphate (Islamic religious rule) throughout the Muslim world—has yet to come to pass. Although there appears to be a nearly unlimited supply of disaffected young (mostly male) Muslims willing to give their lives to suicide missions, many more Muslims have been turned off by bin Laden's tactics, which increasingly seem to include killing other Muslims.

5 **ANTHRAX ATTACKS** are the crime around which the *Criminal Minds* episode "Amplification" (424) revolves. The anthrax killer in this episode proves to be a scientist who was fired from his position at Fort Detrick. The 9/11 attacks are also mentioned in this episode, and the Amerithrax attacks (so named because they were suspected to have been caused by terrorists on U.S. soil) also come up in the episodes "Lessons Learned" (210) and "100" (509).

The first wave of letters containing anthrax spores—coarse brown granules—were mailed in Trenton, New Jersey, on September 18, 2001, just a week after the 9/11 attacks. They were sent to the *New York Post*, NBC News, ABC News, CBS News, and the *National Enquirer*. On October 9, two more letters were mailed, also from Trenton, addressed to Democratic senators Tom Daschle, the Senate majority leader, and Patrick Leahy, the head of the Senate Judiciary Committee.

When a Daschle aide opened the letter and found the substance inside, government mail service was immediately shut down; as a result of that and a misread zip code, the Leahy letter didn't turn up for more than a month. While it languished in Sterling, Virginia, a postal worker there contracted anthrax poisoning. The anthrax that was sent to the senators was more potent than the first batch, a highly refined white powder described as "weaponized." The media letters caused cutaneous (through the skin) anthrax poisoning, whereas the purer powder caused inhalational (through the breath) anthrax poisoning, which is much more severe.

Crude letters accompanied the anthrax. The ones sent to the senators read as follows:

09–11–01
YOU CANNOT STOP US.
WE HAVE THIS ANTHRAX.
YOU DIE NOW.
ARE YOU AFRAID?
DEATH TO AMERICA.
DEATH TO ISRAEL.
ALLAH IS GREAT.

The Daschle and Leahy letters each contained enough refined spores to kill a hundred thousand people if appropriately dispersed.

The first person to die from these attacks was Robert Stevens, sixty-three, a photo editor at the tabloid newspaper the *Sun* (published by the *National Enquirer*'s parent company, American Media, in Boca Raton, Florida). He developed inhalational anthrax and died on October 5.

Some in the media and politics were already casting blame on Osama bin Laden and al-Qaeda or Saddam Hussein and Iraq, acting either independently or in concert. Others suspected domestic terrorists on the far right, observing that the two senators who were targeted were both political liberals who held key positions in determining whether the post-9/11 U.S. Patriot Act would be brought to the Senate floor for a vote. The FBI launched a massive investigation of the attacks, now called Amerithrax, that would continue for years.

On October 21 and 22, two more victims, both postal employees, died. A hospital employee died on October 31, and the fifth fatality, a ninety-four-year-old woman in Connecticut, died on November 21. No anthrax was found in her home, but it was believed that she was exposed to some carried by the mail.

The strain of anthrax that was killing people was determined to have come from the U.S. Army Medical Research Institute of Infectious Diseases at Fort Detrick, Maryland. A "person of interest," Dr. Steven Hatfill, who worked at the facility, was named, and the FBI searched his home. He was later cleared, but not before the accusations and the publicity devastated his life. The government settled a lawsuit brought against it for ruining Hatfill's reputation.

In late July 2008, the FBI notified another Fort Detrick scientist, Dr. Bruce Edward Ivins, that it was going to charge him with the attacks. On July 27, Ivins committed suicide before the charges could be filed. The FBI concluded that Ivins had acted alone. He had helped to develop an anthrax vaccine and was upset that it was about to be taken off the market. He also had a long history of making homicidal threats and had struggled with anxiety, paranoia, and depression. He was a Catholic with strong anti-abortion feelings, and it was speculated that he sent anthrax letters to the two Democratic senators because they were known to be prochoice.

Not everyone is convinced that Ivins was the perpetrator or that he acted alone if he was. The investigation continues on some fronts, but as far as the FBI is concerned, it had identified its man, was able to prove its case to the bureau's satisfaction, and was ready to go to court. The presumption of innocence until proven guilty in a court of law evidently did not apply, with Dr. Ivins dead, and no more definitive answer may ever be known.

6 **ANOTHER CRIMINAL** who is frequently brought up in the show is the Unabomber. He's mentioned by that moniker in "Amplification" (424) and "100" (509) and by his real name, Ted Kaczynski, in "Won't Get Fooled Again" (103) and "A Real Rain" (117).

The Unabomber was first heard from on May 25, 1978, when a crude bomb exploded in the hands of a University of Chicago campus police officer. The victim's injuries were minor because the bomb was a primitive device constructed in a wooden box.

Another bomb went off at Northwestern University on May 9, 1979, again slightly injuring the person who found it. On November 12, a bomb exploded on an American Airlines flight from Chicago to Washington, D.C., and twelve passengers suffered from smoke inhalation. Both of these bombs were also in wooden boxes, but the composition of the bombs was becoming more sophisticated. The airplane bomb had been sent through the mail, so it wasn't meant to target a specific airline or flight, because the bomber couldn't know on which flight his package would end up.

United Airlines president Percy Wood received a package, purportedly containing a book, at his Chicago-area home on June 10, 1980. When he opened the package, the book proved to have been hollowed out to conceal a bomb. Wood received minor injuries. The package held a wealth of clues, including the letters FC engraved on a metal part of the bomb. The package had been sent to Percy Wood, there were bits of *wood shrapnel* inside the package, the book had been published by *Arbor* House, and the phony return address was on *Ravenswood* Street. The bomber was displaying his signature, loud and clear.

The FBI launched a task force that included representatives from the Bureau of Alcohol, Tobacco, and Firearms and the U.S. Postal Inspection Service. Their code name for the case was Unabom, which stood for the "*un*iversity and *a*irline *bom*bing" targets.

The investigators didn't have much to go on yet. They knew how the Unabomber constructed his bombs, but he made them from scrap material that could have been found almost anywhere. His targets had been selected, it turned out, almost at random.

Over the next few years, additional bombs turned up. Some were defused before they went off; others caused injuries of various degrees of severity. The signature FC became commonplace.

On December 11, 1985, the Unabomber's efforts claimed their first life, that of Hugh Sutton, a computer store owner in Sacramento, California.

The next incident, on February 28, 1987, provided what might have been a real clue: an eyewitness saw a hooded man in sunglasses placing an object on the ground. The object turned out to be a bomb that seriously injured the man who found it.

After that, the Unabomber was silent for six years. He surged back into the public consciousness in 1993, when two of his bombs injured victims on June 22 and 24. On December 10, 1994, and April 24, 1995, he struck again, and each of these bombs killed their victims.

In 1995, the Unabomber sent out a thirty-five-thousand-word manifesto that he claimed would explain his actions. He wanted it widely published, and FBI director Louis Freeh and Attorney General Janet Reno agreed. Their reasons were different from his, however: they believed that someone would recognize the ideas and the writing style and be able to identify the killer. The *New York Times*, the *Washington Post*, and other media outlets cooperated and ran the document in full.

The first line of the manifesto's introduction was "The Industrial Revolution and its consequences have been a disaster for the human race." In the fourth paragraph, the Unabomber spelled out his goal in more detail:

We therefore advocate a revolution against the industrial system. This revolution may or may not make use of violence: it may be sudden or it may be a relatively gradual process spanning a few decades. We can't predict any of that. But we do outline in a very general way the measures that those who hate the industrial system should take in order to prepare the way for a revolution against that form of society. This is not to be a POLITICAL revolution. Its object will be to overthrow not governments but the economic and technological basis of the present society.

The manifesto finally defined the FC signature, which stood for Freedom Club. Throughout, the writer referred to "we" instead of "I," but most experts believe he acted alone.

Thousands of tips poured in to the task force, but one stood out. A man named David Kaczynski pointed to his brother, Ted.

Theodore John Kaczynski was born in Chicago (the site of the first bombs) on May 22, 1942. He was a child prodigy who skipped the sixth and eleventh grades, attended an intellectually rigorous high school, and went to Harvard at sixteen, where he began to view the technologically oriented modern world as crushing to the human spirit. After earning his doctorate in mathematics from the University of Michigan—where he started, then abandoned, the process of getting a sex-change operation—he taught for two years at the University of California in Berkeley (the site of two bombs). After living for a while in Salt Lake City, Utah (the site of two more bombs), he moved into a remote mountain cabin in Montana, where he tried to live off the land.

Kaczynski's handwriting and writing style were compared with the Unabomber's notes, envelopes, mailing labels, and the manifesto itself and believed to be a match. The FBI arrested him and searched his cabin on April 3, 1996. They found a wealth of bomb-making materials; forty thousand handwritten pages of journals and notes, including descriptions of his bomb-making experiments and his mailings; and a live bomb that was ready to be sent out. He pleaded guilty in January 1998 and was sent to a supermax prison in Colorado for the rest of his life. He's an active correspondent from prison, and some of his ideas are embraced today by radical antitechnology activists.

12

Group Dynamics

SOME KILLERS, like Ted Bundy or Ed Kemper, like to work alone. Others prefer to pair up, like Lawrence Bittaker and Roy Norris, whereas still others—Kenneth Bianchi comes to mind— are happy to kill solo or as part of a team. Then there are some who seem to need the security of a group. The same dynamic works for armies and firing squads: if many people are killing, and it seems to be for a reason, then it must be okay.

Armies and firing squads, however, usually have the interests of their government or society in mind. Not so our next batch of murderers.

1 WHEN CHARLES MANSON was born in Cincinnati, Ohio, on November 12, 1934, the name that was put on his birth certificate was "no name Maddox." He was born to a promiscuous sixteen-year-old alcoholic named Kathleen Maddox. After a few weeks, he was named Charles Milles Manson, the surname coming from a man to whom Kathleen was briefly married. She filed a paternity suit in 1936 against a man called Colonel Scott, and a court awarded her a judgment of five dollars a month, which Colonel Scott never paid.

From this inauspicious beginning came one of the most notorious criminals of the twentieth century, a man mentioned more often than anyone but Ted Bundy in the first five seasons of *Criminal Minds*. Manson is mentioned in eight episodes: "Extreme Aggressor" (101), "Won't Get Fooled Again" (103), "The Popular Kids" (110), "The Tribe" (116), "Somebody's Watching" (118), "Children of the Dark" (304), "Memoriam" (407), and "The Performer" (507).

Manson's mother went to jail for robbing a gas station in 1939, and Manson went to live with an aunt and an uncle in West Virginia. The uncle was a sadist who called Manson a sissy and, in a misguided attempt to "make a man" of him, outfitted him in a dress for his first day at school—a cruel stunt that had also been done to Henry Lee Lucas. Kathleen, upon her parole, reclaimed her son, but she was not a good mother. She had a habit of leaving him with other people for days at a time while she indulged her tastes for booze and sex, and one story claims that she once traded him to a barmaid for a pitcher of beer.

In 1947 Kathleen tried to put him in a foster home. None was available, so Manson went into the Gibault School for Boys in Terre Haute, Indiana, where he stayed for ten months before running away. His mother didn't want him back, so he took off again, living on the streets and supporting himself through theft. He was arrested but escaped after a single day in jail. Recaptured, Manson was sent to Father Edward Flanagan's Boys Town, where he lasted four days before skipping out. Arrested again at the ripe old age of thirteen, he was sent to a boys' reform school, where he claims to have suffered frequent sexual abuse at the hands of other inmates and some of the guards.

In "Minimal Loss," Prentiss and Reid are taken hostage by an underground cult during a federal raid.

From there, Manson's life was a collage of crimes and prisons. When he was paroled in 1967, after serving time for pimping and transporting women across state lines for sexual purposes, it was over his own objections. He knew where he belonged and where he felt at home.

Nonetheless, San Francisco during the Summer of Love appealed to Manson. Drugs and sex partners were easy to come by, especially for an older guy who had been around the block a few times and had a certain amount of charisma. Manson was not a big man, but if his incarcerated life had taught him nothing else, it had schooled him in how to be a masterful manipulator of people. Manipulation, domination, and control are the hallmarks of a psychopathic personality, and Manson had all those in spades. He grew his hair long and dressed like a hippie. He could play guitar and was not without talent as a songwriter. Young people flocked to him, seeing him as a sort of guru.

Soon enough, the people, mostly young women, who congregated around him became essentially slaves to his whims. They became known as "the Family." As the 1960s wound down, Manson spun a web of words and dope and sex, free love and revolution and apocalypse, and he led the Family onto an old school bus and out of San Francisco. Manson wound up in Los Angeles, where he hooked up with Beach Boys drummer Dennis Wilson, and for a while the Family lived at Wilson's estate.

A man named Charles Watson, eventually nicknamed Tex, met Manson at Wilson's. The Family caused tens of thousands of dollars in damage before Wilson kicked Manson and his friends out. They moved to new digs at Spahn's Movie Ranch, which had been built primarily as a set for western movies, and Watson joined them there. Manson then set his sights on Terry Melcher, Doris Day's son, who sang with a surf band called the Rip Chords and produced records. Manson wanted Melcher to record his music; Melcher listened to it but passed. Manson fumed.

Toward the end of 1968, Manson established a new headquarters near Death Valley, at the Myers and Barker ranches. Manson had more on his mind than making it in the music business. Some of the ideas he riffed on to his Family concerned a coming apocalypse and a race war between blacks and whites. When the Beatles released their album *The Beatles*, which would come to be known as the White Album, one of the tracks, "Helter Skelter," spoke to Manson, seemingly confirming his most psychotic hopes and fears. He began using that song title as the name for his imagined race war. Blacks would win the war, he believed, but he and the Family would be safe underneath Death Valley. The Family would grow until its members outnumbered the victorious blacks, then they would emerge from hiding and take over.

As 1969 wore on, the Family's activities grew darker and more destructive. Instructed to raise money for the Family, Watson ripped off a drug dealer named Bernard Crowe. When Crowe threatened retaliation, Manson shot him in the stomach, believing that he had killed the dealer. Crowe lived, however, but he didn't report the shooting.

Still after money, three Family members dropped in on Manson acquaintance Gary Hinman. Hinman refused to turn over any cash, so they held him hostage for a couple of days. During this time Manson sliced Hinman's ear with a sword. After Manson left, Bobby Beausoleil, a Family associate, stabbed Hinman to death, and one Family member wrote "Political piggy" on a wall in Hinman's blood. Someone also drew a panther's paw, the symbol of the Black Panthers; Manson, who wanted to fan the flames of his desired race war, hoped that the radical black group would be blamed for the crime. Hinman's murder was the Family's first definite murder—although there were others that might have involved members of the Family—but not its last.

Beausoleil was arrested while driving the car he had stolen from Hinman, and he still had the murder weapon with him. Two days later, on August 8, 1969, Manson told the Family, "It's time for Helter Skelter to begin."

Terry Melcher had lived for a while on Cielo Drive, a road that wound up through a canyon above Beverly Hills. He had moved out, and that house was now occupied by actress Sharon Tate and her husband, director Roman Polanski. Manson had been by the house a couple of times since Melcher moved out, and he knew that the record producer no longer lived there. He instructed Watson to take three other Family members to the house and "totally destroy everyone" inside. Watson later said that Manson had not given specific orders to kill but that this was how he interpreted the directions. Watson, at the time, was seeking more power and influence in the Family, and killing for Manson was a step in that direction.

The Family members did as they were told. Polanski was working in London, but Tate, nearly nine months pregnant, and her unborn child were slaughtered, along with four guests: Jay Sebring, Abigail Folger, Voytek Frykowski, and Steven Parent. The murders were brutal and bloody. One victim, Frykowski, was stabbed fifty-one times, clubbed in the head thirteen times, and shot twice. Tate was stabbed sixteen times. On the way out, the murderers wrote "Pig" on the front door in blood.

The next night, Manson wanted more. This time he accompanied the four killers, and two more Family members joined them. They went into the home of Leno and Rosemary LaBianca, husband-and-wife entrepreneurs who lived next to a house where Manson had attended a party. Manson and Watson tied up the LaBiancas, and Manson left the premises.

While he was out of the house, the others stabbed Leno twenty-six times, some of those with a carving fork, and Rosemary forty-one times. Watson carved "WAR" on Leno's abdomen, and Patricia Krenwinkel wrote "Rise" and "Death to pigs" on the walls and "Healter Skelter"—misspelling what had become Manson's raison d'etre, by this point—on the refrigerator in Leno's blood.

The double whammy of vicious home-invasion murders terrified Los Angeles, but it took police a long time to connect the dots. After three months, the detectives with the L.A. County Sheriff's Office who were working the LaBianca case decided that the two assaults were connected, and among their suspects was Charles Manson. Their investigation led to Spahn's Movie Ranch and the Family, and ultimately to the Death Valley ranch, where Manson was found hiding under a bathroom sink.

On his first day of testimony, Manson arrived in court with an X carved into his forehead (which he later turned into a swastika), which was a statement that he had "Xed" himself out of the establishment world. Most of the other family members, including the female defendants, copied the mark on themselves. The prosecution argued that the murders were meant to trigger Helter Skelter.

On January 25, 1971, Manson and the other three defendants were convicted of first-degree murder and other crimes—twenty-seven separate counts against each one. All four were sentenced to death, but their sentences were commuted to life in prison when California abolished the death penalty in 1972. Manson, who had never actually killed anyone himself, was convicted on the basis of the joint-responsibility rule, which holds all of the participants in a conspiracy guilty for the crimes committed in pursuit of the conspiracy's goal.

On September 5, 1975, Family member Lynette "Squeaky" Fromme tried to assassinate President Gerald Ford in Sacramento, where she had moved in order to be close to Manson's new home at Folsom State Prison. Sentenced to life, she was released after serving thirty-four years in prison. Manson is currently ensconced at Corcoran State Prison, where he has applied for parole and been denied eleven times. He'll be eligible to apply again in 2012.

2   **IN CONTRAST** to Charles Manson, Kevin Foster rates only one mention on *Criminal Minds*, in the episode "3rd Life" (312), about a pack of teenage killers.

After a night of vandalism that earned scant coverage in the newspapers, four teenagers in Fort Myers, Florida, led by high school dropout Kevin Foster, decided to present an organized face to the world. They would be the Lords of Chaos. In their manifesto, they wrote, "During the night of April 12, the Lords of Chaos began a campaign against the world. Be prepared for destruction of Biblical proportions. The games have just begun, and terror shall ensue."

The other core members of the group were three high school seniors: comic book nerd Pete Magnotti, computer geek Chris Black, and band member Derek Shields. Other kids moved about the group's periphery and were involved in some of the escapades. Foster, eighteen and described as smart and strong, was their natural leader. His mother owned a pawnshop, and he seemed to have access to an almost limitless supply of guns.

The teenagers began their campaign of terror on April 20, 1996, by blowing up an old Coca-Cola bottling plant. Six nights later they carjacked and robbed the landlord of one of the group's hangers-on.

Their big night came on April 30. They had planned to steal clothing from a department store and then wear the stolen clothes to a senior night event at Walt Disney World, where Foster hoped to steal a character costume and use it as a disguise that would enable him to shoot minorities in the park. When the smoke bomb they wanted to use as a distraction at the department store failed, they gave up that effort and instead went to their high school. After setting the auditorium on fire, they were spotted by Mark Schwebes, the school's thirty-two-year-old band director. He confiscated some items they had stolen from the school and warned them that he would alert the police. After Schwebes left, Black said, "He's gotta die tonight."

Some of the teens went home, but the four original Lords of Chaos members went to Schwebes's home and rang the doorbell. When Schwebes opened the door, Foster fired a Mossberg 12-gauge shotgun into his face at close range, killing him instantly. Foster, believing Schwebes to be gay, fired a second blast at the band director's buttocks. The killing made Foster feel as though he was on top of the world.

That feeling didn't last long. Foster bragged about the murder to other members of the group. One of those told his girlfriend, and soon enough word reached the police. While the boys were on their way to rob a Hardee's restaurant, the police closed in and took them into custody.

Some of the hangers-on weren't charged, or they turned state's evidence and walked. Shields, Magnotti, and Black pleaded guilty to first-degree murder. Black and Shields got a life sentence, and Magnotti was sentenced to thirty-two years. Foster had a three-day trial; it took the jury slightly more than two hours to reach a verdict of guilty. He was sentenced to death on June 17, 1998.

At this time, Foster remains on death row at Florida State Prison. He and his mother—who testified that he was home with her at the time of the murder—were later convicted of conspiring to murder some of the Lords of Chaos who had testified against Foster.

3   **IN "THE POPULAR KIDS"** (110), which features a pack of teenagers who appear to be engaged in satanic ritual activity, there is a reference to the satanic panic of the 1980s. During the 1980s and the early 1990s, there was a rash of claims, mostly in the mass media, about satanic rituals, sacrifices, and abuse. Most of these claims vanished into nothingness when exposed to the light of day, but talk-show hosts like Geraldo Rivera fed the scare for as long as they could, because satanism meant big ratings.

Cult "experts" at the time claimed that fifty thousand to two million children in the United States were ritually sacrificed to Satan every year. In fact, the entire murder rate in the country at that time was around twenty-five thousand a year. Under leading questions by investigators, children told horrific stories of ritual abuse at day-care centers. No proof of this abuse ever turned up, but evidence that the kids were only telling the investigators what they wanted to hear was abundant. Teenagers sometimes turned to the occult and satanism, but out of boredom and alienation, rarely with real seriousness of intent. Without a smoking gun, the media moved on to other pursuits, and the whole panic fizzled.

4 **IN "THE POPULAR KIDS"** (110), profiler Spencer Reid uses Jim Jones and his People's Temple as an example of a murderous cult. Jonestown, Jim Jones's Guyana hideaway, is referred to again in the episode "Minimal Loss" (403), about a cult's disastrous standoff with government officials.

James Warren Jones was born in Indiana and began his career as a preacher there in the 1950s. He developed a large, mixed-race congregation, which was very rare at that time and place. He moved his temple, which practiced what he called "apostolic socialism," to California after the government started looking into his claims of cures for cancer, heart disease, and arthritis.

Fearing an imminent nuclear war, Jones took his congregation to Ukiah, California, which had been described as a place that could withstand a nuclear attack. Later he opened branches in San Francisco and Los Angeles and set up headquarters in San Francisco. Jones was prominent in local and national Democratic political circles.

Rumors of illegal activities surfaced, however, and in 1974 the People's Temple, as Jones called his congregation, acquired land in Guyana. Jones wanted to establish a model communist community there, and by 1977 he and several hundred members of the congregation lived there full-time. In 1978, almost a thousand people lived in the community.

Jones constantly warned his flock about its capitalist enemies. He isolated his congregation from the rest of the world, forcing its members to sign over their possessions to the church. He even made them sign confessions of having sexually molested their children, in order to give him ammunition to use against them if they ever turned on him.

Nevertheless, people did leave the congregation, and the stories they told back home circulated quickly. In November 1978, California congressman Leo Ryan went to Jonestown on a fact-finding trip, accompanied by his staff, the media, and others. On November 18, as he was preparing to leave Guyana to return to the United States, a couple of families asked to be allowed to go with the congressman's party. At the airstrip, a tractor-trailer carrying armed temple members drove up, and the members started shooting. Five people, including Congressman Ryan and one of the temple defectors, were killed, and nine others were injured.

That night, fearing reprisals, the temple members met in their pavilion. Some of Jones's aides had prepared a vat of Flavor-Aid spiked with Valium and cyanide, among other additives. Some in the congregation argued against suicide, but once word of Ryan's death spread, they knew their options were limited. They'd had suicide rehearsals before, so the procedure was familiar. People used syringes to squirt poison into the mouths of infants and children because they weren't cooperating. Once the adults had poisoned their own children, they weren't likely to back out. The poisoned began to die within about five minutes.

Jones, who did not drink his own poison, was found with a gunshot wound to the head, either self-inflicted or at close contact. Nine hundred followers joined him in death.

5 **LIKE JIM JONES,** David Koresh kept his disciples in a contained environment. When you're asking people to believe that you're a prophet—a common thread in the lives of megalomaniacs for whom people are willing to kill and die—it's essential that you control what they see and hear and think about. Some members of

Koresh's Branch Davidian sect believed him to be God Incarnate, so it was not difficult for him to persuade them to do whatever he wanted.

According to reports from inside the sect's ranch compound, about ten miles from Waco, Texas, Koresh wanted a lot. He fathered at least fifteen children by many different "wives," some of whom were as young as twelve. When he wanted to marry someone who was already married, he simply used his authority to annul her existing marriage. Then he could marry the woman or girl, and her "former" husband was expected to live in celibacy. Koresh was, he said, entitled to 140 wives, according to his interpretation of the biblical Song of Songs. Koresh dictated all of the rules by which his flock would live. He required them to relinquish their material possessions, which he could keep or redistribute at will.

The discipline he administered was often harsh. He was said to paddle infants, even those as young as eight months, for forty-five minutes. He made adults go into a sewage pit, then refused them permission to bathe afterward. He made children call their parents "dogs." Only Koresh was to be their "father," just as he was to be the "husband" of any girl he found attractive, however young she might be. Despite these stories, a child abuse investigation by the state failed to turn up any evidence against him.

Vernon Wayne Howell was born in Houston, Texas, on April 17, 1959, to a fourteen-year-old girl. He never knew his father, and at the age of four he was left with his maternal grandmother, who raised him. Dyslexic and barely literate, the boy grew up lonely and isolated and dropped out of high school in his junior year. He was not unintelligent, however. Before he left school, he had memorized the entire Bible, and throughout his life he was able to talk about it at great length, convincing others that he was spiritually wise. He could usually come up with a biblical passage that would excuse any behavior in which he wanted to indulge. He was also a reasonably good musician who, like Manson, considered a rock music career.

At age twenty, Howell joined the Seventh Day Adventist Church, leaving only when a dispute with the pastor, over Howell's interest in the pastor's daughter, soured his relationships there. He moved to Waco in 1981 to join the Branch Davidians, an apocalyptic sect that had splintered off from the Seventh Day Adventists in the 1930s. In 1955, the sect had established a ranch outside Waco, which they called the Mount Carmel Center.

The group's prophet was an elderly woman named Lois Roden. Her adult son, George, expected to be the next prophet, but Howell claimed the gift of prophecy and began a sexual affair with Lois. She declared that God meant for her to have a child with Howell and that this child (who never came along—no surprise, given Lois's age) would be the Chosen One. George Roden objected, and the group was divided in its loyalties.

Howell took some of his followers and set up a splinter of the splinter ninety miles away in Paradise, Texas. For the next several years he worked on building that group. There he began his controlling ways, forcing people to break bonds and attachments made on the outside and show loyalty only to him. He also developed his interest in polygamy—for himself, but not for anyone else—after Lois died.

When George Roden saw his own support fading, he challenged Howell to a contest to see which one of them could raise the dead. Roden dug up a corpse to practice on, and Howell, sensing an advantage, alerted the authorities. Told that he had to supply proof that Roden was abusing a corpse, Howell and some of his followers went into Mount Carmel, armed, to take photographs. A shoot-out ensued in which Roden was wounded and Howell, among others, was arrested. A mistrial freed Howell, but Roden was soon arrested for the murder of another rival. With Roden in a mental institution and a large amount of unpaid back taxes, Mount Carmel was put up for sale by the state. Howell bought it, renamed it Ranch Apocalypse, and brought his followers to live there.

In 1990, Howell legally changed his name to David Koresh. He claimed (erroneously) that *koresh* meant "death" and that he was the rightful heir to the biblical House of David. He also claimed to be the son of God, who could open the Seven Seals of the Book of Revelation. He reiterated this belief to FBI agents during the Waco siege.

Having taken over the group, Koresh made several improvements to the facilities and started up new commercial ventures to provide funding, including a gun business.

The Branch Davidians had always believed in imminent apocalypse, and Koresh wanted to be ready. Although his supporters explained their massive weapons stockpiles as simply being wares bought and sold for their business, the fact was that the compound had laid in quantities of weapons and explosives that the Bureau of Alcohol, Tobacco, and Firearms (ATF) found disturbing.

On February 29, 1993, the ATF finally made its move. A "surprise" attack failed to be a surprise—which was not all that surprising in itself, since a mile-long convoy of more than eighty government vehicles had been required to stealthily approach a compound in rural Texas, far from any town. Koresh, alone and unarmed, opened the door and asked the agents what they wanted. He was told to get down, and he closed the door. Shots were fired, but heated debate over who fired first continues to this day.

The Branch Davidians called 911 and reported the shooting as it was happening, and eventually a cease-fire was ordered. Four ATF agents were dead, and more were wounded. Six Davidians died, although it's possible that two were shot by their fellow members to put them out of their pain when it appeared that medical help would not be coming soon. Among the wounded inside the compound was Koresh.

The FBI's Hostage Rescue Team (HRT) took over the scene, and the cease-fire became a siege. During the first week, twenty-two children and two elderly women voluntarily left the compound, but the rest were determined to stay put, and they released video messages explaining their loyalty to the sect. The FBI tried various means of driving them out, including loud music played over public address systems and bright lights blasted at the compound all night.

The siege lasted fifty-one days. During that time, Koresh was busy inside, dictating a final explanation of his beliefs about the

Seven Seals that would bring about Armageddon. Before he was finished, the FBI received approval from Attorney General Janet Reno to breach the walls and begin spraying gas into the compound. On April 19, the agents moved armored vehicles in to do that. They announced that no one would enter the buildings, but they were met with gunfire nevertheless.

Somehow—and this is a source of controversy—a fire started. The FBI and official reports claim that the Davidians themselves started it; the Davidians claim that the FBI fired an incendiary device into a building they had already filled with gas.

At least seventy-five Davidians died in the blaze. Some were shot, and again there's disagreement over the circumstances of those shootings. Some say that the FBI shot people who were trying to escape the fire, and others say that the Davidians shot one another and themselves to avoid burning to death. Koresh was one of those shot.

The Waco siege was badly conceived and executed. Although no one can say with certainty exactly what mistakes were made, it's obvious that there were many, and the whole tragedy is a black mark on the FBI's record. April 19 became a day that antigovernment activists remember as a day of infamy, and it has been commemorated with other major attacks, such as the Oklahoma City bombing.

The episode "Minimal Loss" (403), in which a standoff at a polygamist compound called the Separatarian Sect Ranch, prompted by allegations of child abuse, ends in a bloody gunfight and a fire, is reminiscent of Waco as well as the investigation into child abuse complaints at the fundamentalist Mormons' Yearning for Zion polygamist compound near Eldorado, Texas, in 2008. The Waco siege is also mentioned in the episode "Identity" (307), which recalls the Ruby Ridge standoff of 1992.

6 **AS WITH WACO,** the events of the Ruby Ridge standoff are fraught with controversy. Ruby Ridge, which was mentioned in the episode "Minimal Loss" (403), was the Idaho home of self-declared white separatist and ex–Green Beret Randy Weaver and his wife, Vicki, and their three children.

As extreme fundamentalist Christians, the Weavers had, over the years, become convinced that the so-called end times were near and that organized religions refused to acknowledge this truth. They started their own small church, preaching the gospel as they saw it.

At the same time, Vicki had a vision of a mountain refuge where she and her family would be safe from the coming apocalypse. In her vision, Vicki, who had only one child, saw two more, a boy named Samuel and a girl named Rachel. The Weavers feared what white supremacists and neo-Nazis call ZOG, the "Zionist Organized Government"—by which they mean the U.S. government. The Weavers believed that their refuge would be safe from that evil as well.

The Weavers had a son, Samuel, in 1978, and a daughter, Rachel, in 1982. The pieces were falling into place, just as in Vicki's vision. They sold their home in Iowa and went west, looking for safe harbor. They found it at Ruby Ridge, Idaho.

After a while they took in a troubled teenager named Kevin Harris, whose father had died and whose mother couldn't control him. Many of their Idaho friends held views just as racist as theirs, but even so, their constant proselytizing got on people's nerves. In January 1985, Randy, who was associated with white-supremacist organizations, was investigated by the Secret Service for threats against the president and other officials. He reportedly had a large cache of weapons at home and was convinced that the world would end in two years.

At a 1986 World Aryan Conference, Randy met an ATF informant who stayed in contact with him during the next few years. The informant was invited to the Weavers' home in 1989 to discuss ways to fight ZOG. Randy sold the man two shotguns. The informant said the barrels were sawed off—an illegal alteration—but Randy insisted that they were of legal length when he sold them.

Randy was arrested, and when he declined to act as an informant for the ATF, he was indicted for manufacturing and possessing an illegal firearm. After his arraignment and the setting of a trial date, Randy was released on a personal-recognizance bond. There's some evidence that an unclear explanation of the process caused Randy to believe that the government would take his cabin and his land, regardless of the outcome of the trial. Vicki sent two letters to the U.S. Attorney's Office declaring that the "blood of tyrants will flow" and promising, "We will not bow to your evil commandments."

Another mistake complicated things further. A letter was sent to Randy giving a date of March 20, 1991, for his trial—but it was really scheduled for February 20, 1991. A clerical error was blamed. In any event, the trial date came and went and Randy Weaver didn't show up, so a warrant was issued for his arrest. Randy sent the sheriff's office a letter stating that he would not come out and that law enforcement would have to take him out by force. U.S. marshals held off on enforcing the warrant because of concerns over the possible danger of approaching the Weaver home.

For the next sixteen months, nobody left the Weaver cabin unarmed. The government explored a number of avenues to take Randy without bloodshed, but they knew that the Weavers had plenty of weapons and apparently longed for a war against the government. Given Randy's Green Beret background, they believed that the area around the cabin was probably booby-trapped. Nothing had yet come to fruition on August 21, 1992, when a surveillance team was chased by one of the Weavers' dogs.

The marshals saw Kevin Harris, Sammy Weaver, and the two daughters, all armed, following the dog. Then Randy came out. The marshals identified themselves and told Randy to halt, but he turned and ran back toward the cabin. The dog caught up to one of the marshals, who held it at bay but didn't shoot because he didn't want to antagonize the family.

Two marshals rose from cover to identify themselves, and Harris opened fire. The marshals returned the fire. The dog looked ready to attack, so one of the marshals shot and killed it. Harris then shot and killed Marshal William Degan.

At least, that's the way the marshals tell it. The Weaver family's supporters have a different version; they say that the marshals showed up in ninja outfits and face masks and ambushed Sammy Weaver and Kevin Harris. The first shot fired was the one that killed the dog; after that, gunfire blazed in both directions, Degan went down, and Sammy was shot in the back while retreating and died on the scene. Only after Sammy fell did any marshal identify himself, in the white supremacists' version.

The marshals called for help while Randy and Vicki Weaver took their son's body into a guest cabin near their main cabin. The gunfight brought the county sheriff's officers, the FBI's HRT, the Idaho State Police, the National Guard, and the U.S. Border Patrol to the scene. A command post was established, and Degan's body was retrieved.

The next day, the HRT commander on the scene issued a proposed amendment, applicable only in this particular case, to the unit's standard rules of engagement. Ordinarily agents are supposed to use deadly force only if someone is in imminent danger of death or serious bodily harm. Among the revised rules was this one: "If any adult male is observed with a weapon prior to the announcement, deadly force can and should be employed, if the shot can be taken without endangering any children."

FBI headquarters didn't approve the amendment, but the assistant director of the bureau's criminal affairs division told the local field commander that it *had* been approved and that the agents had been briefed accordingly. Some of the bureau's SWAT members later admitted that they thought the amended rules were "crazy," and they decided not to follow them.

The next morning, the FBI wanted to get a phone to the cabin, since it didn't have one and the agents wanted to be able to negotiate a surrender. They were still getting into place when a sniper named Lon Horiuchi saw someone he thought was Harris, apparently moving around an outbuilding to get a shot at a bureau helicopter. Horiuchi fired and wounded the man, who turned out to be Randy Weaver. The man ran back into the cabin, along with his daughter Sara and the actual Kevin Harris. Horiuchi fired again. This bullet passed through the cabin door, killing Vicki Weaver and seriously wounding Harris. Vicki was holding the couple's fourth child, ten-month-old Elisheba, in her arms when she was shot.

The FBI was unaware that either Vicki or Sammy Weaver had been killed. After a few more days, when Randy and the rest of the family refused to come out of the cabin, the HRT warned that it would start removing the outbuildings. When the agent took down the one called the "birthing shed," they found Sammy's body and assumed that Randy Weaver had killed his own son.

Randy still wouldn't come out or even answer the telephone that an unarmed robot had taken to the cabin. Finally, the bureau brought in Colonel Bo Gritz, a decorated Vietnam veteran and a hero of the antigovernment movement. Randy agreed to talk to Gritz, and they conferred for two days, initially through the cabin's closed door. On the second day, when Randy opened the door, Gritz became aware of a horrific odor: Vicki had been lying on the kitchen floor, her skull shattered by the bullet, for seven days. Randy agreed that Gritz could take her body out. When Gritz returned the next day, he managed to talk Randy into letting the badly wounded Harris go as well. Next, Gritz made a deal with celebrity lawyer Gerry Spence, who agreed to represent Randy, and with that in place, Randy finally surrendered on August 31.

The trial had its share of missteps as well, including the revelation that at no time did federal agents bother to simply knock on the cabin door. During his closing statement, the prosecutor collapsed in court. The defense, which had called no witnesses, largely prevailed. Harris was declared not guilty of any counts, and Randy Weaver was convicted only on the counts of failing to appear in court and violating bail conditions. After a short prison stretch, he filed a wrongful death lawsuit against the government, which was settled out of court with an offer of a hundred thousand dollars and a million dollars to each of his daughters. Several FBI agents were disciplined for their actions during the siege.

Similarly, the Freemen Standoff was an eighty-one-day ordeal in Montana. A group of antigovernment "Montana Freemen" lived in a self-declared town called Justus Township and rejected the authority of the federal government. They refused to pay taxes or renew their driver's licenses, and they created their own counterfeit checks to pay for merchandise. When foreclosure proceedings were initiated against the land on which Justus Township stood, they refused to vacate, held mock trials, and issued a writ of execution against a federal judge. On June 13, 1996, at the end of a peaceful standoff, they surrendered to the authorities.

David Rossi tells the team it was these failures—at Ruby Ridge and Waco and with the Freemen—that made him leave the FBI, but now he has returned.

13

Safe at Home

A **PERSON'S HOME** is supposed to be a sanctuary. It's not for nothing that the home is often referred to as a "castle." Figuratively, at least, one can close the door and keep out the rest of the world. The threshold can, of course, be crossed by door-to-door peddlers and proselytizers, and it's a rare human being these days who doesn't bring some of the daytime cares of the world into the house at night. Nevertheless, most of us do feel safe when we're inside our homes; we feel safe, at a remove from the world beyond the walls.

So when our homes are attacked—*invaded*, in law enforcement parlance—it's even more shocking than being assaulted on a street corner or a subway platform. Murder victims are often involved in some activity that makes them vulnerable, that puts them into the category of high-risk victims. The most obvious are prostitutes, who regularly go to private places with men they don't know. Hitchhikers also rank high on the list of high-risk victims. But an individual or a family at home, enjoying the evening meal or unwinding in front of a fireplace—these people are supposed to be left alone.

George Foyet, Aaron Hotchner's nemesis in the fourth and fifth seasons of *Criminal Minds*, has some home invasions on his record (including Hotchner's home). So does Karl Arnold, the Fox, from the episodes "The Fox" (107) and "Outfoxed" (508). Other episodes that focus, at least in part, on home invasions include "Plain Sight" (104), "The Big Game" (214), "Ashes and Dust" (219), "Children of the Dark" (304), "Catching Out" (405), "Bloodline" (413), "Hopeless" (504), and "The Slave of Duty" (510).

1 **A MAJOR** home-invasion case in this country that looms large in the minds of many Americans began on November 14, 1959, outside the town of Holcomb, on the windswept plains of western Kansas. The home belonged to successful farmer Herbert William Clutter, one of the bedrocks of Holcomb society, and his wife, Bonnie. They worked the River Valley Farm with the help of a resident hand (who lived in a separate house with his family), their son, Kenyon, and their daughter Nancy. Two older daughters were married and lived away from the farm.

On that cold autumn night, two men who had briefly been cellmates in the Kansas State Penitentiary at Lansing drove up to the farm. They saw someone awake and moving about—the farm hand, tending to a sick child—and almost turned around. But they had been thinking about this burglary for months. It was their big score, their main chance to get the money they needed to buy a boat and go diving for treasure off the coast of Mexico.

Shortly after midnight, Herb Clutter woke up with a flashlight beaming into his eyes. Two intruders were in his bedroom, armed and angry. One was a bowlegged little man with his jeans rolled up at the ankles; the other was taller (but still not large), lithe, and athletic and had a scarred, lopsided face. They took Herb to his office and demanded to know where his safe was. He didn't have a safe, so he couldn't point one out, but the taller of the two men called him a liar. Herb stuck to his guns, insisting that there was no safe.

Upstairs, Nancy, sixteen, heard strangers in the house. Worried about thieves, she hid her most valuable possession, a watch that her father had given her, in a shoe. But the intruders heard her moving about, and they forced Herb to lead them back upstairs and show them where the other family members were. Herb pointed out the doors to Nancy's and Kenyon's rooms, then took them into Bonnie's room. Bonnie was an invalid, thin and frail.

The intruders consulted briefly, then took Bonnie into the bathroom adjoining her bedroom, put a chair in it so she could sit, and locked her in. Next they went into fifteen-year-old Kenyon's room, and the taller man punched Kenyon. The boy was then taken into another bathroom and locked inside. Nancy came out into the hall, and they grabbed her and put her in the bathroom with Kenyon.

Deciding that their captives should be bound, the two men tied Herb's hands, and the smaller man took him down to the furnace room in the basement. Seeing a cardboard mattress box leaning against a wall, he moved it so that Herb could lie on it and wouldn't have to lie on the cold floor. He tied Herb's feet and lashed his hands and feet together. Then he brought Kenyon down and bound him to a couch in the basement's other room, a playroom, and put a pillow under his head. The man went back upstairs, tied Bonnie up in the bathroom, tucked Nancy into her own bed, and tied her up there. The two men taped everybody's mouth except Nancy's.

The intruders discussed their options again, but the plan had been set long before they ever got to the farm. The shorter man started to cut Herb's throat, then handed his partner the knife and told him to finish the job. The partner failed, and Herb fought back. Finally, the short man had his partner hold the flashlight on Herb while he shot him with the 12-gauge shotgun they had brought with them.

The two went back into the playroom and shot Kenyon, then headed upstairs to finish off Nancy and Bonnie.

In "The Slave of Duty," while Agent Hotchner takes a leave of absence from the BAU after his wife's murder, the team must regroup to solve a home invasion case.

That done, they hurried from the house, toting their proceeds for the night's work: between forty and fifty dollars in cash, a portable radio, and a pair of binoculars.

In the morning, a family friend who always went to church with the Clutters came to the house. She couldn't rouse anyone, so her father drove her to a neighboring farm, but the neighbor didn't know where the Clutters might be. They telephoned the family, but no one answered. Together, they returned to River Valley Farm and let themselves in through the never-locked kitchen door.

The police came out in force. Assistant Police Chief Rich Rohleder was a strong believer in the use of scientific techniques for crime busting. He had built his own crime-scene kit, complete with handmade fingerprint brushes, and he carried that and his camera to the Clutter house. Rohleder found two boot prints that belonged to two different men but not to any of the Clutters. He also hatched a theory that almost no one else went along with at first: that robbery had been the motive for the murders.

By the end of the week, almost everyone in the country had heard about the vicious crime. Mass media in the United States were just becoming truly "mass," with the rapidly increasing presence of televisions in every home. The radio carried the same information from coast to coast. The nation's first truly notorious murder spree, that of Charles Starkweather and his girlfriend, Caril Fugate, was still fresh in the public consciousness, especially in the Midwest, since that spree had begun in Nebraska. The Clutter murders were on a similar level, in terms of their sensational nature.

Even in the nation's prisons, the story played on the radio. One of the people who heard it was an inmate at Kansas State Penitentiary named Floyd Wells. Wells knew the Clutters. He had worked at the River Valley Farm a decade earlier. Arranging to see the warden, he told a disturbing story.

After convicts Dick Hickock and Perry Smith had been in a cell together for two weeks, Smith had been paroled with instructions not to return to Kansas. Hickock's new cell mate was Floyd Wells. Cell mates talk, and one of the things Wells had talked about was Herb Clutter, the wealthy farmer who kept plenty of cash in the safe of his old house—at least ten thousand dollars, Wells had insisted.

Hickock, an athletic man with a face left deformed by an automobile accident, had been impressed by these stories and had come up with the idea of teaming up with his paroled pal Perry Smith to rob the house, take the cash from the safe, and then kill everyone in the house so there couldn't be any witnesses. Wells hadn't thought that Hickock would go through with it—he put it down to jailhouse boasting and forgot about it. Now he was convinced that Hickock and Smith had done it.

This fit Rohleder's theory to a T. An all-points bulletin was put out for the arrest of Hickock and Smith.

After the murders, Hickock and Smith had gone to Mexico for a while, stopped in Florida, and then returned to Kansas, paying their way with robberies and bad checks. Finally, at the end of 1959, they were in Las Vegas. On December 30, a couple of patrol officers ran an out-of-state license plate, and the information came back that the plate number belonged to a car that had been stolen in Kansas. The officers watched the car and saw Hickock and Smith return to it. They had mug shots of the Clutter family's killers, and the pictures matched the men. They moved in and arrested the suspects.

Back in Kansas, Hickock and Smith confessed. Initially Smith blamed Hickock for two of the killings, then later changed his story and took credit for all four. It didn't matter—they had acted together, making both equally responsible under the law. They were found guilty and sentenced to hang, and on April 14, 1965, the mismatched killers took their final walk together to the gallows.

Although there had been a safe in the Clutters' old house—the house Wells had been to—the house that Hickock and Smith had invaded was new. Herb Clutter, a college-educated businessman, did most of his business by check and had seen no need to put a safe in the new house. When the killers demanded to be shown the safe, he answered truthfully. He no longer kept large amounts of cash on hand, and he and his family were murdered for pocket money.

The case became famous as the basis for Truman Capote's "nonfiction novel" *In Cold Blood*. Capote underplayed the contributions of Rohleder and combined him and other officers into a composite character based on Alvin Dewey, a detective with the Kansas Bureau of Investigation. Dewey was the bureau's lead investigator on the case and was certainly deeply involved in the manhunt for Hickock and Smith, but in overemphasizing Dewey's role, and in certain other aspects of the story, Capote took creative liberties. Still, his version of the facts is widely considered the truth, and it's because of his book (and the movie adapted from it) that the Clutter home invasion still carries such emotional heft half a century later. The crime is also mentioned in the episode "The Big Game" (214) when Jason Gideon discusses why serial killers kill.

2 **FIFTEEN YEARS** after Hickock and Smith murdered the Clutters, another home invasion in Kansas made the news.

Charlie Otero, fifteen, returned to his Wichita home after school on January 15, 1974, to find his parents, Joseph and Julie, dead in their bedroom. Joseph was on the floor, bound at the wrists and ankles; he had been strangled. The same was true for Julie, but she had also been gagged. Joseph Jr., Charlie's nine-year-old brother, was in his room, at the foot of his bed, strangled and with his head covered by a hood. Downstairs, Charlie's eleven-year-old sister, Josephine, was hanging by the neck from a pipe, partly nude. Two other siblings, Daniel and Carmen, weren't home from school yet.

The police found semen throughout the house. The killer had not sexually assaulted his victims, but he appeared to have masturbated on some of them. The police were at a loss for clues, and the case went unsolved.

On April 4 of the same year, brother and sister Kevin and Kathryn Bright came home to their Wichita house to find a man pointing a gun at them as they entered. The man forced them into a bedroom. Kathryn, twenty-one, was tied up. While Kevin, nineteen, was being bound, he fought back and was shot twice in the head. The man returned to Kathryn, who fought as well, so he gave up on trying to strangle her and instead stabbed her three times. Meanwhile, Kevin, who was not dead after all, ran out into the street and called for help.

The attacker raced from the house. Kathryn died later at the hospital.

That October, a reporter for the *Wichita Eagle* received a phone call alerting him to a letter that had been left in a textbook at the public library. The police retrieved the letter, which contained details about the Otero family homicides that had never been released to the public. At the letter's end was this postscript: "P.S. Since sex criminals do not change their M.O. or by nature cannot do so, I will not change mine. The code word for me will be: Bind them, torture them, kill them, B.T.K., you see he at it again. They will be on the next victim."

After the letter, the killer went silent until March 17, 1977, when a five-year-old boy named Steve Relford met a man on the street outside the boy's home. The man showed him pictures of a woman and a child and asked if Steve knew them. Steve told him he didn't, then went inside his house. A short while later, the same man knocked on the door. Claiming to be a private detective, he forced his way into the home, which was occupied at the time by Steve and two siblings and their mother, Shirley Vian, twenty-four. The man put the kids in a bathroom, then took Shirley into her bedroom. He intended to rape her, but she was sick that day, and he wound up strangling her and masturbating into her panties. The phone rang before he could kill the children, and he fled the house.

The BTK Killer murdered one more victim, Nancy Fox, in 1977. In 1978 he sent another letter to authorities, admitting to murdering the Oteros, Vian, Fox, and another woman (presumed to be Kathryn Bright). He suggested then that the initials he had used in the earlier letter be given to him as a name. He seemed aware of his place in the pantheon of serial killers, as indicated here: "The same thing that made Son of Sam, Jack the Ripper, Havery Glatman, Boston Strangler, Dr. H. H. Holmes Panty Hose Strangler OF Florida, Hillside Strangler, Ted of the West Coast and many more infamous character kill." Finally the police admitted that there was a serial killer in Wichita, and they warned people to be on their guard.

After another pause, the BTK Killer broke into the home of sixty-three-year-old widow Anna Williams in April 1979. He waited, but she came home late, after he had already left. In June, he mailed her a poem titled "Oh Anna Why Didn't You Appear."

He went underground again, only to resurface on April 27, 1985. This time he broke into the home of Marine Hedge, fifty-three. After cutting her phone line, he waited in a back bedroom of her house until she came home. When she did, there was a man with her, so the killer hid until the man left, then emerged and strangled Hedge. That wasn't enough for him, so he put her body in the trunk of her car and drove to his church, where he covered the basement windows with black plastic and spent some time with her, posing her and taking pictures. Finally, he dumped the body and returned the car.

The BTK Killer entered the home of Vicki Wegerle, twenty-eight, on September 16, 1986, by posing as a telephone repairman, complete with hard hat. He strangled her, photographed her death throes, and left in her car. As her husband, Bill, approached their home, he saw his own car driving away. He found his two-year-old son, Brandon, still alive and by himself in the living room, then he found Vicki in the bedroom. The BTK Killer hadn't been heard from in years, so he wasn't suspected in the Hedge murder, and now Wegerle was the initial suspect in his wife's murder.

Dolores Davis, sixty-two, was home alone on January 19, 1991, when she heard the noise of a concrete block crashing through a glass patio door. The killer let himself in, bound and strangled Davis, then drove her body away in her own car and placed it under some trees. He took the car back, got into his own, and returned for her, then he drove her around a while longer and finally dumped her under a bridge.

Again he was gone. FBI profiler John Douglas thought that he either had been arrested or had died. Perhaps the BTK Killer's photographs, drawings, and memories were now sufficient to complete his fantasy. In January 2004, the *Wichita Eagle* ran stories about the murders that had begun thirty years before, and a Wichita lawyer wrote a book about the case.

Possibly afraid that others would tell his story and get it wrong, the BTK Killer began communicating again. The BAU provided a strategy to keep him reaching out by issuing press releases, and it worked. He sent multiple letters, some containing souvenirs and copies of photographs he had taken—items that only the real killer could have had. Some of the packages contained dolls that were bound in ways that suggested the deaths of Nancy Fox and Josephine Otero. The BTK Killer asked whether the police would be able to trace a computer floppy disk back to him if he sent one. The police responded in a classified ad that they wouldn't.

On February 16, 2005, a floppy disk arrived at a TV station. The police checked it out and found traces of software from the Christ

Lutheran Church in Wichita and the name Dennis. The church's current president was Dennis Rader. The investigators obtained a DNA specimen from Rader's daughter, Kerri, and matched it to the DNA found in the semen left at many of the BTK Killer's scenes. Dennis Rader was their man. He was arrested on February 26, thirty-one years after his first murders.

During the decades in which Dennis Rader was killing, his life appeared, from the outside, to be fairly normal. Born on March 9, 1945, he was twenty-nine when he began to murder. At his arrest he was fifty-nine and still hoping to kill again. Rader was employed by ADT Security Systems from November 1974 until July 1998. He held several positions there, including installation manager—a job that took him into many private homes and taught him how to get around security systems.

Rader also worked for the U.S. Census Bureau, and he was the compliance director for Park City, Kansas. He married Paula Dietz in 1971 and had two children. Paula was shocked when her husband was arrested; she had no inkling that she might be married to a serial killer who had ten murders to his credit. Neither did the members of his church, who had voted for him as president. Rader had been a Cub Scout leader, and by the time of his arrest, his son had become an Eagle Scout.

On August 18, 2005, Rader was sentenced to ten life sentences, eligible for parole after 175 years.

Rader is brought up in the episodes "Charm and Harm" (120), "Tabula Rasa" (319), "Zoe's Reprise" (415), and "Omnivore" (418).

3 **THE FIRST TIME** that home invasions come into play on *Criminal Minds* is in the episode "Plain Sight" (104), in which the Tommy Killer enters women's homes in San Diego, murders them, and glues their eyes open. The name *Tommy Killer* comes from the line from the Who's rock opera *Tommy*, "See me, feel me."

San Diego dealt with its own rash of home-invasion murders in 1990, when the Clairemont Killer murdered six women in their own homes.

The first victim was Tiffany Schultz, a twenty-one-year-old student and part-time exotic dancer who had been sunbathing on the balcony of her second-floor apartment in San Diego's Clairemont neighborhood on January 12, 1990. Later that day, her roommate found her. Schultz was wearing just the bikini bottoms and had been stabbed forty-seven times, mostly around her left breast.

Janene Weinhold was next. She lived in a complex across the street from Schultz's, and the two complexes shared a garage. Weinhold was discovered in her second-floor apartment, naked except for a bra, and stabbed multiple times, centering on her right breast. She had been sexually assaulted, and semen was collected from her body.

On April 3, eighteen-year-old Holly Tarr, visiting from Michigan with her friend Tammy, became the third victim. Holly and Tammy were staying with Holly's brother in the same complex that Weinhold had lived in. They were at the pool, and when Holly went back to the apartment before Tammy, she was attacked. Tammy returned to the apartment a few minutes later, but the door was locked. Hearing a scream, she cried for help. A maintenance man opened the door, and as he did, an African American man fled with a knife in his hand. Tammy found her friend wearing panties and a bra, with a deep stab wound in her heart.

The man she had seen looked like someone Tammy and Holly had noticed in the complex's weight room earlier. A check of the weight room's sign-in log revealed the name Cleophus Prince Jr. The police interrogated Prince, but he denied everything and refused to be fingerprinted. They didn't have enough evidence to hold him.

The standard rule of criminal profiling is that killers tend to murder within their own race. But Prince was black and all of his victims white. In other ways, however, he fit the profile. The FBI believed that he lived close by and that he was killing within his comfort zone. It turned out that Prince did live in the complex.

After the Tarr murder, Prince moved away from the complex but not out of San Diego. On May 20, thirty-eight-year-old Elissa Keller was found choked, beaten, and with nine stab wounds in her chest. Prince's next attack was on two women, Pamela Clarkson, forty-two, and her eighteen-year-old daughter, Amber. Each had eleven stab wounds in her chest. All three of these victims lived in the area to which Prince had recently moved.

The police tracked him down again and found several knives in his car. They took a blood sample and fingerprints, then released him, and he rushed to his mother's home in Alabama.

The DNA analysis came back identifying Prince as the killer and rapist. Meanwhile, he was arrested in Alabama, then released on bond while San Diego cops were waiting for DNA results. When the San Diego police asked the Birmingham police to pick him up, the latter called him, and he turned himself in. He was arrested and extradited to California.

The authorities had him cold on the Weinhold case, but they wanted to convict him of all six murders. FBI profiler John Douglas and Special Agent Larry Ankrom of the San Diego field office worked together to provide a profile that would definitively link the crimes. They looked at the similarities among the victims, their residences, their proximity to Prince's residences, and the MO of each murder. Of special note was the killer's focus on stabbing the women in the breast, a psychosexual disorder called piquerism, in which a knife, a pin, or another sharp object acts as a penis substitute and the stabbing stands for sexual penetration. Prince didn't glue his victims' eyes open, but like the Tommy Killer he had a unique signature, and the FBI was able to use it against him.

Over the defense attorney's objections, the profile was introduced in court, and Prince was convicted on all six counts, as well as for twenty burglaries. He was sentenced to death, but as of this writing he is still on death row at San Quentin.

4 **IN SANTA CRUZ** in the late 1960s and early 1970s, with Ed Kemper and Herb Mullin killing coeds and others, mass murder seemed second only to surfing as a favorite leisure-time activity. In "The Last Word" (209), Spencer Reid points out how rare it is to have two serial killers operating in the same city at the same time. In real life, Santa Cruz not only had two serial killers, it also had home invader and mass murderer John Linley Frazier, who helped to put a community that was already on edge even more so.

Frazier, who lived in a tiny shack in the hills outside town, murdered eye surgeon Victor Ohta and his family and his secretary, Dorothy Cadwallader. Frazier had, somewhat halfheartedly, embraced the hippie lifestyle, and he considered the well-to-do Ohta excessively materialistic. At the Ohta home, he shot Victor three times with a .38, then shot Ohta's wife, Virginia, Ohta's sons, Derrick and Taggart, and Cadwallader.

Frazier put the bodies in the swimming pool, set the mansion on fire, and left a note under the windshield of Ohta's Rolls Royce, warning of World War III, "against anything or anyone who dose not support natural life on this planet, materialisum must die, or man-kind will."

Some of Frazier's hippie acquaintances recognized his off-the-wall theories and tipped off the police. His fingerprints were found on the Rolls Royce and on a beer can left at the scene. After Frazier was arrested, he claimed that voices from God had told him to seek vengeance against people who raped the environment. He appeared in court with half his head shaved clean, including an eyebrow.

Despite evidence that Frazier had a long history of paranoid schizophrenia, he was convicted of the murders and sentenced to death on December 30, 1971. He was resentenced to life imprisonment when California abolished the death penalty in 1972. He might have been paroled some day, but on August 13, 2009, Frazier hanged himself in his jail cell.

His story, with its environmentally motivated murders and arson, is similar to the episode "Ashes and Dust" (219), in which the unsub burns families inside their own homes under the guise of avenging the environmental damage caused by leaking underground storage tanks.

Celebrity Stalkers

MOST MURDER VICTIMS know their killers. During an investigation, the detectives dig into the victims' lives to find out why they in particular were attacked, since there's almost always some link between a victim and a perpetrator. In a very few cases, people like JonBenét Ramsey become famous in death when the crimes against them become part of the national landscape.

But every now and then, crimes are committed against people who are already famous. Celebrities, the rich, the powerful—these people can also be victimized, and in some cases, as with Patty Hearst's kidnapping, who they are makes them targets.

1 **MARK DAVID CHAPMAN**, mentioned in the episode "The Last Word" (209), became inextricably linked with former Beatle

John Lennon on December 8, 1980. Chapman, twenty-five at the time, was born in Fort Worth, Texas. His father was a physically abusive air force staff sergeant, and his mother was a nurse. Soon after his birth, the family moved to Georgia. Chapman tried to escape the fear he felt at home by imagining a race of "Little People" over whom he had godlike power. He was often depressed, which he dealt with by retreating into his fantasy world or listening to the Beatles. During his first two years of high school, he experimented with marijuana, LSD, and heroin.

At age sixteen he became a born-again Christian and met girlfriend Jessica Blankenship, also a born-again Christian. He was angered by John Lennon's 1966 comment that the Beatles were more popular than Jesus. Chapman gave up drugs, but soon he fell under the influence of something else: J. D. Salinger's novel *The Catcher in the Rye*. An engaging story of young Holden Caulfield's alienation, *The Catcher in the Rye*, like *The Collector* by John Fowles, seems to be a favorite novel of murderers.

The two things that Chapman had going for him were his girlfriend and his career working as a camp counselor for the YMCA. He went to Beirut, Lebanon, through a YMCA international program. After civil war broke out there, he returned to the United States and was offered a position working with Vietnamese refugees in Fort Chaffee, Arkansas.

At Fort Chaffee, he had a sexual fling with a coworker. After the summer ended, Chapman was at college in Tennessee with Blankenship, and his guilt over the affair (because he believed that premarital sex was a sin) drove him into a deep depression. He dropped out of school, and Blankenship ended their engagement. Back in Georgia, Chapman took a job as an armed security guard.

Chapman's sights changed again when he started daydreaming about Hawaii. He flew there, stayed till his money nearly ran out, returned to Georgia, then used the last of his savings to go back to Hawaii. This time he tried to commit suicide by running a vacuum hose from the tailpipe of his car through one of its windows, but the exhaust pipe melted the hose. The next day, he checked into a mental health clinic. He was discharged after just a couple of

In "Broken Mirror," the BAU, using Garcia's high-tech skills, must find a wealthy politician's kidnapped daughter with the help of her identical twin sister.

weeks, but he stayed on as an employee, working for the clinic in various capacities.

Once Chapman was making money again, he took a six-week trip to various cities in Asia and Europe. When he returned to Hawaii, he began a relationship with Gloria Abe, a Japanese American woman who was his travel agent. She converted from Buddhism to Christianity for him, and they were married on June 2, 1979.

The darker side of Chapman's nature soon came back. He spent money irresponsibly, went into debt, and lost his job. He got another security guard gig and started drinking again. His obsessions shifted with terrible speed, frightening Gloria. He wanted to change his name to Holden Caulfield. He read a biography of his one-time hero John Lennon and complained about Lennon's wealth. He prayed to Satan, outlining his reasons for wanting to kill Lennon.

The Little People had returned. They tried to talk him out of carrying out his plan, but he silenced them.

On October 27, 1980, Chapman bought a Charter Arms .38. Three days later, he flew to New York. When he learned he couldn't easily buy bullets there, he flew to Georgia, spent a few days visiting, and loaded up on ammo.

Then he watched the movie *Ordinary People*, about a suicidal young man. When it was over he called Gloria, and she told him to come home. He did, but not for long. Soon he flew back to New York. He arrived on December 6 and immediately visited the Dakota, the luxury Manhattan apartment building in which John Lennon and Yoko Ono lived.

Two days later he left his hotel room carrying a copy of the new Lennon and Ono album, *Double Fantasy*, with his revolver in his pocket. He stopped at a bookstore and bought a copy of *The Catcher in the Rye*, in which he wrote, "This is my statement," and signed it "Holden Caulfield."

Outside the Dakota, Chapman saw celebrities come and go: Paul Simon, Lauren Bacall, Mia Farrow, and others. He was even introduced to the young Sean Lennon.

Finally, at about 5 p.m., Lennon and Ono emerged. Chapman asked Lennon to sign his copy of *Double Fantasy*, and Lennon gladly complied. Chapman thanked him, and the ex-Beatle got into a car. Chapman was amazed at the man's politeness and sincerity. He said later that he wanted to take the record and leave.

Instead, he stayed. Shortly before 11 p.m., Lennon and Ono returned home and walked past Chapman to enter the building. Some accounts say that Chapman called out to Lennon and Lennon turned and saw him holding a gun. Chapman insists that it didn't happen that way—that he didn't speak, he simply shot Lennon in the back without warning. He fired five times; four of the bullets hit Lennon, who still managed to climb six steps before falling.

The doorman snatched the gun away. Instead of fleeing, Chapman took off his coat and hat to show that he wasn't further armed. Then he paced on the sidewalk, reading *The Catcher in the Rye*, until the police came.

The world mourned. Tributes to Lennon were held everywhere. In New York's Central Park on December 14, between fifty thousand

and a hundred thousand people turned up to celebrate Lennon's life and mark his passing. (John Hinckley Jr. was among them.)

Despite an initial inclination to plead not guilty by reason of insanity, at the last minute Chapman changed his mind. He pleaded guilty and was sentenced to twenty years to life. For his own protection, he's in solitary confinement at Attica Correctional Institution in New York. He has been denied parole five times and is eligible again in 2010.

2 **A COUPLE OF** *Criminal Minds* episodes deal with the issue of erotomania, a delusion in which someone believes that another, usually a stranger and a celebrity of some sort, is in love with him or her. The deluded party interprets meaningless or unintentional stimuli as "signals" from the loved one. It's also called De Clerambault's syndrome, after the psychologist who first described it. Erotomania first comes up in the episode "Broken Mirror" (105) and returns in "Somebody's Watching" (118).

The most notorious U.S. example of erotomania gone terribly wrong is that of John Hinckley Jr., who was obsessed with the actress Jodie Foster. On March 30, 1981, Hinckley, in what he called "the greatest love offering in the history of the world," tried to assassinate President Ronald Reagan outside the Washington Hilton Hotel. He succeeded in wounding Reagan, Press Secretary James Brady, a police officer, and a Secret Service agent.

John Warnock Hinckley Jr. was born into a life of privilege on May 29, 1955. His father was the chairman of the Vanderbilt Energy Corporation, and his mother, JoAnn, was a homemaker who especially favored John Jr. They lived in Oklahoma, Texas, and then Colorado. After graduating from Vanderbilt University, Hinckley's older brother, Scott, became a vice president of the family business. Everyone expected John Jr. to do the same.

But Hinckley dropped out of college in April 1976, and the lifelong Beatles fan went to Hollywood to try to become a songwriter. Martin Scorsese's movie *Taxi Driver* came out that year, and Hinckley watched it over and over. In the movie, Robert De Niro plays Travis Bickle, a violent, alienated cab driver who develops a fascination with a campaign volunteer who works for a senator who is seeking the presidential nomination.

As his fascination turns to obsession, Bickle encounters Iris, a twelve-year-old prostitute played by Jodie Foster. Their relationship deepens, and as the movie roars to its shattering conclusion, Bickle sends Iris money and a letter telling her that he'll be dead soon. He tries to assassinate the candidate, but that effort is unsuccessful. Finally he kills Iris's pimp and is hailed by the media as a hero.

The movie was in part inspired by the case of Arthur Bremer, who stalked and tried to assassinate Alabama governor and presidential candidate George Wallace. The incident put Wallace in a wheelchair.

Hinckley identified with Bickle. He started dressing like the character, favoring army surplus fatigue jackets and combat boots. Like Bickle, he kept a diary and drank peach brandy.

Giving up on Hollywood, Hinckley bounced around, dropping in and out of college and living in Colorado, Texas, and California. In August 1979, seemingly inspired by Bickle's firearms collection, he bought his first gun and took up target shooting. Hinckley added to his collection regularly and started buying ammunition called Devastator rounds, which explode on impact.

A *People* magazine article in May 1980 described Jodie Foster's enrollment at Yale University. Hinckley headed for New Haven.

He had written to Foster before and had received polite responses from her or a publicist—the sort of thing that any movie star sends out by the bucketload to adoring fans. Hinckley, lost in the throes of erotomania, read more into them. He was convinced that Foster needed him to "rescue" her, as Bickle had rescued Iris.

In New Haven, Hinckley made contact with Foster a couple of times. She was polite but firm, telling him that she didn't interact with people she didn't know. In addition to calling her on the phone, he sent her letters and poems.

Hinckley thought he loved Foster. He believed that he just needed to demonstrate it with an act that would get her attention. And thanks to *Taxi Driver*, he knew exactly what to do. It was 1980—election year. President Jimmy Carter was running for reelection against Ronald Reagan.

Hinckley went to a couple of Carter's campaign appearances. Once he left his gun collection in his hotel room, and another time he was stopped at the airport for having guns in his luggage. He was fined, his guns were confiscated, and he was released. Soon he was shopping for more weapons.

After Mark David Chapman assassinated John Lennon on December 8, 1980, Hinckley took a train to New York and joined in the vigil for Lennon in Central Park, describing himself as "in deep mourning." Soon he added a Charter Arms revolver, just like the one Chapman had used, to his gun collection.

On March 30, Hinckley, staying in a Washington, D.C., hotel, wrote Foster a letter explaining his plan to win her love—a letter he never mailed—and took a cab to the Washington Hilton, where Reagan was going to address a labor conference.

As Reagan left the hotel at 2:25 p.m., Hinckley fired six shots. The last ricocheted off the bulletproof presidential limousine and hit the president under his left arm. Press Secretary James Brady was wounded more seriously and became partially paralyzed from the attack. He became a powerful activist against gun violence. Some Secret Service agents immediately apprehended Hinckley.

When First Lady Nancy Reagan arrived at the emergency room, the president got off the famous line, "Honey, I forgot to duck." Later, as he was wheeled into the operating room, he looked up at the surgical team and said, "Please tell me you're all Republicans." The surgery was successful, and Reagan recovered fully.

After a trial that concluded with a screening of *Taxi Driver*, Hinckley was found not guilty by reason of insanity and sent to St. Elizabeth's Hospital in Washington, D.C. He is allowed occasional visits with his parents, but his claims that he has recovered from his obsession with Jodie Foster are belied by the photographs of Foster in his room as well as his attempts to mail-order nude photos of her.

3 **JODIE FOSTER** wasn't the only actress to be stalked by an ero-tomaniac. Theresa Saldana, another actress (who, coincidentally, had also appeared in a Robert De Niro film, *Raging Bull*), was also stalked and attacked by a "fan." On March 15, 1982, when Saldana was twenty-seven years old, a stranger approached her as she unlocked her car in West Hollywood. He asked if she was Theresa Saldana, and when she answered in the affirmative, he slashed and stabbed her multiple times with a hunting knife.

Saldana survived the attack, and her stalker, Arthur Jackson, was subdued by a water deliveryman who saw the assault from a second-floor apartment. Jackson was from Aberdeen, Scotland, and had undergone several stints at mental hospitals. In between those, he had moved to the United States, served in the army, and been deported back to Scotland for threatening President John F. Kennedy. He had a habit of latching onto strange women in obsessive ways, and after seeing Saldana in the movie *Defiance*, she became the object of his obsession.

In 1982, Jackson reentered the country illegally and, with the help of a private detective he hired, tracked Saldana down. His plan was to shoot her, but without proper identification he was unable to buy a gun. That fact probably saved Saldana's life, and her survival has allowed her career to continue and flourish. Jackson served fourteen years in a U.S. prison, then was extradited to England, where in 2004 he died of heart failure in a mental hospital.

4 **ROBERT JOHN BARDO**, who is mentioned along with Hinckley in "Somebody's Watching" (118), was twelve years old when Jackson attacked Saldana. The son of an alcoholic air force non-commissioned officer and a Korean woman, Bardo, along with his six older siblings, grew up in classic military fashion, moving frequently until the family finally settled in Tucson, Arizona, when Bardo was thirteen.

He was a troubled boy who was abused by at least one of his siblings. After he threatened suicide, he was temporarily placed in a foster home and then institutionalized at fifteen years of age.

He was diagnosed as severely emotionally handicapped, and his family was deemed pathological and dysfunctional. After a month his parents brought him home again, and soon he quit high school for good.

Bardo had been earning straight A's, but as a dropout the only job he could get was as a janitor at a Jack in the Box restaurant. With nothing mooring his life, his attention was easily captivated by a fresh-faced young actress named Rebecca Schaeffer. Schaeffer had modeled and appeared on the soap opera *One Life to Live*, but her real break came as Pam Dawber's younger sister on the TV sitcom *My Sister Sam*.

That's where Bardo saw her, in 1986, and he was instantly obsessed. Although his attention drifted to other young performers, Schaeffer remained his primary interest. He sent fan mail, but that was intercepted by her agent and handlers, who didn't let the creepiest letters get to her. Bardo headed to Los Angeles and, clutching a teddy bear and a letter, tried to get onto the Warner Bros. lot to find Schaeffer. The lot's security fended him off. He tried again, this time with a concealed knife, and was reportedly escorted back to his hotel by the security chief.

After Schaeffer's series ended in 1988, she made a movie called *Scenes from the Class Struggle in Beverly Hills*, in which the seemingly innocent young actress shot a fairly adult love scene. Bardo saw it, and his juvenile obsession took on an angry tone. It was time to meet the object of his affection.

Bardo had Arthur Jackson's example to follow. He hired a private detective, who was able to obtain Schaeffer's address from the Department of Motor Vehicles for four dollars. Bardo, still underage, got an older brother to buy him a handgun and hollow-point bullets.

On the morning of July 19, 1989, Schaeffer, then twenty-one, had an appointment with Francis Ford Coppola to discuss a possible role in *The Godfather, Part III*. When the doorbell of her apartment rang, a stranger stood there, holding a paper bag. He drew a gun from the bag and shot Schaeffer once in the chest, then ran. Schaeffer died at the hospital thirty minutes later.

A friend of Bardo's in Tennessee told the Los Angeles police that Bardo had been obsessed with Schaeffer. The day after the shooting, the police in Tucson responded to a report of a young man acting strangely at an intersection. When they picked him up, they sent his picture to Los Angeles, where people in Schaeffer's neighborhood identified him as someone they'd seen around her apartment.

Found guilty of first-degree murder in October 1991, Bardo was sentenced to life without possibility of parole. In July 2007, Bardo was attacked at the Mule Creek State Prison and stabbed eleven times. Unlike Rebecca Schaeffer, he survived.

Blood Suckers and Flesh Eaters

MOST OF THE CRIMES DEPICTED on *Criminal Minds* are acts that violate societal taboos, those social prohibitions against activities that are particularly objectionable to our Western society: murder, rape, and kidnapping, for example. But as awful as these acts are, there are twists to them, violations of even more serious taboos, in our culture that have—in other cultures, other times and places—not only *not* been taboo but, within certain ritual contexts, have been considered sacred acts.

Humans have been known to drink human blood for a variety of reasons. Long before Bram Stoker wrote *Dracula*, making famous the eastern European legend of the vampire, ancient Gauls drank the blood of their vanquished enemies. So did the Moche of Peru. The *Mahabharata*, a Sanskrit epic poem of ancient India, includes scenes of warriors drinking their enemies' blood, and the German epic the *Nibelungenlied* describes the same practice among the Burgundians. This widespread ancient practice stemmed from the belief that it would give the warriors strength in future battles. King Louis XI of France reportedly drank the blood of children in his dying days because he believed that it had healing properties. In more modern times, the practice has persisted in some areas.

Cannibalism, the eating of human flesh, was also practiced for various reasons (e.g., by warriors to gain strength). Nor is cannibalism taboo in all cultures, even today. Some Melanesian tribes still practice it, as do the Korowai of Papua New Guinea. Some scientists believe that cannibalism was normal human behavior at one time, accounting for genes that protect human brains from diseases that can be contracted by eating contaminated human flesh. In recent history, cannibalism has been resorted to as a means of self-preservation when starvation was the only other option, such as in the case of the survivors of a plane crash in the Andes Mountains in 1972.

In contemporary Western civilization, however, both practices are not only illegal but are seen as among the most heinous acts a person can commit. These two taboos crop up on *Criminal Minds* with some regularity.

1 **IN THE EPISODE** "Blood Hungry" (111), the term *anthropophagy*—feeding on human flesh—is mentioned. Spencer Reid brings up the case of Richard Trenton Chase, the so-called Vampire Killer of Sacramento.

On January 27, 1978, at about 12:30 p.m., Chase tried to open the door to a house in north Sacramento. Finding it unlocked—which he believed was an invitation—he walked into the house. Four people were inside at the time: Evelyn Miroth, thirty-eight; her six-year-old son, Jason; her twenty-two-month-old nephew, David; and a neighbor, Daniel Meredith, fifty-one. Dan was watching the kids while Evelyn took a bath. He went to see who was at the door, and Chase shot him in the head with a .22 at point-blank range.

In "The Uncanny Valley," Dr. Reid tries to talk with a woman suspected of turning real-life women into her own personal doll collection.

Chase turned over the body and took Meredith's wallet and car keys, then continued into the house. First he came upon David, who was in his crib, and shot him in the head. Then he followed Jason, who was running into his mother's bedroom, and killed him with two head shots.

Chase entered the bathroom, where he shot Evelyn, then hauled her body from the tub into her bedroom. There he cut the back of her neck and sodomized her, drinking the blood from the slashes in her neck at the same time. When he was finished, he stabbed her anus multiple times. He sliced her abdomen open with a cross cut; the blood that had pooled there flowed freely. Chase collected it in a bucket and drank it.

He went back for the baby, which he took into a bathroom. Cracking David's skull, Chase ate some brain matter and drank more blood. When a six-year-old girl, a friend of Jason's, knocked on the door, Chase panicked, grabbed David's corpse, and fled the house, escaping in Meredith's car. The little girl told a neighbor that she had seen a man leave, and the neighbor came and discovered the grisly scene. The police arrived shortly thereafter and found Chase's fingerprints, handprints, and shoe prints in his victims' blood.

At home, Chase continued his dismemberment of young David. He cut off the boy's head and drank blood from the neck. Slicing the body open, he removed some internal organs and ate them. Others went into the blender to be made into smoothies. What was left Chase put into a box and deposited in a nearby church. A church janitor found the box on March 24, the remains partly mummified. Meredith's car was located, abandoned, near where a dog had been found shot and disemboweled.

Richard Chase was born on May 23, 1950. As a young boy, he exhibited the triad of sociopathy: bed-wetting, fire-starting, and cruelty to animals. By the age of eight, he was over the bed-wetting. But other problems waited around the corner.

When Chase was twelve, his parents started fighting often. His mother, later identified as "highly aggressive" and "hostile," accused her husband of infidelity, of poisoning her, and of using drugs. The hostility continued for a decade, when the couple finally divorced.

Chase took to using drugs and drinking heavily. He had a few girlfriends, but he couldn't maintain an erection, and his relationships ended when intercourse proved unsuccessful. He had no close male friends. After he graduated from high school, he got a job that he held for a few months, but after this job he would never again keep a job longer than a few days. He couldn't handle the workload or the social pressures of junior college. He was arrested once for drunk driving and again for carrying an unlicensed gun and resisting arrest. Unable to support himself, he drifted between his parents' separate homes. His life was locked in a downward spiral.

His adolescent hypochondria worsened, and as he imagined diseases for himself, he also imagined possible cures. Chase caught or purchased rabbits, which he disemboweled, then ate their entrails whole or processed them in a blender. He grew convinced that his heart was shrinking and that he needed to resupply it with blood or it would disappear. He thought that his own blood was turning to powder. He believed that someone had stolen his pulmonary artery and that his head was changing shape. When he injected rabbit blood into his veins as a "cure," he got a bad case of blood poisoning. Diagnosed as schizophrenic, he was committed to a mental institution. Even there he found prey, capturing birds on the grounds, biting their heads off, and drinking their blood. The hospital staff called him Dracula.

Medication seemed to help, and in 1976 he was released into the care of his parents. Soon, though, he was living in his own place again. He returned to old habits, catching animals, including dogs and cats, killing them, and drinking their blood. He also bought guns and started practicing with them.

His mother decided that he no longer needed medication and weaned him off it. From that point on, his course was predictable.

Chase committed his first murder on December 29, 1977. He was practicing with his .22 pistol, shooting from his car. He hit the wall of one house and fired through the kitchen window of another. Then he saw Ambrose Griffin and his wife taking groceries from their car into their house. Chase fired twice and Ambrose fell dead. All of these incidents were in the same Sacramento neighborhood.

On January 23, 1978, a woman saw Chase trying the door and windows of her house as she approached. She stood and watched him. He saw her, lit a cigarette, and eventually wandered off. Locked doors meant he wasn't welcome, he later admitted.

Down the street a short while later, someone else had left a door unlocked. The owners, approaching their home, saw someone exit the house and run away. He had stolen a few things, had urinated into a drawer of baby clothes, and had defecated on a child's bed.

Another hour passed, then Chase encountered an acquaintance from high school in a shopping center parking lot. She was shocked at his appearance. He was frighteningly thin and disheveled. His cheeks were sunken and his eyes were bulging. He had a yellowish crust around his mouth. His sweatshirt was bloody. Anxious, she got into her car and tried to leave. When Chase grabbed at her car door, she stepped on the gas and zoomed away. Hearing about the murders four days later at the Miroth house, the young woman reported her encounter to the police and gave them Chase's name.

Meanwhile, after being left behind by his high school acquaintance, Chase kept wandering the neighborhood, checking doors. He found another opportunity at the home of David and Teresa Wallin. David was at work. His wife, three months pregnant, was taking out the garbage. Chase shot Teresa three times, killing her. Taking her into her bedroom, he had sex with her corpse while stabbing it repeatedly. He disemboweled her, then got a used yogurt container from the kitchen and filled it with blood, which he then drank. Before leaving the property, he picked up dog feces from the yard, went back inside, and shoved it into Teresa's mouth.

The Sacramento police called in the FBI, and profiler Robert Ressler flew out to work on the case. He suggested that the offender would be a white male between twenty-five and twenty-seven, extremely thin, and slovenly. He would have a history of mental illness and drug use. He would be a loner and unemployed, living on a disability payment or off his relatives. He was a disorganized offender, too mentally unstable to hold a job or function in society.

Chase lived less than a mile from where Dan Meredith's car had been abandoned. Now that the police had Chase's name, detectives went to his apartment. When he didn't come out, the cops split up, one heading for the manager's apartment while the other walked away from the building. Taking advantage of the moment, Chase darted for his truck, carrying a box, but the police grabbed him. He wore his .22 in a shoulder holster, and Meredith's wallet was in his back pocket. The box contained bloody rags.

What the police found inside Chase's apartment was far worse: three food blenders, coated with blood; body parts in the refrigerator, including a container of human brain tissue; a calendar with the dates of the Wallin and Miroth-Meredith murders marked on it, along with forty-four more dates marked throughout the rest of the year.

A jury found Chase guilty of six counts of homicide on May 8, 1979, and he was sentenced to die in the gas chamber. Ressler, who believed that Chase was clearly insane and should have been institutionalized rather than imprisoned, interviewed him extensively while he was on death row. Chase insisted that his killings were done in self-defense. He was suffering from soap-dish poisoning (an imaginary ailment), he said, and had been victimized by Nazis and UFOs.

In prison, Chase was given antidepressants to control his continuing hallucinations. He saved up his pills for several weeks, and on December 26, 1980, he took them all at once. A guard found Chase on his bunk, dead.

2   **VAMPIRISM** bares its blood-soaked fangs in "The Performer" (507). In that episode, the condition known as Renfield syndrome, or clinical vampirism, is discussed. A real-life example of this phenomenon is John Brennan Crutchley, who was known as the Vampire Rapist (*rapist* only because none of his probable murders was ever proven).

Crutchley was arrested because a helpful motorist stopped when he saw a teenage girl crawling on the side of a Florida road, naked and weak, in late November 1985. The motorist took her home and called the police and an ambulance. The girl had lost 40–45 percent of her blood.

She had been hitchhiking, she told the police. A man had picked her up, then said he had to get something from his house. When they arrived there, he got into the back of the car and threw a rope around her throat.

The girl came to on the man's kitchen counter, her arms and legs bound. The man had a video camera and lights mounted. As the camera ran, he raped her. After he was done, he drew blood from her with needles and drank it, claiming that he was a vampire. He handcuffed her and put her in a bathtub, and kept coming back for more. Finally he left the house, and she was able to escape. The doctors who examined her believed that she would have died if the man had drawn any more blood.

The house belonged to John Brennan Crutchley, a thirty-nine-year-old computer engineer who was married and had one child. His family was in Maryland for the Thanksgiving holiday. Crutchley was arrested and his home was searched, but the search was haphazard. The videotape in the camera had been partly erased, so the documentary evidence of the victim's rape was gone. A stack of credit cards several inches thick appeared in a photograph, but the cards themselves were gone when the police returned to look for them. Identification cards belonging to two other women were in the house; Crutchley claimed that those women had given him their IDs. There were bodies in his past, and plenty of them, but no evidence tied him to the murders that seemed to follow him from state to state.

Crutchley had participated in kinky sexual activities with what must have been several dozen women and couples, some with his wife's participation. He was a sexual sadist. When he was a boy, his mother had dressed him in girls' clothes until he was five or six. According to FBI profiler Robert Ressler, Crutchley had all the hallmarks of a serial killer. Ressler believes that Crutchley did indeed kill many women, but in the end Crutchley was convicted only of sexual battery, kidnapping, and aggravated battery against the teenage hitchhiker and sentenced to twenty-five years to life.

He was released after eleven years for good behavior, but he was arrested again the next day for violating his parole after he tested positive for marijuana use. That was his third strike, and he went back to prison for life. Crutchley died in prison on April 2, 2002, after putting a plastic bag over his head. His death was ruled a case of autoerotic asphyxiation.

3 **AS INFAMOUS** as Richard Trenton Chase is, he's a nobody compared to the most notorious modern cannibal, Milwaukee's Jeffrey Dahmer. Dahmer is one of those killers whose name pops up frequently on *Criminal Minds*, beginning with the very first episode, "Extreme Aggressor" (101), and again in "Plain Sight" (104), "The Boogeyman" (206), "Fear and Loathing" (216), "Jones" (218), "In Name and Blood" (302), and "Zoe's Reprise" (415).

In "Fear and Loathing," the BAU agents believe they're looking for a smooth-talking killer who easily wins the trust of his victims. Spencer Reid points out that Jeffrey Dahmer was so calm and self-assured that he convinced the police not to look at a bag full of body parts.

Reid is correct. The incident he mentions was Dahmer's first murder, and it was only one of many occasions on which the authorities could have stopped him before he racked up a total of seventeen known murders.

Dahmer, then eighteen, had for years had fantasies of meeting an attractive male hitchhiker and having sex with him. He had grown up in Bath, Ohio, where, he said, people just didn't talk about homosexuality. He called it the biggest taboo in town; others might insist that there were greater taboos and that Dahmer eventually broke most of them.

His parents had divorced the year before. His father was living in a motel, and Dahmer lived with his mother and David, his younger brother. One night in June 1978, when his mother and his brother were out of town for a week, Dahmer took the car and drove around town. He spotted Steven Hicks, also eighteen, the hitchhiker of his dreams, or a close enough approximation. Dahmer picked up Hicks and took him to the empty house. They drank beer and smoked pot, but Dahmer realized that Hicks wasn't gay and wasn't going to fulfill the rest of Dahmer's fantasy. Not wanting Hicks to leave, Dahmer hit Hicks in the head with a barbell. Then he placed the barbell across Hicks's throat and strangled him to death.

This was another thing that Dahmer had fantasized about. Like Bob Berdella, the Kansas City Butcher (see chapter 2), Dahmer longed for complete control over others. If he couldn't control people in life, he would control them in death. After killing Hicks, Dahmer masturbated, then took the body to a crawl space under the house.

The next day, he had to dispose of Hicks in a more permanent fashion. He bought a hunting knife and went back into the crawl space. Slicing open Hicks's belly and seeing his internal organs got him aroused again. He cut Hicks's body into pieces and triple-bagged each piece in garbage bags. Around 3 a.m., while he was driving to dump the pieces in a ravine ten miles from his house, the police stopped him for crossing the centerline.

Dahmer passed an inebriation test, but while the police were talking to him, one officer shined a flashlight into the backseat of Dahmer's car and asked about the plastic bags. Dahmer said it was garbage that he hadn't yet taken to the landfill. Despite the smell—or maybe because of it—the officers believed him and let him go. He decided to take the bags back home instead of dumping them. At home he broke the bones up into tiny pieces and burned the clothes.

For Dahmer, the cooling-off period after that first homicide was nine years long. But when he started up again, he didn't stop.

Jeffrey Lionel Dahmer was born on May 21, 1960, in Milwaukee, Wisconsin. His father, Lionel Dahmer, was an analytical chemist. He noticed that Jeffrey had a fascination with the bones of dead animals at an early age. He didn't think anything of it at the time, but later he would see it as a dark premonition.

Otherwise, Jeff was a cheerful child, until an operation for a double hernia at the age of four. His natural happiness never seemed to return after that; instead, he seemed solemn, distant, and apathetic. Between the ages of ten and fifteen, even the way he carried himself changed; he became rigid and tense, with a blank face and a shy manner.

Dahmer had also developed an unsettling habit of collecting dead animals and dissecting them. He stripped the skin off a large dog he found by the road and mounted its head on a stick, which he set out in the woods as a prank.

His later high school years were filled with nightmarish fantasies and a growing alcohol problem. These reached their culmination in the murder of Steven Hicks, and they never went away again.

After high school, Dahmer tried college, but after staying drunk for a semester at Ohio State University, he dropped out. Next, he went into the army, which discharged him after two years for habitual drunkenness.

Back home in 1982, after being arrested for drunk and disorderly conduct, Dahmer moved in with his paternal grandmother in West Allis, Wisconsin. He tried to straighten out his life, tried to push away the sexual fantasies and the booze. He attended church with his grandmother and thought that he was doing a good job of regaining control of himself.

Eventually, though, the compulsion to have sex with men began to rule him again. He started going out to gay bars, bookstores, and bathhouses. He bought a male mannequin, which he kept under his bed, hoping that by playing with it and controlling it he would satisfy the urge to do the same with real men. It didn't work. There were more arrests, for indecent exposure. In 1986, after the second arrest, he served ten months in jail. He was soon arrested again, for fondling a thirteen-year-old boy.

In 1987, while Dahmer was on probation for that crime, he met Steven Tuomi, twenty-six, outside a gay bar. They went to a hotel room rented in Dahmer's name and drank together. Dahmer claimed that he blacked out, and when he woke up, Tuomi was dead. Sure that he had beaten the young man to death, Dahmer bought a large wheeled suitcase and put the body in it, then took it to his grandmother's house and put it in the fruit cellar for a week. At the end of the week, he cut the corpse open, masturbated, and "defleshed" the body. He smashed the skeleton with a sledgehammer—except for the skull, which he kept—and put the flesh and the broken bones out with the garbage. The skull he soaked in undiluted bleach, to clean it, but it became too brittle, and he eventually had to throw that away, too.

The next year, Dahmer moved out of his grandmother's house. He was making a living working at a chocolate factory in Milwaukee, so he rented a one-bedroom apartment, figuring that would give him more freedom for what he must have already known was coming. His next brush with the law came when a young Laotian man he had drugged and photographed got away and reported the assault. The police came to the apartment, but once again they failed to find the clues, including a skull in one of Dahmer's drawers.

From there, a routine developed. Dahmer would go out to a bar or a bathhouse and pick up a man. Since sex with live humans wasn't as enjoyable for him as sex with corpses, he drugged the man with sleeping pills, then strangled him. He photographed each stage of murder and dismemberment to use later for sexual stimulation. As time went on, he became more creative in his methods of disposal, such as by dissolving body parts in chemicals or acids. He kept some bones and several skulls, planning to build an altar with them to use for some vague ritual, in the hope of receiving special powers.

Ultimately, killing men and having sex with their corpses wasn't enough. To feel closer to them, to feel some continuing control over them, he began eating their flesh. Also like Berdella, he experimented with ways to turn them into zombies, such as by drilling a hole in their heads and pouring or injecting acid into their brains. He claimed that most victims died right away but that one remained somewhat functional for a couple of days. The ideal would have been for one of them to live on, completely under his control, with no thoughts but to serve Dahmer in whatever way he wanted. The idea that a lover might reject or leave him was too horrible to bear.

Samantha Malcolm, the "doll"-collecting unsub in "The Uncanny Valley" (512), wants her victims completely controlled as well, only in her case most of them are treated with enough care that they live for months as human dolls. Malcolm kidnapped and drugged her victims into paralysis, but, unlike Dahmer, she didn't rape, murder, or cannibalize them.

As Dahmer got better at dismembering, his cooling-off period became shorter and shorter. In 1989 he killed only once. In 1990, living in a different Milwaukee apartment, he murdered four young men. In 1991 there were eight homicides, at a rate of one a week.

In May 1991, the police missed yet another chance to catch him. Dahmer picked up a fourteen-year-old Laotian—by sheer chance, the little brother of the man he had molested who had gotten away and reported him—and photographed him, drugged him, and drilled a small hole in his skull. He gave the boy an injection of boiling water, then went across the street to get a beer before the bar closed. While he was gone, the boy woke up and left Dahmer's apartment.

When Dahmer returned, he saw the boy sitting on the sidewalk, disoriented. Someone had called the police, and they were trying to interrogate him. Dahmer stepped up and told the police that the boy was his lover (he told them that the boy was older, that Laotians just look young) who had gotten very drunk and ran away after an argument. Once again, Dahmer was persuasive. The officers helped Dahmer get the boy back into the apartment. There they saw the photos that Dahmer had taken earlier, which seemed to confirm Dahmer's story. They left the boy there. Had they looked in the bedroom, they would have found the body of Dahmer's previous victim, still on the bed three days after his murder.

That simple act could have saved five lives. Instead, Dahmer killed the boy as soon as the police left, and, as if inspired by his near miss, set a frantic pace for the rest of the summer.

On another occasion, detectives interviewed Dahmer about a different homicide—not one of his—in the building. Despite the terrible smells that always lingered in Dahmer's apartment now, the detectives didn't question him about his own activities. Yet another would-be victim escaped and reported Dahmer's assault, but the police interpreted it as a tiff between gay men and didn't even question Dahmer.

On July 22, 1991, Dahmer took a man named Tony Edwards home. He tried to handcuff Edwards, but he got the cuffs locked around only one wrist. When Edwards fought back, Dahmer threatened him with a large knife. Edwards got away and ran into the street, where he flagged down a police car. He convinced the cops to return to Dahmer's apartment with him and told them to look in the bedroom for the knife that Dahmer had brandished.

The cop who went into the bedroom saw more than just a knife. He saw some of Dahmer's collection of photographs that documented the stages of death and dismemberment. He told his partner to cuff Dahmer.

Photos weren't even the half of it. Once the police started looking at the apartment, they found a decomposing severed head in the refrigerator, along with three bags of human organs. Three more heads and other body parts were stored in a freestanding freezer. A sealed oil drum contained three torsos soaking in acid. Still more body parts, in various stages of decomposition, were scattered around the apartment, along with all the skulls.

Dahmer tried to deny the crimes, but only briefly. Of his seventeen victims, most were black, and some were Asian or Hispanic. Three were Caucasian, like Dahmer. Since serial killers usually murder within their own race, there was speculation that Dahmer's homicides had a racial motive behind them. Dahmer denied this; he said it was due to the neighborhood he lived in and the mix of people who frequented the bars he went to. He would have murdered white men if they had been available, but they weren't.

Dahmer was ultimately charged with fifteen homicides. He first pleaded not guilty by reason of insanity, then changed his plea to guilty but insane, a variation allowed under Wisconsin law. After a two-week trial, the jury took five hours to find him guilty and sane, and he was sentenced to 957 years in prison.

In prison, Dahmer felt threatened by the African American inmates, who believed that his murders had been racially motivated. In July 1994, slightly more than two years after his sentencing, he and another inmate were attacked by Christopher J. Scarver, a delusional schizophrenic who heard voices telling him he was the son of God. Scarver bludgeoned Dahmer and the other inmate to death with the rod from a set of weights—poetic justice, perhaps, considering that Dahmer's first murder had been committed with a barbell.

4 **FOR ALL OF THE MENTIONS** of Dahmer on *Criminal Minds*, none of them occur in the two episodes that focus on cannibalism. These are "Blood Hungry" (111) and "Lucky" (308). The cannibal in "Lucky," barbecue restaurant owner Floyd Ferrell, feeds one of his victims to the search party that is looking for her.

What's particularly creepy is that Ferrell isn't unique among cannibals in his choice of profession. Hadden Clark, a former student at the Culinary Institute of America and a professional chef, was a cannibal who killed at least two people in Maryland and is suspected of several more. His older brother, Bradfield, was convicted of strangling and dismembering a dinner guest in California, and cannibalism is believed to have been a factor in his crime as well.

German serial killer and cannibal Georg Grossman was a professional butcher who sold meat on the black market during World War I, and he had a sausage stand at a train station. Upon his arrest, evidence of at least three dead women was found in his apartment; it's believed that up to fifty may have disappeared at his hands and that the meat he served was often human.

Elsewhere in Germany during the same period, cannibal Fritz Haarman preyed on young boys, murdering between twenty-four and fifty of them. Like Grossman, he sold some of his human meat on the black market.

Finally, as recently as November 2009, three homeless Russian men were arrested for killing a man, eating part of him, and selling the rest as meat to a local kebab kiosk.

16

On Other Shores

AS FRITZ HAARMAN AND GEORG GROSSMAN demonstrate all too awfully, grisly murder is not strictly a U.S. phenomenon. Every continent, with the possible exception of Antarctica, has had its share of killers, some well known and others more obscure, and some of their stories are reflected in *Criminal Minds* episodes.

Most serial killers like to get close to their victims. For this reason, knives are a far more popular weapon with these murderers than guns are. Killers who use fire as a weapon, however, don't really have the proximity option.

Clara Hayes, in the episode "Compulsion" (102), says, "I do this for Charon." The "this" to which she refers is the setting of a series of fires at Bradshaw College in Tempe, Arizona, the most recent with fatal results. Discussing the unsub's motive, the BAU's Spencer

Reid says, "When asked about his motives, Peter Dinsdale said, 'I am devoted to fire. Fire is my master.'"

The full quote, in fact, is "I am devoted to fire and despise people." Dinsdale did say these things, but not until a law enforcement fluke brought in one of the most prolific—and unnoticed—serial killers in English history.

1 **KINGSTON UPON HULL**, an industrial city 150 miles north of London along England's east coast, couldn't be more different from Tempe, in the Phoenix metropolitan area and, in real life, the home of Arizona State University. But beginning in 1973, Hull, as it's known, was the site of arson fires that went unsolved until 1979. They were set by Peter Dinsdale, who had, by the time of the 1979 blaze, changed his name to Bruce George Peter Lee, in honor of his hero, martial arts star Bruce Lee.

Dinsdale, who was physically and mentally disabled and subject to epileptic fits, could never have been a martial arts star. He was born in Manchester, England, in 1960, to a prostitute who turned him over to his grandmother to raise when he was six months old. In his lower-class neighborhood in Hull, he became a familiar figure, going to a special school for the disabled and becoming widely known as "Daft Pete." He was a constant target of mockery by the town's other children. Sometimes he seemed intent on avoiding attention, keeping to himself while warning others that they had no idea what he'd been up to. Most assumed that he couldn't have been up to much. They were wrong.

Dinsdale set his first fatal fire at the age of twelve, although he might well have begun committing arson before that. Richard Ellerington, six years old, attended the same special school as Dinsdale. On June 23, 1973, Ellerington's parents went out for the evening, leaving Richard and their five other children home with babysitter Carol Dennett and her own baby. All of the children were in bed by the time the couple returned, and because of the late hour, Dennett slept over.

Billows of smoke awakened the family around 7 a.m. The house was in flames, but everyone escaped except young Richard. The firefighters found his body after the blaze had been extinguished. When the school bus stopped outside the smoldering Ellerington house, word spread that Richard had died in the fire. Dinsdale sat on the bus, looking out the window and saying nothing.

On October 12 of that year, he set a fire that killed seventy-two-year-old Arthur Smythe, who had gangrene in both legs and couldn't get out of the house in time to save himself. The fire was blamed on a faulty kerosene heater. On October 27, David Brewer, who was at home because of an industrial injury, died in a fire that would be attributed to clothes hanging to dry before an open fireplace. The next year, fire claimed the life of eighty-two-year-old widow Elizabeth Rokahr. An inquest concluded that she had been smoking in bed. Two years passed before Dinsdale's next arson homicide: he set a fire that killed thirteen-month-old Andrew Stevenson in 1976.

By this time, Dinsdale had a regular MO. He either entered a house through an unlocked door and poured kerosene, then lit it, or he poured the kerosene inside through the mail slot and stuffed burning paper in to ignite the accelerant.

During his teen years, Dinsdale wasn't just setting fires. He worked at a racetrack and a pig market, sometimes babysat for younger children, and earned extra cash as a "rent boy," a young man who loiters around public restrooms to provide sexual services for older men.

His fire-setting habit continued, however. He severely injured Ros Fenton, who spent months in the hospital and lost her unborn baby, as well as her daughter, Samantha. In another incident, six-month-old Katrina Thacker was killed.

Dinsdale's worst attack might have been at the Wensley Lodge retirement home. Eleven elderly men perished in the blaze, making it one of Britain's worst mass murders. This fire was blamed on a plumber who had been using a blowtorch in the boiler room earlier that day.

All of these fires were attributed to accidents, so the police never got involved. Only the Brewer and the Thacker fires were

In "Zoe's Reprise," Morgan and the team pursue a copycat serial killer who is re-creating the techniques used by past famous murderers.

the results of some slight, real or imagined; Dinsdale set the others simply because he could.

The end of Dinsdale's reign of fire came after he set a fire at the home of Tommy and Edith Hastie. Tommy was a small-time criminal who was in prison for burglary. His oldest son had been involved in the robbery with him, and the other children were frequently in trouble. The night of the fire, the couple's three daughters were staying with relatives, and Edith Hastie was home with her four sons. She woke up when the house was almost fully engulfed in flames. Charlie, fifteen, managed to push Edith out a second-story window. She broke an ankle, but she lived. Only one of her sons survived his burns.

This time, arson was easily confirmed. Detective Superintendent Ronald Sagar discovered a ring of kerosene and some used matches near the door. Dinsdale later admitted that he had tried to start the fire with matches and, failing that, had shoved lit newspaper inside.

Sagar had a hard time making progress in the case. In that neighborhood, talking to the police was frowned upon. Every apparent lead turned into another dead end.

Only one tip seemed promising. A witness had seen two men running away from the Hastie house and getting into a Rover 2000. Drug dealers favored those cars, and the Hastie family was known to have crime connections. Perhaps one of the Hasties had angered a dealer. This, too, led nowhere, and after a couple of months of the police watching everyone in the area who drove a Rover 2000, the witness declared that he'd made a mistake—the occurrence he had seen had taken place on a different night, not the night of the fire.

Sagar was running out of ideas, and the case was growing colder. Because one of the Rover 2000 drivers he'd followed had been a frequent customer of rent boys, Sagar decided to haul some of them in for questioning.

One, Bruce George Peter Lee, admitted not only to knowing Charlie Hastie but also to having engaged in sexual activity with him. The case had been open six months, and Sagar's superiors wanted to shut the investigation down. Sagar read Dinsdale his rights, then accused him of starting the fire, suggesting that their "indecency" was behind it.

"I didn't mean to kill them," Dinsdale said of the Hasties. He admitted that Charlie had demanded money or else he'd tell the police what they'd been up to. Dinsdale had a crush on Angie Hastie, Charlie's older sister, but she wouldn't give him the time of day. These two factors made him angry enough to burn down the house.

Once he started confessing, Dinsdale told Sagar about the other fires and pointed out houses that he'd burned. He had, he said, started at least thirty fires around Hull. By the time he was finished confessing, he had accepted the blame for twenty-six deaths. "I like fires," he said. "I do. I like fires."

Dinsdale pleaded guilty to twenty-six counts of manslaughter on the grounds of diminished capacity, with some arson counts thrown in for good measure. He was sentenced to the Rampton Secure Hospital, a high-security mental institution.

In 1981, the *Sunday Times* of London investigated Dinsdale's claims and concluded that he could not have started the fire at

Wensley Lodge. A justice agreed and struck those eleven deaths from Dinsdale's record, setting his body count at only fifteen—still a major figure in the annals of British murderers.

At Rampton, Dinsdale married a fellow patient, Ann-Marie Davison. He's legally entitled to be married, but he and his wife are not allowed to consummate their marriage.

Although Dinsdale could theoretically be released if he's ever judged sane, given his record it's unlikely that he will ever be free to start fires again or to enjoy relations with his bride.

2 **WHEN THE BAU** profilers travel to Mexico in "Machismo" (119), they discuss the apparent discrepancy between the number of serial killers that Mexico has had and the number that the country admits to having. Jason Gideon blames the "Chikatilo syndrome." Spencer Reid elaborates a bit, explaining that Andrei Chikatilo, a Russian, murdered more than fifty people before he was caught, largely because the Soviet Union believed that serial killers were a decadent Western phenomenon and therefore wouldn't admit that it had one.

Not only did that attitude make it hard for the Soviet police to track down the killer, it also meant that potential victims didn't take steps to protect themselves, because the state-run media weren't allowed to warn the public that a serial killer was on the loose.

After Chikatilo's first murder, on December 22, 1978, the Soviet bureaucracy made it easy for him to get away with it. He lured a nine-year-old girl into an old house and tried to rape her, but he was unable to achieve an erection. He choked her to death and stabbed her, which finally brought him to a climax.

Evidence could have connected Chikatilo to the murder, but the authorities focused on another man who had a previous conviction for rape and murder. They arrested this man and tortured him until he confessed. He was sentenced to fifteen years, but when the victim's relatives pressured the courts for harsher justice, the wrong man was retried and executed. Chikatilo had killed, but he would not be punished for it.

Andrei Romanovich Chikatilo was born in Ukraine on October 16, 1934. He was born with hydrocephalus, an excess of cerebrospinal fluid in the brain, which caused him to have a misshapen head and other physical ailments. A terrible famine racked Ukraine from 1932 to 1933, thanks to Joseph Stalin's desire to crush Ukrainian nationalism. In 1932 Stalin raised Ukraine's grain procurement quotas by 44 percent. This meant that there would not be enough grain for the peasants, because Soviet law required that no grain from a collective farm could be given to the residents of the farm until the government's quota was met. The result was that at least six million people died. Some turned to cannibalism to survive.

Chikatilo's mother told Andrei and his sister that their older brother, Stepan, had been a victim of cannibals. There is no independent evidence that Stepan ever existed, and he might have simply been a figment of her imagination. When the USSR entered World War II, Chikatilo's father was conscripted, and Chikatilo spent those years sleeping in his mother's bed. He was a chronic bed-wetter, and she beat him every time he soiled her sheets.

During the war, Chikatilo witnessed the effects of German bombing, and later he said that the bodies in the street both frightened and excited him.

Chikatilo was a lonely child, partly blind and given to violent fantasies. His first sexual experience was at fifteen, when he grabbed a ten-year-old friend of his sister's and wrestled with her, which caused him to ejaculate. For most of his life thereafter, he was impotent, although he could achieve orgasm through the violent abuse of his victims.

Despite his physical and emotional problems, Chikatilo was intelligent, and he tried to get into Moscow State University. He failed the entrance exam, so he fulfilled his mandatory military service and then became a telephone engineer. His sister moved in with him and arranged a meeting with a girlfriend, Fayina, whom Chikatilo subsequently married. Even with her he couldn't achieve an erection, but he could ejaculate and inseminate her by hand; in this way they had two children and the semblance of a normal life.

Chikatilo changed careers and became a schoolteacher. That didn't last long, because there were complaints about his inappropriate behavior toward the children. He moved from school to school and town to town as he kept being fired from each teaching job. He finally ended up as a factory clerk near the city of Rostov-on-Don, and he held this position until his arrest. It was there that he began killing, at the advanced age of forty-two.

Enough trust was put in him by the company that Chikatilo was sent all over the country by himself, and he did this frequent travel by train or bus. Although many of his homicides occurred close enough to home to earn him the nickname the Rostov Ripper, he frequently picked victims near bus depots and train stations in the cities he traveled to—making him even more difficult to pin down.

After his first victim in 1978, Chikatilo didn't kill again until 1981. That year he took one victim, a seventeen-year-old student whom he enticed to have sex but who laughed at his inability to become erect. Between June and December 1982, he killed six girls between the ages of ten and nineteen as well as a nine-year-old boy.

His pattern was to lure them from a rail station or depot into nearby woods, where he would stab and slash and mutilate, some with as many as seventy separate wounds. He often slashed or cut out the eyes. Sometimes he ate internal organs, and possibly sexual organs, which he frequently removed from his victims. Later he took to slicing off the upper lip or nose and leaving it inside the victim's mouth or slashed-open stomach.

The next year, 1983, Chikatilo again took a break until June. Between then and the end of the year, he murdered six more women and girls, who ranged in age from thirteen to twenty-five, and two boys, ages seven—his youngest victim yet—and fourteen. Chikatilo murdered fifteen victims in 1984, including his oldest yet, a forty-five-year-old woman, and a mother-daughter combination. Two of the year's victims were male, the rest female.

Chikatilo was arrested twice during these years, once when a police officer observed suspicious behavior around the bus stops and saw Chikatilo receiving oral sex from a prostitute. When Chikatilo was arrested, he had a knife and a length of rope under his coat, but his blood type didn't match what the authorities were looking for, based on semen samples from other crime scenes, so he was released. Another time he served three months in prison for petty thefts.

In 1985, Chikatilo was relatively quiet, killing only twice: both victims were eighteen-year-old girls. He didn't kill again until 1987, when his victims were three boys, ages twelve, thirteen, and sixteen. In 1988 he committed three more murders, two boys and a young woman, and that pattern repeated in 1989. During this period, the authorities learned that semen samples don't always match up to blood types.

As if a dam had broken, in 1990 Chikatilo broke his own record, killing eight victims: six boys and two women. The Soviet investigators were drawing nearer, and during that year they developed a plan to place obvious officers at certain stations and depots, forcing their unsub to take his victims from the stations where they had plainclothes officers positioned.

Their plan worked, and they came up with a suspect. He was someone they had talked to before and had released, but now they knew that their science had been faulty. Chikatilo was picked up again, in spite of a lack of solid evidence. He could be held for ten days, and nine passed before he finally confessed. The police thought they had him on thirty-six homicides, but there were far more, as many as fifty-five or fifty-six, Chikatilo claimed. Some could not be corroborated, and he was charged with fifty-three counts of murder.

While Chikatilo was studied, judged sane, and waiting for trial, the Soviet Union collapsed. He went on trial in Russia and was placed in a large cage. Sometimes he drooled, sang, or rolled his eyes, and on two occasions he exposed himself in court. His trial stretched from April to August 1992, and the jury took two more months to reach a verdict. He was convicted of fifty-two counts of murder and five of molestation and was sentenced to be executed. That happened on February 15, 1994, with a single shot to the head—a much more merciful end than he had given his victims.

Chikatilo is also brought up in the episode "Jones" (218), in which it's pointed out that he fantasized that the males he killed were his captives whom he was responsible for torturing. That torture and mutilation, in his imagination, made him a hero.

Andrei Chikatilo is a classic example of an organized killer—up until the actual murder begins, at which point he lost control and attacked savagely. Fired from all of his teaching jobs, once his killing spree began, he held the same factory clerk's job until his arrest, with enough trust put in him by the company that he was sent all over the country by himself. He kept his admittedly unusual marriage going and raised two children. Despite his odd appearance, he was able to quickly grasp what would entice people of various genders and ages—sweets, money, sex—and sweet-talk them into accompanying him into the woods.

Toward the end, Chikatilo might have been undergoing a final mental disintegration. This could account for the frequency of attacks in 1990 and the fact that even though he must have known he was the subject of a massive search (given the increased police presence around his usual hunting grounds), he could not seem to take a break from killing as he had done in earlier years. It's possible that if he had maintained his rate of killing one or two a year, he might have stayed on the loose for even longer. People all over Russia are no doubt thankful that he didn't.

3 **WHETHER OR NOT** the Mexican authorities admit it, they have had their share of serial killers, as has South America. FBI profiler Robert Ressler has been invited to Ciudad Juárez to try to help solve the murders of four hundred to eight hundred women that have taken place there since the early 1990s. All of these murders, often called the "femicides" of Juárez, are not believed to be the work of a single killer, but it's theorized that a serial killer could be contributing to the overall total. Juárez is one of the fastest growing cities in the world, with a murder rate exceeding that of any city not in a war zone. With the continuing femicides and the drug-related killings, the number of murders there in 2009 topped than twenty-six hundred.

In 1999, Fernando Hernandez Leyva, from Cuernavaca, Mexico, was arrested—again; he had been arrested in 1982 and 1986 and had escaped both times. This time he was accused of 137 murders, along with several kidnappings and robberies. Hernandez Leyva reportedly admitted to more than a hundred murders. If this number is true, he would be the worst-known individual serial killer in Mexico's history. In custody, he tried to commit suicide by hanging himself, but his more than three-hundred-pound bulk broke the rope.

In South America lives the man called the Monster of the Andes. At least, we can presume that he lives; the Ecuadorian authorities released him from prison in 1998, and he hasn't surfaced again. Wherever he is, however, Pedro Alonzo Lopez is probably still killing.

Lopez was born in Colombia in 1949, the seventh child of thirteen. His mother, a prostitute, caught him fondling his sister's breasts at the age of eight and turned him out onto the street. Terrified, the boy turned to the first kindly stranger he met, but that man took the boy into a building and repeatedly sodomized him.

After a brief interlude at a day school ended with molestation at the hands of a male teacher, Lopez returned to the streets, making his living by petty crimes and car theft. Arrested in 1969 for auto theft, he had been in prison for just two days when he was gang-raped by four older inmates. He took revenge on them with a handmade knife and killed the first four victims of what would become a very long list.

By the time he was arrested for the second time, in 1980, he confessed to having raped and murdered more than 350 girls throughout Colombia, Peru, and Ecuador. The authorities didn't believe him until he started showing them his crowded dump sites. Having had his innocence stolen at such a young age, Lopez claimed, made him determined to do the same to as many people as he could. He swore, in his only prison interview, that he would kill again when he was freed.

The facts are in dispute, but most reports say that Lopez served twenty years in solitary confinement in Ecuador. That was the country's legal limit, and Ecuador has no death penalty. So even though Lopez was wanted in Colombia and Peru, he was taken to the Colombian border during the night, in 1998 or 1999, and released. Other reports say that he was delivered into the hands of the Colombian authorities. Either way, no one seems to know where he is today.

4 **PROBABLY THE MOST** famous serial killer worldwide is Jack the Ripper. He is also one of the earliest known murderers to meet the modern criteria for the term *serial killer*. Before Jack, stranger murder was all but unheard of; except during war, people killed personal enemies or family members, but not people they had never met.

As one might expect, references to Jack crop up occasionally on *Criminal Minds*. In the episode "Jones" (218), a female killer patterns her murders of men after the Ripper's crimes against women. He comes up again in "Zoe's Reprise" (415), in which the killer's crimes resemble those of a number of famous murderers.

Because Jack was never caught or identified, all we really know about him are his crimes (and the inferences that can be drawn from those crimes, which have been the subject of debate ever since). His five murders (possibly as many as eleven, but five are definitely agreed upon) have formed the basis for entire libraries of books that purport to examine the case and, often, to reveal the "real" Jack the Ripper. In fact, even the name might well be fraudulent, because it came from a letter to London's Central News Agency that is widely considered to have been the work of an impostor.

Taken as a whole, the eleven murders, which occurred from April 3, 1888, to February 13, 1891, are termed the Whitechapel Murders, after the district of London's East End where they occurred.

The five victims who are believed to have been killed by a single murderer are Mary Ann Nichols, Annie Chapman, Elizabeth Stride, Catherine Eddowes, and Mary Jane Kelly.

Nichols was the first of the five to be killed. When her body was found on August 31, 1888, her throat had been slashed with two cuts, and her abdomen was sliced open. There were other, less severe incisions on her abdomen.

Chapman's throat also had two cuts when she turned up on September 8. Again, the abdomen of the victim was slashed open, and in this case her uterus had been removed.

Stride and Eddowes were both murdered on September 30. Stride had a single slash to the throat and no abdominal mutilation; it is presumed that the Ripper was interrupted and thus went on to take a second victim. Eddowes had her throat severed and her abdomen opened, and her left kidney and most of her uterus were gone.

Kelly, the last certain Ripper victim, was found in her apartment on November 9, 1888. Her throat had been cut to the spine, her abdomen was opened wide, and nearly all of her internal organs, including her heart, were missing.

Suspects in the Ripper murders were in no short supply and included people from high society, such as Prince Albert Victor, royal physician Albert Gull, and a wealthy man named Francis Tumblety. Modern profilers don't know if the real Ripper was ever named as a suspect, but they speculate that the killer was a highly disorganized type. He may have had more in common with Richard Trenton Chase than with a skilled medical doctor or a member of the royal family. His murders were sexually motivated. He was someone who would not have stood out among the vagrants and prostitutes of Whitechapel (as a member of the royal family certainly would). He was mentally deranged and became more so with each woman he killed. He used a blitz-style attack because he was not someone who could charm anyone into a vulnerable position. He was a quiet loner, he probably returned to the scenes of his murders, and he was most likely questioned during the investigation.

Today, it's all guesswork, of course, and the real answers—short of the discovery of a contemporary diary or journal confessing to the crimes in enough detail to be persuasive—will never be known. It's this air of mystery, in addition to the brutality and the novelty, at the time, of the murders, that keeps people reading and writing about Jack the Ripper even now.

The Strangest of
the Strange

SOME CRIMES AND CRIMINALS defy easy categorization. Murderers are a dime a dozen, it seems, especially on prime-time television. But every now and then, *Criminal Minds* turns toward the truly bizarre, the once-in-a-lifetime—one hopes—cases that stand out among all the serial killers, home invaders, and family annihilators. Those cases are the subject of this chapter, a roundup of some of the oddest incidents.

In "Won't Get Fooled Again" (103), Jason Gideon has to ask for help from his old nemesis, bomber Adrian Bale, whose treachery got six FBI agents killed in Boston and sent Gideon into a psychological tailspin. But when a different bomber locks a collar bomb around a victim's neck and sends him into a police station, the BAU team is short on options and time.

The events of this episode are reminiscent of an incident in Pennsylvania on which the FBI's real BAU consulted—an incident that, like many on *Criminal Minds*, was more complex than it appeared at first.

1 **AT 2:40 P.M.** on August 23, 2003, in Erie, Pennsylvania, a man named Brian Douglas Wells walked into the PNC Bank branch at Summit Towne Center with a homemade shotgun in his hand and a bomb around his neck, under his T-shirt. He carried several detailed notes—a script, according to the FBI: one to give to the bank teller, one for the teller to give to the police, and one describing the steps that Wells had to follow to have the bomb removed. He had been given fifty-five minutes to accomplish these tasks. His note said, in part, "This powerful, booby-trapped bomb can be removed only by following our instructions. Using time attempting to escape it will fail and leave you short of time to follow instructions. Do not delay."

Wells got the money and raced back to his car. He drove to a nearby McDonald's, where his note led him to another note—the first stop in a bizarre, desperate scavenger hunt with survival as the goal. He started off again, but the police pulled him over and ordered him out of the car. They handcuffed him and sat him down on the curb. When he explained that there was a bomb locked around his neck, they evacuated the area and called the bomb squad.

Panicking, Wells spent the next thirty minutes begging the officers to save him. Before anything could be done, the bomb exploded. Far from the end of the investigation, this was only the beginning.

Brian Wells was hardly the sort of man one would expect to be involved in such a strange, dramatic plot. By all accounts he was a naive, gentle forty-six-year-old who worked on his old car, took care of his cat, watched videos with his mother, and delivered pizzas for a living.

It was the pizzas, apparently, that got him in trouble. Wells had worked for Mama Mia's Pizzeria for ten years. On that fateful

August day, he was about to go off duty when an order came in for two small sausage and pepperoni pizzas. Wells agreed to deliver them in his own car, then take off for the day.

The address Wells had been sent to wasn't a home at all, but a secluded, wooded area. The next thing anybody knew, he was walking into the bank with a gun shaped like a cane.

From the start, the authorities wondered if Wells had been involved in the plot. His family and his friends insisted that he was an innocent pawn who had been captured and forced to rob the bank for fear of his life. One source told Wells's brother John that Brian Wells had found himself surrounded by people with guns. They locked the bomb around his neck, and Wells started running. A gunshot stopped him, convincing him that they would do whatever it took to get him to cooperate. Another witness in the area confirms having heard a shot. Wells repeated the same basic tale in the half hour he spent with police before the bomb went off.

For the next year, the FBI investigated the case without reaching any conclusions. A witness named William Rothstein, who lived in the wooded area near the spot where Wells was supposed to deliver the pizzas, died of cancer, but not until after he swore on his deathbed that he was not involved with the bank job. Coincidentally, he just happened to have a dead body stashed in his freezer when the FBI interviewed him, hidden there to help a friend get away with murder. Another witness, who also drove for Mama Mia's, died of an overdose within hours of talking to FBI agents.

On the first anniversary of the crime, the FBI released a detailed profile of the unsub they called Collarbomber. The profile stated, "According to these FBI and ATF experts, this is a very complex crime, and most likely involves more than one person. However, it is the 'mastermind,' that person who oversaw its design and implementation, that has left the blueprint of his personality on every aspect of the crime.

"To the general public," the profile continued, "this crime may appear to be an elaborate bank robbery. However, it continues to be the opinion of the BAU that this is much more than a mere bank robbery. The behavior seen in this crime was choreographed

In "To Hell . . ." ". . . And Back," the BAU tracks a serial killer who chooses junkies, prostitutes, and the homeless off the streets of Detroit as his victims.

by 'Collarbomber' watching on the sidelines according to a written script in which he attempted to direct others to do what he wanted them to do. This is very unusual and complex criminal behavior. Because of the complex nature of this crime, the BAU believes there were multiple motives for the offender, and money was not the primary one."

The profile then reveals that the note that was intended for the police would have put them in the same area as Wells when the bomb went off, if Wells had not been spotted and stopped. The idea was to kill as many people as possible—ideally, police officers—and Wells had been instructed that while inside the bank he should stay close to as many bank employees as he could, presumably for that reason.

The authorities suggested that Wells was in on the plot all along. He might have believed that the bomb was simply a fake meant to fool the bank employees. At some point he realized it was genuine, which explains his very real panic during the last minutes of his life.

More time passed. In August 2006, the authorities claimed to be closing in on the real killers. One of the people they looked at was Kenneth Barnes, a convicted drug dealer, described by an acquaintance as "a very smart guy who could make or rebuild anything." Barnes knew Rothstein, the witness with the corpse in his freezer. Barnes also knew, and occasionally worked for, Marjorie Diehl-Armstrong, who had been convicted in 2003 of killing her boyfriend. It was her boyfriend's body that Rothstein had been keeping on ice.

In July 2007, the authorities finally brought indictments in the case, and the conclusions they had reached startled some and outraged Wells's family and friends. The FBI concluded that Wells really was in on the plot, except that he believed the bomb was a fake; that's why he went along willingly.

The mastermind behind the plot was deemed to be Diehl-Armstrong, fifty-eight. A federal grand jury indicted her and Barnes, fifty-three, in the case. A third person, Floyd Stockton, sixty, was given immunity in exchange for his testimony against the other two. Diehl-Armstrong and Rothstein hatched the scheme, investigators said, in order to raise enough money to have Diehl-Armstrong's father killed. Barnes would do the murder for $125,000, but Diehl-Armstrong had less than $9,000. Her father's death, she believed, would net her a big inheritance, but she was unaware that the man had spent most of what she expected to gain. Brian Wells was allegedly roped into the plot through a prostitute who knew Barnes.

Diehl-Armstrong was already in prison for her previous boyfriend's murder (the one whose corpse had been found in Rothstein's freezer), but there was controversy over whether, due to severe bipolar disorder, she was competent to stand trial in the bank robbery case. Various judges ruled that she was not, but in September 2009 another judge determined that she was. Barnes, who had already been tried, was sentenced to forty-five years for his role in the crime.

John Wells doesn't believe the official story. He's created a Web site on which he pleads for anyone with further knowledge to come forward. He asks some reasonable questions. If money was the goal, he wants to know, then why put his brother through a complicated scavenger hunt after the robbery? Why try to set up an encounter between Brian and the police in the hope of killing some cops? If Diehl-Armstrong was after quick cash, there would have been easier ways to go about getting it. And if she was too bipolar to stand trial, would she have been able to conceive of such a devious plan?

These questions might never be answered, and we might never know for certain if the pizza deliveryman realized, when he left Mama Mia's that day, what the rest of his afternoon would hold.

2   **IN THE EPISODE** "Derailed" (109), BAU profiler Elle Greenaway is held hostage on a train, along with the other passengers, by a paranoid schizophrenic who believes that the government has implanted a microchip in his body to monitor him. In this episode, Spencer Reid mentions the real-life case of Ralph Tortorici.

Tortorici had suffered delusions for years before the incident took place. He had been born with a defective urethra, and it had taken a series of operations to correct the problem. Somewhere along the way he became convinced that during his final operation, the government put a tracking device in his body. In 1992, at the age of twenty-four, he told doctors at the university health center at State University of New York–Albany that a microchip had been implanted in his penis. He was referred for psychiatric help, but his delusions didn't go away. He turned to drugs to quiet his fear, but they didn't do the job, either.

Finally, on December 14, 1994, Tortorici interrupted a professor and thirty-five students in an ancient history class on campus. He carried a high-powered rifle and a hunting knife. He announced that he had a computer chip in his brain, and that he wanted the professor to leave the classroom and summon the press and the state's congressional representatives. He wanted President Clinton's intervention as well, because it was the government, he was convinced, that was responsible for the chip. Once the professor was gone, Tortorici used a fire hose to secure the doors.

The professor called the police, who negotiated with Tortorici over a PA system. Tortorici fired his rifle once to show that he was serious. When it appeared that the negotiations were breaking down, a sophomore named Jason McEnaney rushed Tortorici and tried to get the gun. It discharged, seriously wounding McEnaney. Other students charged, and in the ensuing struggle, Tortorici was injured with his own knife.

Upon his arrest, Tortorici was charged with multiple counts of kidnapping, aggravated assault, and attempted murder. Found competent to stand trial, he asked to be excused from being present in the courtroom, which is almost unheard of in a criminal trial. Without him there, all the focus was on the facts of the case rather than on a defendant who might have come across as somewhat sympathetic.

In February 1996, the jury found him guilty on eleven counts of kidnapping and aggravated assault, and he was sentenced to fifteen to forty-seven years in prison. After an unsuccessful suicide attempt in 1996, Tortorici succeeded on August 10, 1999, in hanging himself with a bedsheet.

3 **THE UNSUB** in the episode "The Eyes Have It" (506), a taxidermist, is described as an *assaultive enucleator* because he removes the eyeballs from his murder victims. The surgical removal of an eyeball is a process called enucleation of the eye, and it is usually done only when an eyeball is seriously damaged or diseased. It's a very uncommon practice among murderers; far more common is simply to stab or otherwise attack the eyes.

One assaultive enucleator's first victim was a streetwalker who worked near the Star Motel in Dallas, Texas. When Mary Lou Pratt's body was found dumped on a suburban street on the morning of December 13, 1980, she had a bullet from a .44 in the back of her head. It wasn't until she was on the medical examiner's slab that anyone discovered that her eyeballs had been surgically removed.

A couple of months later, another hooker, Veronica Rodriguez, told patrol officers John Matthews and Regina Smith, who worked the hooker stroll, that she had been raped and assaulted by a white trick, who had left a gash on her forehead and a slice across her throat. She had escaped him and run away, she said, to a friend's house.

On February 10, prostitute Susan Peterson was found, dumped just outside Dallas city limits. She'd been shot three times. As in the case of Pratt, her eyeballs were gone. She had worked in the same neighborhood as Pratt, so the police knew they had a serial killer on their hands. Both victims were white, so the killer probably was, too, and so would any future victims be.

But the next body was an African American prostitute named Shirley Williams. Her eyeballs had been removed, but with less care. The broken tip of an X-Acto blade was found in one eye. The killer had been rushed, perhaps.

When Matthews and Smith returned to the neighborhood, yet another black hooker, Brenda White, told them a story about a white john who had scared her so much she had jumped from his car and run away. He'd shouted that he hated whores and wanted to kill them all.

The patrol officers heard too many stories from too many hookers about a scary white man, so they started trying to run the man down. Rodriguez had identified the friend whose house she had run to as Axton Schindler, a truck driver. When they ran his address, however, it came up as belonging to someone named Fred Albright. But Albright was dead. Even so, he owned other property, very close to where the first two bodies had been dumped. Schindler's real address was nearby, in one of Albright's other houses.

An officer at the police department had heard the name Albright before, in an anonymous tip from someone who had known Pratt. The late Fred Albright's adopted son, a man named Charles Albright, the tipster had said, had a thing for eyes. Running Charles Albright's name, they discovered a man with multiple arrests on his record, for theft, burglary, forgery, and sexual intercourse with a child—a girl who had been fourteen when he was fifty-one. They showed Albright's photo to White and Rodriguez, and they both identified him as the man who had attacked them.

Born on August 10, 1933, Charles Albright had been given up by his birth mother and adopted when he was three weeks old. His adoptive mother doted on him, but she was strange and unstable. Sometimes she would make him wear dresses and play with dolls, and she would tie him to his bed when he wouldn't nap.

When he was eleven she enrolled him in a mail-order taxidermy course. He was fascinated by the taxidermy eyes he saw in stores, but those, his penny-pinching mother insisted, were too expensive. He proved to be a good student and a skilled taxidermist, even as a boy, but animals with buttons sewn in place of eyes never looked quite right.

Albright overcame his unusual upbringing to become a cultured, educated man, fluent in several languages; a skilled artist and a science teacher; a husband and a father. He was also a frequenter of prostitutes, a thief, a liar, and, eventually, a murderer.

He never admitted to the crimes, and the investigators were able to gather only enough physical evidence to tie him to one, the murder of Shirley Williams. For her murder, Albright was sentenced to life in prison.

4 **THREE CRIMINALS**, mentioned by name on *Criminal Minds* one time each, have a great deal in common. In the episode "North Mammon" (207), an unsub abducts three high school girls and imprisons them in a concrete cellar, telling them that if they can select one girl to die, the other two will be set free. Spencer Reid refers to the sophisticated complex that John Jamelske built under his suburban home, where he kept careful track of the lives of the victims he imprisoned there for years. (Indeed he did have such a lair, although "sophisticated" might be a stretch.) In "Cradle to Grave" (505), the unsub has a more specific goal for the women he imprisons in his house: he wants to get them pregnant. That episode brings up the crimes of Gary Heidnik and Josef Fritzl.

John Jamelske was a handyman who had become a millionaire real estate investor from the Syracuse, New York, suburb of DeWitt.

During the 1980s, when he was in his fifties, Jamelske went through what some called a midlife crisis. He lost weight, grew a ponytail, and started wearing designer jeans. His wife suspected that he was having an affair but didn't pursue the matter.

What she didn't know was that from 1988 until his capture in 2003, Jamelske kept women and girls captive in his underground dungeon. He raped them on an almost daily basis and required them to keep detailed records of when they had sex, when they brushed their teeth, and when they bathed.

His first victim was a fourteen-year-old Native American girl, whom he kept until she was seventeen. He warned her that her family would be killed if she told what had happened to her. When she returned home, she told no one what she had been through, and she let her family think she had simply run away.

In 1995, Jamelske took a fourteen-year-old Latina and kept her for thirteen months, then let her go with the same kind of threat. She told her family but was afraid to tell the police.

In August 1997, he snatched a fifty-two-year-old Vietnamese woman. She stayed in the dungeon until May 1998. When she was finally freed, she went to the cops, but she was unable to identify her captor or take authorities to the place she'd been held. The investigation stalled.

Jamelske's wife, Dorothy, died in August 1999, after a battle with colon cancer. Jamelske waited until May 2001 to select his dungeon's next occupant, a young white woman whom he kept for only two months. She also reported her abduction and described the inside of the dungeon, but she, like the previous victims, was unable to pinpoint its location. He took them out of the house blindfolded, or in the dead of night, and dropped them off in far-flung parts of the city.

In October 2002 he abducted a sixteen-year-old black girl. During the time they spent together, Jamelske grew to trust her. He let her have access to parts of his house, although he secured those sections so she couldn't get out. He took her out bowling and to karaoke bars. He seemed to think that they had a regular, romantic relationship.

The morning of April 8, 2003, he took the girl along on an errand. She asked to be allowed to telephone a church about the times for services, but instead she called her sister and told her what had been going on. The sister alerted the police, and Jamelske was arrested. At the time, he remembered thinking, "I did something wrong, but I figured it's like unlawful imprisonment, maybe [I'll get] thirty hours of community service or something of that nature."

Given his capacity for denial of such epic proportions, his sentence of eighteen years to life probably came as a surprise to him. At the time of this writing, he is serving hard time at Dannemora, where it's unlikely that he'll ever be set free.

By contrast, Josef Fritzl of Amstetten, Austria, didn't abduct perfect strangers to keep in his secret dungeon. Instead, in an even more perverse crime, his captive was his daughter Elisabeth. He kept her in his dungeon for twenty-four years and repeatedly raped her, which resulted in the births of seven children, whom he also kept in the dungeon.

Fritzl was a native son of Amstetten, born there on April 9, 1935. In 1956, he married, and he and his wife had seven children, including Elisabeth, who was born in 1966. Fritzl's childhood was ravaged by war and by family abuse. He claimed that during World War II bombing raids, his mother would take the rest of the family to a shelter but would leave him alone at home.

In 1967, the year after Elisabeth's birth, Fritzl was convicted of rape. He was, he told officials, "born to rape." He began raping Elisabeth when she was eleven. On August 29, 1984, when she was eighteen, he took her into the dungeon he had built in the cellar and locked her away. He forced her to write occasional letters saying that she was alive and well but asking her family not to search for her. These letters seemed to convince Elisabeth's mother, who remained unaware of her daughter's proximity.

The dungeon was a remarkable construction. A person had to pass through eight doors, one of which had an electronic lock for which only Fritzl knew the password, to reach the outside world. Inside were four windowless rooms, including a full bathroom, a kitchenette, and two sleeping areas with beds.

One of Elisabeth's babies, a boy with a twin brother, grew ill shortly after birth. Despite his daughter's pleadings, Fritzl refused to take the infant to get medical care. When the boy died, Fritzl cremated him in the furnace.

Fritzl took three of his daughter's children upstairs into the house, claiming that Elisabeth had dropped them off to be raised by their grandparents. Fritzl's wife, who was forbidden to set foot in the basement, apparently never knew that her daughter was so close or that her grandchildren's father was her husband.

The end of Elisabeth's captivity came on April 19, 2008, when her daughter Kerstin, nineteen, became very ill. This time Fritzl was willing to take the sick young woman to the hospital, but the doctors needed the medical history of her mother. Fritzl took Elisabeth in, and the whole sick secret unraveled. Kerstin and her brothers Stefan, eighteen, and Felix, five, had never before seen daylight.

At his trial, Fritzl pleaded guilty to murder, rape, enslavement, and more and was sentenced to life in prison. Given that he was seventy-three at the time, chances are that his imprisonment will not be as long as his daughter's was.

Gary Heidnik was born on November 22, 1943. His early childhood in Cleveland, Ohio, was marked by the divorce of his parents. Heidnik and his brother, Terry, after living briefly with their alcoholic mother and her new husband, moved in with their father, who had also remarried. The boys hated their "wicked" stepmother, and their father took her side in their frequent spats. An unpleasant living situation was made worse by Heidnik's bed-wetting; his father punished Heidnik severely on these occasions, hanging his soiled sheets in the boy's bedroom window for the neighbors to see. According to Heidnik, his father sometimes dangled him out the window as well, holding him by the ankles and shaking him.

When Heidnik fell from a tree, his skull was smashed, and his misshapen cranium is believed to have caused some behavioral aberration, as well as earning the boy the nickname "football-head" from his schoolmates. Heidnik was intelligent and driven, but he suffered psychological disorders that kept him from achieving his full potential. He was discharged from the army after a year, earning a full disability pension and a diagnosis of "schizoid personality disorder."

Heidnik's mother's suicide in 1970 prompted his first suicide attempt, one of many unsuccessful attempts resulting in frequent hospitalizations. A religious "epiphany" resulted in his becoming ordained by the United Church of the Ministers of God, and as Bishop Heidnik he founded the "Church of Heidnik." With a fif-teen-hundred-dollar investment in a Merrill Lynch account, the church amassed a fortune of half a million dollars.

Brushes with the law became commonplace for Heidnik, who was charged with aggravated assault after attacking a tenant of one of his properties, then with a multitude of charges for his kid-napping and rape of his mentally handicapped "girlfriend." The aggravated assault charges were dropped, and in the other case he served most of his sentence at a hospital rather than in prison. In April 1983 he was released into the community once again.

Soon, Heidnik married a mail-order bride from the Philippines. That marriage was short-lived and marked by violence. His wife had a son, the existence of whom she kept from Heidnik until she sued him for paternal support. Other "girlfriends," mostly mentally disabled women with whom he struck up relationships, also had children whom they then kept away from their father. The idea that he had yet another child to whom he had no access sent Heidnik into a spiraling rage, which ultimately resulted in the crimes for which he was arrested a final time: the kidnap, torture, and rape of six women whom he kept in the basement of his Philadelphia home, and the murder of two of them.

Heidnik's first victim was a twenty-five-year-old African American prostitute named Josefina Rivera. On November 26, 1986, she was picked up by a white man driving a Cadillac Coupe de Ville.

He took her back to his house; it didn't look like much to her, inside or out, but she spotted a Rolls Royce in the garage. She and the john had sex, and as she started to get dressed, he attacked her, choking her and locking handcuffs around her wrists. Half naked, she was led into the cold basement room that was to be her new home.

Heidnik glued clamps around her ankles, then connected them to a length of chain and secured that to a pipe. Rivera wasn't going anywhere. She watched him work on a pit in the basement floor, digging it wider and deeper, explaining as he did that he meant to have ten slaves and would need a much more substantial pit. He had four children by different mothers, but none of them lived with him. He wanted company, but without the niceties of an actual relationship. He wanted sex slaves to do his bidding. He wanted to get them all pregnant and create a large, mixed-race family.

If Rivera "misbehaved," she was put into the pit, which was covered by a weighted board, so she tried not to upset her captor.

The next captive, Sandra Lindsay, was another African American woman. She was mentally disabled and had known Heidnik long enough to have become pregnant with his child and have it aborted. For Heidnik, it was payback time. He fed the women irregularly, kept them half-naked, and raped them whenever he wanted.

That December, he brought nineteen-year-old Lisa Thomas home and drugged her wine, and when she woke up, she was in the basement with the other women. A week later Heidnik grabbed Deborah Dudley, twenty-three. Dudley fought and challenged him at every opportunity, so she got more beatings and pit time than the others. Now Heidnik began to indulge himself in other ways, such as by forcing the four women to have sex with one another while he watched. Instead of continuing to feed them scraps from his own meals, he brought them dog food.

On January 18, 1987, he brought Jacquelyn Askins, eighteen, into the basement. Now he was halfway to his goal.

Heidnik became angry with Lindsay for some reason on February 7, and he punished her by hanging her by one wrist from a roof beam for two days. When he took her down, she had a high fever, and by morning she was dead. He took her body upstairs, cranked up a power saw, and dismembered her. He put her head into a large cooking pot, and he cut flesh (which he never admitted to eating) from wherever he could. Some of it he fed to his two dogs, and some went into the dog food that he gave his other captives.

After a couple of days, the police knocked on the door, wanting to know what the terrible smell was. The neighbors had complained. Heidnik said that he had burned his dinner, and the police took the explanation at face value.

Next in Heidnik's repertoire was to tell the women that they would be rewarded for informing on one another. Rivera told Heidnik that the others planned to jump him; his response was to deafen the accused plotters by driving screwdrivers through their eardrums. He also took to applying electric shocks to everyone but Rivera. She had become his favorite, and sometimes he used her to help him torture the others. She had other "privileges," such as occasionally being allowed upstairs to watch a movie or be raped in a more comfortable environment.

Dudley died while suffering electric torture. Heidnik and Rivera disposed of the body, then Rivera recruited a friend and sometime coworker, Agnes Adams, as Dudley's replacement. On March 24, 1987, Rivera asked Heidnik's permission to visit her family. As astonishing as it sounds, Heidnik agreed. Rivera raced home and told her anxious boyfriend where she had been. Then she told the police, and Heidnik was arrested. All of the stories Rivera told, however, couldn't prepare the police for the horrific scenes they would discover in that Philadelphia home.

Heidnik was convicted of two counts of first-degree murder, five of kidnapping, six of rape, four of aggravated assault, and one of involuntary deviant sexual intercourse. On July 6, 1999, after surviving several suicide attempts in prison, he was executed by lethal injection.

5 THE FOURTH SEASON of *Criminal Minds* ends with a two-part story, "To Hell . . ." (425) ". . . And Back" (426). In these episodes, the team heads to Detroit to catch a killer who is abducting homeless people, drug addicts, and prostitutes from the city's Cass Corridor. Such places as skid rows, havens for the destitute full of drug users, sex workers, and the homeless, have been the hunting grounds for serial killers since Jack the Ripper lurked in Whitechapel.

Canada's Low Track in Vancouver, British Columbia, is no different. In 1983 prostitutes started disappering from there. The police didn't seem to pay attention until a sex worker advocate made the disappearances a personal crusade in 1998. Once the police began investigating, they eventually identified sixty-three missing women. Prostitutes are notoriously hard to keep track of, since they tend not to favor official scrutiny, and when they disappear they are often not missed because they are already societal outcasts. In this case, however, given the large number of missing prostitutes, it was evident, even to those who usually wouldn't notice, that something was going on. Some women turned up, either alive or dead from an identifiable cause, so they were crossed off the list. But even as the list shrank, more women were taken off the streets.

A tip pointed police in the direction of Robert William Pickton, who, with his brother David, owned a pig farm in Port Coquitlam, British Columbia. The Picktons also owned a salvage yard, which the tipster said was patrolled by a ferocious six-hundred-pound pig who ran with the guard dogs. Another side business, the Piggy Palace Good Times Society, was listed as a nonprofit charity that supposedly organized special events on behalf of worthwhile groups. The special events were actually drunken raves featuring prostitutes from the Low Track. David had been convicted of sexual assault once, and Robert had been charged with the attempted murder of a prostitute. Even though those charges had been dropped, the brothers were no strangers to police.

The pig farm was searched but nothing was found, and prostitutes kept disappearing. Another search, in early 2002, yielded more concrete results. Robert, fifty-four, was arrested on weapons charges. After being released on bail, he was then rearrested on murder charges because the investigators had finally found evidence of some of the victims on the farm, beginning with heads and bodies stored in freezers—victims that had all been taken after the tipster had fingered the brothers. By mid-2004, after two years of extensive searching, the authorities identified the remains of thirty women. There was evidence that a wood chipper had been used to dispose of some of the bodies by turning them into pig feed. There was also some speculation that human meat might have been mixed in with pork and sold for human consumption.

Because there were so many victims, a Canadian judge decided to try Robert Pickton in several trials. The first trial would be for six murders, then he would be tried for an additional twenty. After the longest criminal trial in Canadian history, Pickton was found not guilty of first-degree murder, but guilty of second-degree murder on all six counts. He was sentenced to life in prison with no parole for twenty-five years, the maximum sentence allowed.

The British Columbia attorney general decided that if Pickton's appeal was denied, he wouldn't bring Pickton to trial for the other twenty victims, since no harsher sentence could be imposed. At this writing, the pig farmer is still in prison, waiting for the Canadian Supreme Court to hear his appeal.

6 **THERE ARE** a few serial killers whose names are so familiar that even people who shy away from news coverage or fictional depictions of crime know them. Jack the Ripper and Ted Bundy certainly fall into that category. One whose name is slightly less well known, even though his crimes are at least as notorious, is the shy, soft-spoken Ed Gein, whose case was fictionalized by Robert Bloch in his novel *Psycho* and made famous by Anthony Perkins's character Norman Bates in Alfred Hitchcock's film adaptation.

Gein also provided inspiration for the movies *The Texas Chainsaw Massacre* and *The Silence of the Lambs*, and his supposed Oedipus complex is referenced in the *Criminal Minds* episode "Cold Comfort" (414), in which the unsub is trying to re-create someone he loved and lost.

Edward Theodore Gein was born on August 27, 1906, in Plainfield, Wisconsin. His father was an alcoholic who beat Ed and his brother, Henry. Augusta, Gein's mother, ran a grocery store in La Crosse. After her boys were born, she bought a farm outside the town so that she could control their exposure to the world she hated. She worked hard to convince the boys of the evils beyond their own land, including the fact that all women—except for her—were good-for-nothing whores. She delighted in reading them the most graphic descriptions of murder and divine retribution from the Old Testament. She discouraged them from making friends, and she was convinced that her sons would turn out to be failures, just like their father.

Nonetheless, Gein loved his mother. After their father's death, both boys took occasional odd jobs in town, and Henry was exposed to new ideas, which he brought back to Ed. Some of these were critical of their mother; Ed didn't like it when Henry spoke ill of her.

On May 16, 1944, the brothers were fighting a brushfire on their land when they became separated. After the fire was controlled, Ed couldn't find Henry, and he reported the disappearance to the police. When a search party was formed, Ed led the party directly to his brother's body, which had bruises on the head and was lying on land the fire had passed over. Still, no one in the community believed that Ed Gein was capable of murdering his brother.

Now Gein had no one at home except Mother.

That year, Augusta had a stroke. Although Gein nursed her, on December 29, 1945, a more severe stroke took her away for good. Now Gein was alone.

He kept the farm, but thanks to government farm subsidies, he didn't have to work it. Instead, he lived on his government checks and did occasional odd handyman work or babysitting for extra money. He sealed off the parts of the house his mother had enjoyed the most, and he used only the kitchen and an adjoining room that he turned into a bedroom.

Alone in his small part of the big house, Gein's mind turned to strange pursuits. He read pulp magazines, horror and crime comics, anatomy texts, and accounts of Nazi atrocities. He had never been with a woman, but he found himself fascinated by their bodies. At the graveyard, he found that with some digging, he had a ready supply of available female bodies for closer examination. Examination alone wasn't good enough, however, and he began to take parts from middle-aged women who resembled his mother.

Gein had long been enthralled by the power women had over men; his mother had, after all, controlled her husband and her two adult sons. Gein had dreamed of being a woman, and with the parts he took from the cemetery, he played at being one. He danced around the yard in the moonlight wearing skins he removed from the women's bodies, and he even made a vest out of a pair of women's breasts. He put female genitalia in his mother's underwear and wore that. He preserved heads, which he kept around the house and which some of his rare visitors saw and commented on.

Dead women were soon no longer fresh enough for Gein. In November 1957, he was a frequent visitor to the Worden Hardware Store, owned by Bernice Worden and her adult son, Frank, a deputy sheriff. Deer-hunting season was upon them, and Gein kept asking Frank when he was going hunting. Finally, on November 15, Frank told Gein that he would be hunting the next day. Gein said he would be back in the morning for a gallon of antifreeze.

Sure enough, when Frank made it back to the store, the last sale Bernice had written up was of antifreeze. But when Frank made that discovery, late on a Saturday—after being surprised to find the store locked up and his mother not there—he also found a pool of blood. He called the sheriff and reported the exchange with Gein. Frank didn't trust Gein, who seemed to spend a lot of time staring at Bernice.

Lawmen went out to Gein's farm. Gein wasn't home, but as the authorities were looking around the property, someone beamed a flashlight into a shed and saw Bernice's body hanging upside down, disemboweled and decapitated, slit from crotch to sternum like a deer.

Gein had been home that afternoon when Bob and Darlene Hill, teenage acquaintances, came by the house. Bob was the closest thing Gein had to a friend—he sometimes showed the boy his pulp magazines and comic books, and he had even revealed a shrunken head that he said was a relic of South Seas headhunters. That day the teens were hoping for a lift into town to buy a new car battery. Gein came to the door in a blood-spattered leather apron, with blood spray on his face. He said he had just finished dressing a deer, and he drove Bob and Darlene on their errand. When they arrived back at the Hill residence after dark, their mother, Irene, invited Gein to stay for dinner.

He was still there when a neighbor came in to tell them the news that Bernice Worden had disappeared. After dinner, Gein was on his way to his car when some police officers picked him up. Gein immediately insisted that somebody had framed him for Bernice's murder—even though the police had not yet mentioned the dead woman.

None of the men who went inside Gein's house that night ever forgot what they saw. The house was a cluttered wreck, full of trash, mildewed seed bags, and farm implements amid the furniture. Far worse were Gein's souvenirs: a belt made of female nipples; a box of salted female genitalia; and chair cushions, wastebaskets, and lamp-shades made out of human skin. Gein's bed had a skull on each of the four posts, and other skulls, some with hair still attached, were scattered about. One skull was being used as a bowl. His refrigerator contained wrapped human organs and flesh.

The walls of his makeshift bedroom were decorated with crudely fashioned death masks made from the faces of dead women. He had ten female heads, including that of Mary Hogan, a popular saloon keeper who had disappeared three years earlier. Worden's head had been prepared for hanging, with twine threaded through the ears, but Gein hadn't had a chance to put her up yet. Her heart was in a pot on the stove. The authorities also found Gein's mammary vest, the one he wore to pretend to be a woman. It had straps on the back, and he admitted to wearing it with human "leggings."

When the sheriff and his men tore down the boards that closed off the rest of the house, they discovered that part of it was preserved just as it had been more than a decade before, when Augusta Gein had ruled the home.

Gein denied any murders other than those of Worden and Hogan, although he was suspected of at least nine. He also denied engaging in necrophilia, but there was clearly a sexual component to his crimes, and he was never known to have had a sexual relationship with a living woman. He denied cannibalism as well, but he'd been known to give people "venison" even though he had never hunted deer. His treasures, he insisted, had been dug up from forty different graveyards, but he hadn't killed for most of them.

Gein and the entire locale of Plainfield became instant worldwide sensations. Reporters flocked to the Wisconsin farming community. Children told jokes called "Geiners" (Q: What did Eddie Gein say when the hearse drove by? A: Dig ya later, baby!).

Gein was sentenced to the Central State Hospital for the Criminally Insane in Waupun, Wisconsin. After ten years there, he was deemed competent to stand trial, but he was quickly judged not guilty by reason of insanity and returned to the hospital. He never left again except to be transferred to the geriatric ward of the Mendota Mental Health Institute, where he died from cancer on July 26, 1984. Gein was buried in the Plainfield cemetery, near his mother and the graves he had robbed. Together again, at long last.

The Real Profilers

THE LEGENDARY J. EDGAR HOOVER, director of the FBI from 1924 until he died in 1972, left a mixed but lasting legacy. In some ways, he turned the bureau into his personal investigative agency: running roughshod over the rights of citizens, keeping files on actors and activists alike, and being willing to use the fruits of the bureau's investigations to persuade members of Congress and even presidents to do his bidding.

At the same time, he turned the bureau into the world-class crime-busting operation it is today. He decentralized it, creating field offices around the country so the response to crime could be immediate. He created the FBI laboratory that began in humble digs in a room at the Old Southern Railway Building in Washington, D.C., and has grown into the premier lab of its kind. Long before Miranda was the law of the land, he insisted that suspects be treated with dignity, that they be warned of their rights, and that the reports that agents filed about them be honest. He invented the Ten Most Wanted list. And he believed in the importance of training his agents.

One of Hoover's final and most important acts was the creation of the FBI Academy in Quantico, Virginia. The academy opened its doors in 1972, three days after Hoover's death. It serves to train new FBI agents, to keep agents informed about new developments in criminal investigation, and to train other law enforcement officials in the techniques the FBI has learned.

Before Quantico, police officers could train with FBI agents at the National Academy. The National Academy functioned to instill greater professionalism among police officers and to help the FBI develop a national network of officers with whom it had good relations. One of the academy's instructors, a former California cop named Howard D. Teten, had read Dr. James A. Brussel's accounts of his own experiences with the psychological profiling of criminals, and he was impressed with much of Brussel's approach.

At Quantico, Teten and Patrick J. Mullany, a field agent from New York who had a degree in psychology, together became the driving force behind the bureau's new Behavioral Sciences Unit (BSU), which was established in 1972. They developed a new method of analyzing unknown offenders based on the details of their crimes, particularly through careful analysis of the crime scene. The agents who formed the BSU taught this method to other agents and police officers at Quantico, and they also went out on the road to speak to law enforcement officials wherever they could.

At the same time, the BSU began to get requests from police agencies for assistance with unsolved crimes. One of the earliest requests, a plea from the Bozeman, Montana, field office for help with a kidnapping case, resulted in a profile that eventually helped to pinpoint serial killer David Meirhofer. As more and more requests flooded in, the unit grew. It also, at Robert K. Ressler's urging, created a program that brought agents interested in profiling to the academy for training, then sent

Agent Jareau brings her new baby boy to the BAU offices and introduces him to her colleagues in "Normal."

them back to their field offices, where they could provide profiling expertise and act as coordinators whenever agencies in their areas requested formal assistance.

To further their knowledge about crimes and criminals, the members of the BSU interviewed a series of assassins and would-be assassins, including Arthur Bremer, Sirhan Sirhan, James Earl Ray, and others. Eventually, that program expanded to include interviews with many serial killers, serial rapists, and child molesters. As the profilers' understanding of the psychology of these offenders grew, their profiles became more precise and detailed.

Profilers point out that their profiles can't lead investigators directly to a suspect. They can say what type of person might have committed a given crime, but they can't magically conjure up a name and an address. Moreover, the information they get has to be as complete and as accurate as possible, because mistakes or disregarded facts can alter the profile significantly enough to make it worse than useless. Profilers think of profiling as a science, but not an exact one.

Many of the profilers working in the BSU—which came to be called the Investigative Support Unit during John Douglas's tenure—in those days (the 1970s and 1980s) became household names, at least in households with an interest in crime and law enforcement. In addition to Teten, Mullany, Ressler, and Douglas, Roger DePue, Dick Ault, Roy Hazelwood, and Gregg McCrary all worked in the unit when it was growing into the outfit that would inspire best-selling books, movies, and TV shows—and they were helping to identify some of the worst criminals ever to walk U.S. soil.

Ressler and an agent named Jim McKenzie looked at ways to spread the FBI's work, to make its resources more accessible to police departments around the country. Their idea, which would put the BSU and other aspects of criminal investigation under a single umbrella, became the National Center for the Analysis of Violent Crime, or NCAVC.

Independently, a police detective in Los Angeles named Pierce Brooks—the man who had headed up the Harvey Glatman investigation in the late 1950s—had proposed a computer system that would link all of the police departments in California so that the details of all of the violent crimes that occurred in one jurisdiction would be available to everyone. When Brooks first proposed it, California's budget couldn't accommodate it. But decades later, Brooks, after a distinguished law enforcement career, had brought the idea back and received a U.S. Department of Justice grant to study the feasibility of what he called the Violent Criminal Apprehension Program (ViCAP).

The FBI liked Brooks's idea, but it thought that his proposal for structuring it was too limited. Instead, the bureau convinced him to bring it under the NCAVC umbrella, which he did. Brooks managed ViCAP, which is now, in the FBI's words, "a nationwide data information center designed to collect, collate, and analyze crimes of violence."

Today, NCAVC describes its mission as combining "investigative and operational support functions, research, and training in order to provide assistance, without charge, to federal, state, local, and foreign law enforcement agencies investigating unusual or repetitive violent crimes, communicated threats, and other matters of interest to law enforcement."

The agency is divided into four components: ViCAP; Behavioral Analysis Unit 1 (BAU-1), which deals with terrorist threats; Behavioral Analysis Unit 2 (BAU-2), which is focused on crimes against adults; and Behavioral Analysis Unit 3 (BAU-3), which handles crimes against children.

When agents from the Quantico BAU headquarters do go into the field, as the ones on *Criminal Minds* do, it's usually to consult on-site with local law enforcement officers who have requested the unit's assistance, usually through someone in a local bureau office, not an agent, like the show's J.J. Jareau, stationed at headquarters. The agents visit crime scenes and consider physical evidence, all in the service of coming up with the best, most detailed profile of the unknown offender. But they don't kick down doors, engage in high-speed chases, or make arrests. They're an advisory group, operationally involved in cases, but not, except in very rare instances, with guns drawn. They don't travel in a pack on a Gulfstream jet, as the profilers in the TV show do, but instead they spend much of their time sitting in front of computer screens, reading case files, and talking to law enforcement on the phone.

There is once again a Behavioral Sciences Unit at the FBI, but more like the original BSU than today's BAU, it is a training and research unit, not an operational one.

According to the FBI's Web site, "The mission of the BAU is to provide behavioral-based investigative and operational support by applying case experience, research, and training to complex and time-sensitive crimes, typically involving acts or threats of violence." The unit does this through the process of criminal investigative analysis, which "involves reviewing and assessing the facts of a criminal act, interpreting offender behavior, and interaction with the victim, as exhibited during the commission of the crime, or as displayed in the crime scene. BAU staff conduct detailed analyses of crimes for the purpose of providing one or more of the following services: crime analysis, investigative suggestions, profiles of unknown offenders, threat analysis, critical incident analysis, interview strategies, major case management, search warrant assistance, prosecutive and trial strategies, and expert testimony."

Criminal Minds is not an entirely accurate depiction of the work of real BAU members, but the agents on TV have the same mission as their real-life counterparts. When the BAU is brought into a case, it's because there is a criminal out there who has already struck and will likely strike again. The agents, in cooperation with local law enforcement, want to figure out who the criminal is and to make sure that there are no more victims. Sometimes it takes years, sometimes more people are victimized, and some crimes are never solved.

But the dedicated agents of the Behavioral Analysis Unit— whether on TV or in the real world—don't give up the hunt.

BIBLIOGRAPHY

Adams, Briggs, et al. *Murder and Mayhem*. New York: Signet Books, 1991.

Bruno, Anthony. *The Iceman: The True Story of a Cold-Blooded Killer*. New York: Delacorte Press, 1993.

Brussel, James A. *The Casebook of a Crime Psychiatrist*. New York: Bernard Geis Associates, 1968.

Bugliosi, Vincent, and Curt Gentry. *Helter Skelter: The True Story of the Manson Murders*. New York: Bantam Books, 1995.

Cahill, Tim. *Buried Dreams: Inside the Mind of a Serial Killer*. New York: Bantam Books, 1989.

Capote, Truman. *In Cold Blood: A True Account of a Multiple Murder and Its Consequences*. New York: Random House, 1965.

Carlo, Philip. *The Ice Man: Confessions of a Mafia Contract Killer*. New York: St. Martin's Press, 1996.

Chase, Alston. *Harvard and the Unabomber: The Education of an American Terrorist*. New York: W. W. Norton, 2003.

Cheney, Margaret. *The Co-ed Killer*. New York: Walker, 1976.

DeMeo, Albert. *For the Sins of My Father: A Mafia Killer, His Son, and the Legacy of a Mob Life*. New York: Broadway Books, 2002.

Douglas, John, and Mark Olshaker. *Journey into Darkness: Follow the FBI's Premier Investigative Profiler as He Penetrates the Minds and Motives of the Most Terrifying Serial Killers*. New York: Pocket Books, 1997.

———. *Mindhunter: Inside the FBI's Elite Serial Crime Unit*. New York: Pocket Books, 1995.

———. *Obsession: The FBI's Legendary Profiler Probes the Psyches of Killers, Rapists, and Stalkers and Their Victims and Tells How to Fight Back*. New York: Pocket Books, 1998.

Eftimiades, Maria. *Garden of Graves: The Shocking True Story of Long Island Serial Killer Joel Rifkin*. New York: St. Martin's Press, 1993.

Evans, Stewart P., and Keith Skinner. *The Ultimate Jack the Ripper Companion: An Illustrated Encyclopedia*. New York: Carroll & Graf, 2001.

Duarte, Stella Pope. *If I Die in Juárez*. Tucson: Univ. of Arizona Press, 2008.

Freeman, Lucy. *Before I Kill More . . .* New York: Crown, 1955.

Grant, George. *Killers.* London: Compendium, 2006.

Graysmith, Robert. *Zodiac.* New York: Berkley Books, 2007.

Hazelwood, Roy, and Stephen G. Michaud. *Dark Dreams: Sexual Violence, Homicide, and the Criminal Mind.* New York: St. Martin's Press, 2001.

———. *The Evil That Men Do.* New York: St. Martin's Press, 1998.

Jeffers, H. Paul. *Who Killed Precious? How FBI Special Agents Combine High Technology and Psychology to Identify Violent Criminals.* New York: Pharos Books, 1991.

Jones, Richard Glyn, ed. *The Mammoth Book of Women Who Kill.* New York: Carroll & Graf, 2002.

Keppel, Robert D., and William Birnes. *Signature Killers: Interpreting the Calling Cards of the Serial Murderer.* New York: Pocket Books, 1997.

Kessler, Ronald. *The FBI.* New York: Pocket Books, 1994.

Klausner, Lawrence D. *Son of Sam: Based on the Authorized Transcription of the Tapes, Official Documents and Diaries of David Berkowitz.* New York: McGraw-Hill, 1981.

Leyton, Elliott. *Hunting Humans: The Rise of the Modern Multiple Murderer.* New York: Pocket Books, 1986.

Michaud, Stephen G. *Lethal Shadow: The Chilling True-Crime Story of a Sadistic Sex Slayer.* New York: Onyx, 1994.

Mustain, Gene, and Jerry Capeci. *Murder Machine: A True Story of Murder, Madness, and the Mafia.* New York: Dutton, 1992.

Newton, Michael. *The Encyclopedia of Serial Killers.* New York: Facts on File, 2000.

Norris, Joel. *Arthur Shawcross: The Genesee River Killer.* New York: Pinnacle Books, 1992.

———. *Henry Lee Lucas: The Shocking True Story of America's Most Notorious Serial Killer.* New York: Zebra Books, 1991.

———. *Serial Killers: The Growing Menace.* New York: Doubleday, 1998.

Page, Carol. *Bloodlust: Conversations with Real Vampires.* New York: HarperCollins, 1991.

Ramsey, John, and Patsy Ramsey. *The Death of Innocence: JonBenét's Parents Tell Their Story.* Nashville: Thomas Nelson, 2000.

Randal, Jonathan. *Osama: The Making of a Terrorist.* New York: Alfred A. Knopf, 2004.

Ressler, Robert K., and Tom Schachtman. *I Have Lived in the Monster.* New York: St. Martin's Press, 1997.

———. *Whoever Fights Monsters.* New York: St. Martin's Press, 1992.

Rodriguez, Teresa. *The Daughters of Juárez: A True Story of Serial Murder South of the Border.* New York: Atria Books, 2007.

Rule, Ann. *Green River, Running Red: The Real Story of the Green River Killer, America's Deadliest Serial Murderer.* New York: Free Press, 2004.

————. *The Stranger Beside Me*. New York: Penguin, 1989.

Schechter, Harold. *The Serial Killer Files: The Who, What, Where, How, and Why of the World's Most Terrifying Murderers*. New York: Ballantine Books, 2003.

Smith, Carlton, and Tomas Guillen. *The Search for the Green River Killer*. New York: Signet Books, 2004.

Thomas, Steve, and Don Davis. *JonBenét: Inside the Ramsey Murder Investigation*. New York: St. Martin's Press, 2000.

Wilson, Colin, and Donald Seaman. *The Serial Killers: A Study in the Psychology of Violence*. New York: Carol, 1990.

INDEX

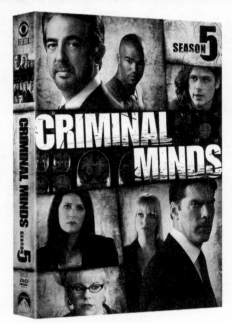